Applied Cloud Deep Semantic Recognition

Advanced Anomaly Detection

Applied Cloud Deep Semantic Recognition

Advanced Anomaly Detection

Edited by
Mehdi Roopaei
Paul Rad

CRC Press
Taylor & Francis Group
Boca Raton London New York

CRC Press is an imprint of the
Taylor & Francis Group, an **informa** business

AN AUERBACH BOOK

Mehdi Roopaei
University of Texas at San Antonio
San Antonio, Texas

Nicu Sebe
DISI
University of Trento
Trentino, Italy

Eli Shechtman
Adobe Research
San Jose, California

Zhangyang Wang
Department of Computer Science and
    Engineering
Texas A&M University
College Station, Texas

Zhaowen Wang
Adobe Research
San Jose, California

Chao Wu
Data Science Institute
Imperial College London
London, United Kingdom

Jianchao Yang
Snapchat Inc.
Venice, California

Guangnan Ye
IBM T.J. Watson Research Center
Yorktown Heights, New York

Yizhe (Ethan) Zhu
Rutgers University
Piscataway, New Jersey

Introduction

Anomaly Detection and Situational Awareness

In data analytics, anomaly detection is discussed as the discovery of objects, actions, behavior, or events that do not conform to an expected pattern in a dataset. Anomaly detection has extensive applications in a wide variety of domains such as biometrics spoofing, healthcare, fraud detection for credit cards, network intrusion detection, malware threat detection, and military surveillance for adversary threats. While anomalies might be induced in the data for a variety of motives, all of the motives have the common trait that they are interesting to data scientists and cyber analysts. Anomaly detection has been researched within diverse research areas such as computer science, engineering, information systems, and cyber security. Many anomaly detection algorithms have been presented for certain domains, while others are more generic.

In the past, many anomaly detection algorithms have been designed for specific applications, while others are more generic. This book tries to provide a comprehensive overview of the research on anomaly detection with respect to context and situational awareness that aims to get a better understanding of how context information influences anomaly detection. We have grouped scalars from industry and academic with vast practical knowledge into different. In each chapter, advanced anomaly detection and key assumptions have been identified, which are used by the model to differentiate between normal and anomalous behavior. When applying a given model to a particular application, the assumptions can be used as guidelines to assess the effectiveness of the model in that domain. In each chapter, we provide an advanced deep content understanding and anomaly detection algorithm, and then we show how the proposed approach deviates from basic techniques. Further, for each chapter, we describe the advantages and disadvantages of the algorithm. Last but not least, in the final chapters, we also provide a discussion on the computational complexity of the models and graph computational frameworks such as Google Tensorflow and H2O, since it is an important issue in real application domains. We hope that this book will provide a better understanding of the different directions in which research has been done on deep semantic analysis and situational assessment using deep learning for anomalous detection, and how methods developed in one area can be applied to applications in other domains.

This book seeks to provide both cyber analytics practitioners and researchers with an up-to-date and advanced knowledge in cloud-based frameworks for deep semantic analysis and advanced anomaly detection using cognitive and artificial intelligence (AI) models. The structure of the remainder of this book is as follows.

Chapter 1: Large-Scale Video Event Detection Using Deep Neural Networks

This chapter aims at the development of robust and efficient solutions for large-scale video event detection systems using a state-of-the-art deep learning approach. Because of the rapid growth of large-scale video recording and sharing, there is a growing need for robust and scalable solutions for analyzing video content. The ability to detect and recognize video events that capture real-world activities is one of the key and complex problems. In particular, the author investigates event detection with automatically discovered event-specific concepts with organized ontology. Specifically, he built a large-scale event-specific concept library named EventNet that covers as many real-world events and their concepts as possible. After an automatic filter process, he ended up with 95,321 videos and 4490 concepts in 500 event categories. A deep neural network was trained on top of the 500 event categories. EventNet represents a video event ontology that organizes events and their concepts into a semantic structure. It offers great potential for event retrieval and browsing. The EventNet system allows users to explore rich hierarchical structures among video events, relations between concepts and events, and automatic detection of events and concepts embedded in user-uploaded videos in a live fashion. The author of this chapter proposes an automatic semantic concept discovery scheme that exploits Internet resources without human labeling effort. To distinguish this work from one that builds a generic concept library, his approach as an event-driven concept discovery provides more relevant concepts for events. In order to manage novel unseen events, he proposes the construction of a large-scale event-driven concept library that covers as many real-world events and concepts as possible. He resorts to the external knowledge base called WikiHow, a collaborative forum that aims to build the world's largest manual for human daily life events.

Chapter 2: Leveraging Selectional Preferences for Anomaly Detection in Newswire Events

In this chapter, the authors introduce the problem of automatic anomalous event detection and propose a novel event model that can learn to differentiate between normal and anomalous events. Events are fundamental linguistic elements in human speech. Thus, understanding events is a fundamental prerequisite for deeper semantic analysis of language, and any computational system of human language should have a model of events. The authors generally define anomalous events as those that are unusual compared to the general state of affairs and might invoke surprise when reported. An automatic anomaly detection algorithm has to encode the goodness of semantic role filler coherence. This is a hard problem since determining what a good combination of role fillers is requires deep semantic and pragmatic knowledge. Moreover, manual judgment of an anomaly itself may be difficult, and people often may not agree with each other in this regard. Automatic detection of anomaly requires encoding complex information, which poses the challenge of sparsity due to the discrete representations of meaning that are words. These problems range from polysemy and synonymy at the lexical semantic level to entity and event coreference at the discourse level. The authors define an event as the pair of a predicate or a semantic verb and a set of its semantic arguments like agent, patient, time, location, and so on. The goal of this chapter is to obtain a vector representation of the event that is composed from representations of individual words, while explicitly guided by the semantic role structure. This representation can be understood as an embedding of the event in an event space.

Chapter 3: Abnormal Event Recognition in Crowd Environments

In this chapter, a crowd behavior detection and recognition is investigated. In crowd behavior understanding, a model of crowd behavior needs to be trained using the information extracted from rich video sequences. In most of the traditional crowd-based datasets, behavior labels as ground-truth information rely only on patterns of low-level motion/appearance. Therefore, there is a need for a realistic dataset to not only evaluate crowd behavioral interaction in low-level features but also to analyze the crowd in terms of mid-level attribute representation. The authors of this chapter propose an attribute-based strategy to train a set of emotion-based classifiers, which can subsequently be used to represent the crowd motion. For this purpose, in the collected dataset each video clip is provided with annotations of both "crowd behaviors" and "crowd emotions." To reach the mentioned target, the authors developed a novel crowd dataset that contains around 45,000 video clips, annotated according to one of five different fine-grained abnormal behavior categories. They also evaluated two state-of-the-art methods on their dataset, showing that their dataset can be effectively used as a benchmark for fine-grained abnormality detection. In their model, the crowd emotion attributes are considered latent variables. They propose a unified attribute-based behavior representation framework, which is built on a latent SVM formulation. In the proposed model, latent variables capture the level of importance of each emotion attribute for each behavior class.

Chapter 4: Cognitive Sensing: Adaptive Anomalies Detection with Deep Networks

In this chapter, the authors try to apply inspirations from human cognition to design a more intelligent sensing and modeling system that can adaptively detect anomalies. Current sensing methods often ignore the fact that their sensing targets are dynamic and can change over time. As a result, to build an accurate model should not always be the first priority. What we need is to establish an adaptive modeling framework. Based on our understanding of free energy and the Infomax principle, the target of sensing and modeling is not to get as much data as possible or to build the most accurate model, but to establish an adaptive representation of the target and achieve balance between sensing performance and system resource consumption. To achieve this aim, the authors of this chapter adopt a working memory mechanism to help the model evolve with the target; they use a deep auto-encoder network as a model representation, which models complex data with its nonlinear and hierarchical architecture. Since we typically only have partial observations from a sensed target, they therefore design a variance of the auto-encoder that can reconstruct corrupted input. Also, they utilize the attentional surprise mechanism to control model updates. Training of the deep network is driven by surprises detected (anomalies), which indicates a model failure or the target's new behavior. Because of partial observations, they are not able to minimize free energy in a single update, but iteratively minimize it by finding new optimization bounds. In their proposed system, the model update frequency is controlled by several parameters, including the surprise threshold and memory size. These parameters control the alertness as well as the resource consumption of the system in a top-down manner.

Chapter 5: Language-Guided Visual Recognition

In this chapter the aim is to recognize a visual category from language description without any images (also known as zero-shot learning). Humans have the capability to learn through exposure to visual categories associated with linguistic descriptions. For instance, teaching visual concepts to children is often accompanied by descriptions in text or speech.

Zero-shot learning in simple terms is a form of extending supervised learning to a setting of solving, for example, a classification problem when not enough labeled examples are available for all classes. The authors use Wikipedia articles of visual categories as the language descriptions. They denote this capability as "language-guided visual recognition (LGVR)." In this chapter, they formally define the LGVR, its benchmarks, and performance metrics. They also discuss the challenges in the zero-shot learning setting and illustrate the difference between two learning settings that they denote as the "super-category shared" setting and the harder, yet less often studied setting that they denote as "super-category-exclusive."

Chapter 6: Deep Learning for Font Recognition and Retrieval

This chapter mainly investigates the recent advances of exploiting the deep learning techniques to improve the experiences of browsing, identifying, selecting, and manipulating fonts. Thousands of different font faces have been fashioned with huge variations in the characters. There is a need for many applications such as graphic design to identify the fonts they encounter in daily life for later use. While they might take a photo of the text of an exceptionally interesting font and seek out a professional to identify the font, the manual identification process is extremely tedious and error prone. Therefore, this chapter concentrates on the two critical processes of font recognition and retrieval. Font recognition is a process that attempts to recognize fonts from an image or photo effectively and automatically to greatly facilitate font organization as a large-scale visual classification problem. Such a visual font recognition (VFR) problem is inherently difficult because of the vast space of possible fonts; the dynamic and open-ended properties of font classes; and the very subtle and character-dependent differences among fonts (letter endings, stroke weights, slopes, size, texture, and serif details, etc.). Font retrieval arises when a target font is encountered and a user/designer wants to rapidly browse and choose visually similar fonts from a large selection. Compared to the recognition task, the retrieval process allows for more flexibility, especially when an exact match to the font seen may not be available, in which case similar fonts should be returned.

Chapter 7: A Distributed Secure Machine-Learning Cloud Architecture for Semantic Analysis

The authors of this chapter have developed a scalable cloud AI platform, an open-source cloud architecture tailored for deep-learning applications. The cloud AI framework can be deployed in a well-maintained datacenter to transform it to a cloud tailor-fit for deep learning. The platform contains several layers to provide end users with a comprehensive, easy-to-use, complete, and readily deployable machine-learning platform. The architecture designed for the proposed platform employs a data-centric approach and uses fast object storage nodes to handle the high volume of data required for machine learning. Furthermore, in the case of requirements such as bigger local storage, network attachable storage devices are used to support local filesystems, strengthening the data-centric approach. This allows numerous compute nodes to access and write data from a centralized location, which can be crucial for parallel programs. The architecture described has three distinct use cases. First, it can be used as a cloud service tailored for deep-learning applications to train resource-intense deep-learning models fast and easily. Second, it can be used as a data warehouse to host petabytes of datasets and trained models. Third, the API interface can be used to deploy trained models as AI applications on the web interface or at edge and IoT devices. The proposed architecture is implemented on bare-metal OpenStack cloud nodes connected through high-speed interconnects.

Chapter 8: A Practical Look at Anomaly Detection Using Autoencoders with H2O and the R Programming Language

In this chapter, the authors have utilized the R programming language to explore different ways of applying autoencoding techniques to quickly find anomalies in data at both the row and cell level. They also explore ways of improving classification accuracy by removing extremely abnormal data to help focus a model on the most relevant patterns. A slight reduction over the original feature space will catch subtle anomalies, while a drastic reduction will catch many anomalies as the reconstruction algorithm will be overly crude and simplistic. Varying the hidden layer size will capture different points of view, which can all be interesting depending on the complexity of the original dataset and the research goals. Therefore, unsupervised autoencoders are not just about data compression or dimensionality reduction. They are also practical tools to highlight pockets of chaotic behavior, improve a model's accuracy, and, more importantly, better understand your data.

Mehdi Roopaei
Paul Rad

Chapter 1

Large-Scale Video Event Detection Using Deep Neural Networks

Guangnan Ye

Contents

1.1 Motivation

The prevalence of video capture devices and the growing practice of video sharing in social media have resulted in an enormous explosion of user-generated videos on the Internet. For example, there are more than 1 billion users on YouTube, and 300 hours of video are uploaded every minute to the website. Another media sharing website, Facebook, reported recently that the number of videos posted to the platform per person in the U.S. has increased by 94% over the last year.

There is an emerging need to construct intelligent, robust, and efficient search-and-retrieval systems to organize and index those videos. However, most current commercial video search engines rely on textual keyword matching rather than visual content-based indexing. Such keyword-based search engines often produce unsatisfactory performance because of inaccurate and insufficient textural information, as well as the well-known issue of semantic gaps that make keyword-based search engines infeasible in real-world scenarios. Thanks to recent research in computer vision and multimedia, researchers have attempted to automatically recognize people, objects, scenes, human actions, complex events, etc., and index videos based on the learned semantics in order to better understand and analyze the indexed videos by their semantic meanings. In this chapter, we are especially interested in analyzing and detecting events in videos. The automatic detection of complex events in videos can be formally defined as "detecting a complicated human activity interacting with people and object in a certain scene" [1]. Compared with object, scene, or action detection and classification, complex event detection is a more challenging task because it is often combined with complicated interactions among objects, scenes, and human activities. Complex event detection often provides higher semantic understanding in videos, and thus it has great potential for many applications, such as consumer content management, commercial advertisement recommendation, surveillance video analysis, and more.

In general, automatic detection systems, such as the one shown in Figure 1.1, contain three basic components: feature extraction, classifier, and model fusion. Given a set of training videos,

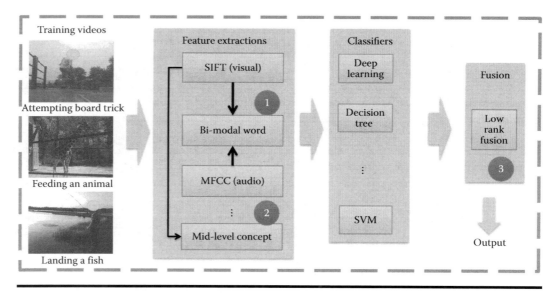

Figure 1.1   Event detection framework.

state-of-the-art systems often extract various types of features [35]. Those features can be manually designed low-level features, for example, SIFT [24], mel-frequency cepstral coefficients (MFCC) [30], etc., that do not contain any semantic information, or mid-level feature representation in which certain concept categories are defined and the probability scores from the trained concept classifiers are considered the concept features. After the feature extraction module, features from multiple modalities are used to train classifiers. Then, fusion approaches [7,10] are applied so that scores from multiple sources are combined to generate detection output. In this chapter, we focus on event detection with automatically discovered event-specific concepts with organized ontology (e.g., shown as #2 in Figure 1.1).

Analysis and detection of complex events in videos requires a semantic representation of the video content. Concept-based feature representation can not only depict a complex event in an interpretable semantic space that performs better zero-shot event retrieval, but can also be considered for mid-level features in supervised event modeling. By zero-shot retrieval here, we refer to the scenario in which the retrieval target is novel and thus there are no training videos available for training a machine learning classifier for the specific search target. A key research problem of the semantic representation is how to generate a suitable concept lexicon for events. There are two typical ways to define concepts for events. The first is an event-independent concept lexicon that directly applies object, scene, and action concepts borrowed from existing libraries, for example, ImageNet [13], SUN dataset [29], UCF 101 [17], etc. However, because the borrowed concepts are not specifically defined for target events of interest, they are often insufficient and inaccurate for capturing semantic information in event videos. Another approach requires users to predefine a concept lexicon and manually annotate the presence of those concepts in videos as training samples. This approach seems to involve tremendous manual effort, and it is infeasible for real-world applications.

In order to address these problems, we propose an automatic semantic concept discovery scheme that exploits Internet resources without human labeling effort. To distinguish the work that builds a generic concept library, we propose our approach as an event-driven concept discovery that provides more relevant concepts for events. In order to manage novel unseen events, we propose the construction of a large-scale event-driven concept library that covers as many real-world events and concepts as possible. We resort to the external knowledge base called WikiHow, a collaborative forum that aims to build the world's largest manual for human daily life events. We define EventNet, which contains 500 representative events from the articles of the WikiHow website [3], and automatically discover 4,490 event-specific concepts associated with those events. EventNet ontology is publicly considered the largest event concept library. We experimentally show dramatic performance gain in complex event detection, especially for unseen novel events. We also construct the first interactive system (to the best of our knowledge) that allows users to explore high-level events and associated concepts with certain event browsing, search, and tagging functions.

1.2 Related Work

Some recent works have focused on detecting video events using concept-based representations. For example, Wu et al. [31] mined concepts from the free-form text descriptions of the TRECVID research video set and applied them as weak concepts of the events in the TRECVID MED task. As mentioned earlier, these concepts are not specifically designed for events, and they may not capture well the semantics of event videos.

Recent research has also attempted to define event-driven concepts for event detection. Liu et al. [15] proposed to manually annotate related concepts in event videos and to build concept models with the annotated video frames. Chen et al. [12] proposed discovering event-driven concepts from the tags of Flickr images crawled using keywords of the events of interest. This method can find relevant concepts for each event and achieves good performance in various event detection tasks. Despite such promising properties, it relies heavily on prior knowledge about the target events, and therefore cannot manage novel unknown events that might emerge at a later time. Our EventNet library attempts to address this deficiency by exploring a large number of events and their related concepts from external knowledge resources, WikiHow and YouTube. A related prior work [34] tried to define several events and discover concepts using the tags of Flickr images. However, as our later experiment shows, concept models trained with Flickr images cannot generalize well to event videos because of the well-known cross-domain data variation [16]. In contrast, our method discovers concepts and trains models based on YouTube videos, which more accurately capture the semantic concepts that underlie the content of user-generated videos.

The proposed EventNet also introduces a benchmark video dataset for large-scale video event detection. Current event detection benchmarks typically contain only a small number of events. For example, in the well-known TRECVID MED task [1], significant effort has been made to develop an event video dataset that contains 48 events. The Columbia Consumer Video (CCV) dataset [37] contains 9,317 videos of 20 events. Such event categories might also suffer from data bias and thus fail to provide general models applicable to unconstrained real-world events. In contrast, EventNet contains 500 event categories and 95,000 videos that cover different aspects of human daily life. It is believed to be the largest event dataset currently. Another recent effort also attempts to build a large-scale, structured event video dataset that contains 239 events [36]. However, it does not provide semantic concepts associated with specific events, such as those defined in EventNet.

1.3 Choosing WikiHow as EventNet Ontology

A key issue in constructing a large-scale event-driven concept library is to define an ontology that covers as many real-world events as possible. For this, we resort to the Internet knowledge bases constructed from crowd intelligence as our ontology definition resources. In particular, WikiHow is an online forum that contains several how-to manuals on every aspect of human daily life events, where a user can submit an article that describes how to accomplish given tasks such as "how to bake sweet potatoes," "how to remove tree stumps," and more. We choose WikiHow as our event ontology definition resource for the following reasons:

Coverage of WikiHow Articles. WikiHow has good coverage of different aspects of human daily life events. As of February 2015, it included over 300,000 how-to articles [3], among which some are well-defined video events* that can be detected by computer vision techniques, whereas others such as "how to think" or "how to apply for a passport," do not have suitable corresponding video events. We expect a comprehensive coverage of video events from such a massive number of articles created by the crowdsourced knowledge of Internet users.

To verify that WikiHow articles have a good coverage of video events, we conduct a study to test whether WikiHow articles contain events in the existing popular event video datasets in the

---

* We define an event as a video event when it satisfies the event definition in the NIST TRECVID MED evaluation, that is, a complicated human activity that interacts with people/objects in a certain scene.

Table 1.1 Matching Results between WikiHow Article Titles and Event Classes in the Popular Event Video Datasets

Dataset	Exact Match	Partial Match	Relevant	No Match	Total Class #
KTH [22]	4	1	1	0	6
Hollywood [20]	6	0	1	0	7
CCV [37]	6	5	8	1	20
MED 10–14 [1]	16	17	5	0	48
UCF101 [17]	58	11	20	12	101
Matched class #	90	34	45	13	182

computer vision and multimedia fields. To this end, we choose the event classes in the following datasets: TRECVID MED 2010–2014 (48 classes) [1], CCV (20 classes) [37], UCF 101 (101 classes) [17], Hollywood movies (7 classes) [20], KTH (6 classes) [22]. Then, we use each event class name as a text query to search WikiHow and examine the top-10 returned articles, from which we manually select the most relevant article title as the matching result. We define four matching levels to measure the matching quality. The first is *exact match*, where the matched article title and event query are exactly matched (e.g., "clap hands" as a matched result to the query "hand clapping"). The second is *partial match*, where the matched article discusses a certain aspect of the query (e.g., "make a chocolate cake" as a result to the query "make a cake"). The third case is *relevant*, where the matched article is semantically relevant to the query (e.g., "get your car out of the snow" as a result to the query "getting a vehicle unstuck"). The fourth case is *no match*, where we cannot find any relevant articles about the query. The matching statistics are listed in Table 1.1. If we count the first three types of matching as successful cases, the coverage rate of WikiHow over these event classes is as high as $169/182 = 93\%$, which confirms the potential of discovering video events from WikiHow articles.

Hierarchical Structure of WikiHow. WikiHow categorizes all of its articles into 2,803 categories and further organizes all categories into a hierarchical tree structure. Each category contains a number of articles that discuss different aspects of the category, and each is associated with a node in the WikiHow hierarchy. As shown in Figure 1.2 of the WikiHow hierarchy, the first layer contains 19 high-level nodes that range from "arts and entertainment" and "sports and fitness" to "pets and animals." Each node is further divided into a number of children nodes that are subclasses or facets of the parent node, with the deepest path from the root to the leaf node containing seven levels. Although such a hierarchy is not based on lexical knowledge, it summarizes humans' common practice of organizing daily life events. Typically, a parent category node includes articles that are more generic than those in its children nodes. Therefore, the events that reside along a similar path in the WikiHow tree hierarchy are highly relevant (cf. Section 1.4). Such hierarchical structure helps users quickly localize the potential search area in the hierarchy for a specific query in which he/she is interested and thus improves concept-matching accuracy (cf. Section 1.7). In addition, such hierarchical structure also enhances event detection performance by leveraging the detection result of an event in a parent node to boost detection of the events in its children nodes and vice versa. Finally, such hierarchical structure also allows us to develop an intuitive browsing interface for event navigation and event detection result visualization [11], as shown in Figure 1.3.

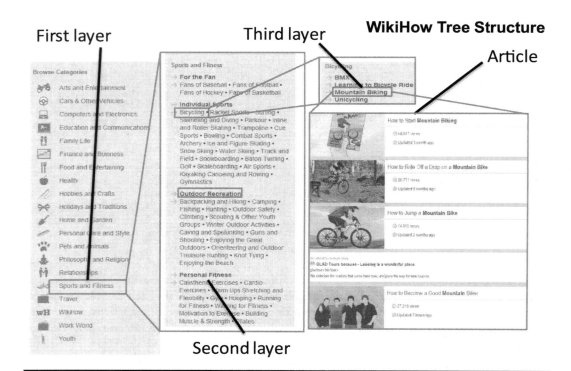

Figure 1.2 The hierarchial structure of WikiHow.

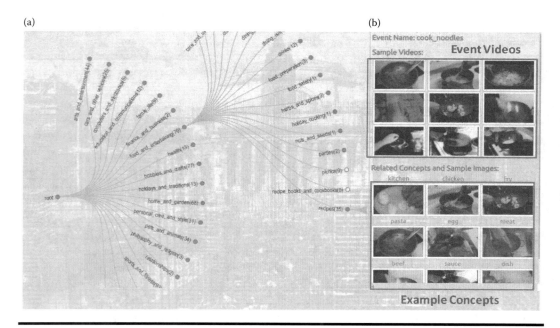

Figure 1.3 Event and concept browser for the proposed EventNet ontology. (a) The hierarchical structure. (b) Example videos and relevant concepts of each specific event.

1.4 Constructing EventNet

In this section, we describe the procedure used to construct EventNet, including how to define video events from WikiHow articles and discover event-specific concepts for each event from the tags of YouTube videos.

1.4.1 Discovering Events

First we aim to discover potential video events from WikiHow articles. Intuitively, this can be done by crawling videos using each article title and then applying the automatic verification technique proposed in References 12 and 33 to determine whether an article corresponds to a video event. However, considering that there are 300,000 articles on WikiHow, this requires a massive amount of data crawling and video processing, thus making it computationally infeasible. For this, we propose a coarse-to-fine event selection approach. The basic idea is to first prune WikiHow categories that do not correspond to video events and then select one representative event from the article titles within each of the remaining categories. In the following, we describe the event selection procedure in detail.

Step I: WikiHow Category Pruning. Recall that WikiHow contains 2,803 categories, each of which contains a number of articles about the category. We observe that many of the categories refer to personal experiences and suggestions that do not correspond to video events. For example, the articles in the category "Living Overseas" explain how to improve the living experience in a foreign country and do not satisfy the definition of a video event. Therefore, we want to find such event-irrelevant categories and directly filter their articles, in order to significantly prune the number of articles to be verified in the next stage. To this end, we analyze 2,803 WikiHow categories and manually remove those that are irrelevant to video events. A category is deemed as event irrelevant when it cannot be visually described by a video and none of its articles contains any video events. For example, "Living Overseas" is an event-irrelevant category because "Living Overseas" is not visually observable in videos and none of its articles are events. On the other hand, although the category "Science" cannot be visually described in a video because of its abstract meaning, it contains some instructional articles that correspond to video events, such as "Make Hot Ice" and "Use a Microscope." As a result, in our manual pruning procedure, we first find the name of a category to be pruned and then carefully review its articles before deciding to remove the category.

Step II: Category-Based Event Selection. After category pruning, only event-relevant categories and their articles remain. Under each category, there are still several articles that do not correspond to events. Our final goal is to find all video events from these articles and include them in our event collection, which is a long-term goal of the EventNet project. In the current version, EventNet only includes one representative video event from each category of WikiHow ontology. An article title is considered to be a video event when it satisfies the following four conditions: (1) It defines an event that involves a human activity interacting with people/objects in a certain scene. (2) It has concrete non-subjective meanings. For example, "decorating a romantic bedroom" is too subjective because different users have a different interpretation of "romantic." (3) It has consistent observable visual characteristics. For example, a simple method is to use the candidate event name to search YouTube and check whether there are consistent visual tags found in the top returned videos. Tags may be approximately considered visual if they can be found in existing image ontology, such as ImageNet. (4) It is generic and not too detailed. If many article titles under a category share the same verb and direct object, they can be formed into a generic event name. After this, we end with 500 event categories as the current event collection in EventNet.

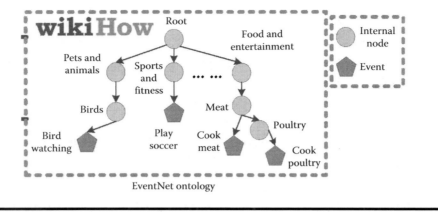

Figure 1.4   A snapshot of EventNet constructed from WikiHow.

1.4.2 Mining Event-Specific Concepts

We apply the concept discovery method developed in our prior work [12] to discover event-driven concepts from the tags of YouTube videos. For each of the 500 events, we use the event name as query keywords to search YouTube. We check the top 1,000 returned videos and collect the ten most frequent words that appear in the titles or tags of these videos. Then we further filter the 1,000 videos to include only those videos that contain at least three of the frequent words. This step helps us remove many irrelevant videos from the search results. Using this approach, we crawl approximately 190 videos and their tag lists as a concept discovery resource for each event, ending with 95,321 videos for 500 events. We discover event-specific concepts from the tags of the crawled videos. To ensure the visual detectability of the discovered concepts, we match each tag to the classes of the existing object (ImageNet [13]), scene (SUN [29]), and action (Action Bank [32]) libraries, and we only keep the matched words as the candidate concepts. After going through the process, we end with approximately nine concepts per event, and a total of 4,490 concepts for the entire set of 500 events. Finally, we adopt the hierarchical structure of WikiHow categories and attach each discovered event and its concepts to the corresponding category node. The final event concept ontology is called EventNet, as illustrated in Figure 1.4.

One could argue that the construction of EventNet ontology depends heavily on subjective evaluation. In fact, we can replace such subjective evaluation with automatic methods from computer vision and natural language processing techniques. For example, we can use concept visual verification to measure the visual detectability of concepts [12] and use text-based event extraction to determine whether each article title is an event [8]. However, as the accuracy of such automatic methods is still being improved, currently we focus on the design of principled criteria for event discovery and defer the incorporation of automatic discovery processes until future improvement.

1.5 Properties of EventNet

In this section, we provide a detailed analysis of the properties of EventNet ontology, including basic statistics about the ontology, event distribution over coarse categories, and event redundancy.

EventNet Statistics. EventNet ontology contains 682 WikiHow category nodes, 500 event nodes, and 4,490 concept nodes organized in a tree structure, where the deepest depth from the

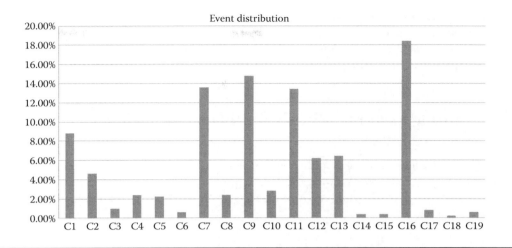

Figure 1.5 Event distribution over the top-19 categories of EventNet. From C1 to C19 are respectively "Arts and Entertainment," "Cars and Other Vehicles," "Computers and Electronics," "Education and Communications," "Family Life," "Finance and Business," "Food and Entertaining," "Health," "Hobbies and Crafts," "Holidays and Traditions," "Home and Garden," "Personal Care and Style," "Pets and Animals," "Philosophy and Religion," "Relationships," "Sports and Fitness," "Travel," "Work World," and "Youth."

root node to the leaf node (the event node) is eight. Each non-leaf category node has four child category nodes on average. Regarding the video statistics in EventNet, the average number of videos per event is 190, and the number of videos per concept is 21. EventNet has 95,321 videos with an average duration of approximately 277 seconds (7,334 hours in total).

Event Distribution. We show the percentage of the number of events distributed over the top-19 category nodes of EventNet, and the results are shown in Figure 1.5. As can be seen, the top four popular categories that include the greatest number of events are "Sports and Fitness," "Hobbies and Crafts," "Food and Entertainment," and "Home and Garden," whereas the least four populated categories are "Work World," "Relationships," "Philosophy and Religion," and "Youth," which are abstract and cannot be described in videos. A further glimpse of the event distributions tells us that the most popular categories reflect the users' common interests in video content creation. For example, most event videos captured in human daily life refer to their lifestyles, reflected in food, fitness, and hobbies. Therefore, we believe that the events included in EventNet have the potential to be used as an event concept library to detect popular events in human daily life.

Event Redundancy. We also conduct an analysis on the redundancy among the 500 events in EventNet. To this end, we use each event name as a text query, and find its most semantically similar events from other events located at different branches from the query event. In particular, given a query event e_q, we first localize its category node C_q in the EventNet tree structure, and then exclude all events attached under the parent and children nodes of node C_q. The events attached to other nodes are treated as the search base to find similar events of the query based on the semantic similarity described in Section 1.7. The reason for excluding events in the same branch of the query event is that those events that reside in the parent and children category nodes manifest hierarchical relationships such as "cook meat" and "cook poultry." We treat such hierarchical event pairs as a desired property of the EventNet library, and therefore we do not involve them in the redundancy analysis. From the top-5 ranked events for a given query, we ask human annotators to determine whether there is a redundant event that refers to the same event as the query. After applying all 500 events as queries, we find zero redundancy among query events and all other events that reside in different branches of the EventNet structure.

1.6 Learning Concept Models from Deep Learning Video Features

In this section, we introduce the procedure for learning concept classifiers for the EventNet concept library. Our learning framework leverages the recent powerful CNN model to extract deep learning features from video content, while employing one-vs-all linear SVM trained on top of the features as concept models.

1.6.1 Deep Feature Learning with CNN

We adopt the CNN architecture in Reference 6 as the deep learning model to perform deep feature learning from video content. The network takes the RGB video frame as input and outputs the score distribution over the 500 events in EventNet. The network has five successive convolutional layers followed by two fully connected layers. Detailed information about the network architecture can be found in Reference 6. In this work, we apply *Caffe* [2] as the implementation of the CNN model described in Reference 6.

For training of the EventNet CNN model, we evenly sample 40 frames from each video, and end with 4 million frames over all 500 events as the training set. For each of the 500 events, we treat the frames sampled from its videos as the positive training samples of this event. We define the set of 500 events as $E = \{0, 1, \ldots, 499\}$. Then the prediction probability of the kth event for input sample n is defined as

$$p_{nk} = \frac{\exp(x_{nk})}{\sum_{k' \in E} \exp(x_{nk'})}, \tag{1.1}$$

where x_{nk} is the kth node's output of the nth input sample from CNN's last layer. The loss function L is defined as a multinomial logistic loss of the softmax, which is $L = (-1/N) \sum_{n=1}^{N} \log(p_{n,l_n})$, where $l_n \in E$ indicates the correct class label for input sample n, and N is the total number of inputs. Our CNN model is trained on an NVIDIA Tesla K20 GPU, and it requires approximately 7 days to finish 450,000 iterations of training. After CNN training, we extract the 4,096-dimensional feature vector from the second to the last layer of the CNN architecture, and further we perform ℓ_2 normalization on the feature vector as the deep learning feature descriptor of each video frame.

1.6.2 Concept Model Training

Given a concept discovered for an event, we treat the videos associated with this concept as positive training data, and we randomly sample the same number of videos from concepts in other events as negative training data. This obviously has the risk of generating false negatives (a video without a certain concept label does not necessarily mean it is negative for the concept). However, in view of the prohibitive cost of annotating all videos over all concepts, we follow this common practice used in other image ontologies such as ImageNet [13]. We directly treat frames in positive videos as positive and frames in negative videos as negative to train a linear SVM classifier as the concept model. This is a simplified approach. Emerging works [18] can select more precise temporal segments or frames in videos as positive samples.

To generate concept scores on a given video, we first uniformly sample frames from it and extract the 4,096-dimensional CNN features from each frame. Then we apply the 4,490 concept models to each frame and use all 4,490 concept scores as the concept representation of this frame. Finally, we average the score vectors across all frames and adopt the average score vector as the video level concept representation.

1.7 Leveraging EventNet Structure for Concept Matching

In concept-based event detection, the first step is to find some semantically relevant concepts that are applicable for detecting videos with respect to the event query. This procedure is called *concept matching* in the literature [12,31]. To accomplish this task, the existing approaches typically calculate the semantic similarity between the query event and each concept in the library based on external semantic knowledge bases such as WordNet [28] or ConceptNet [23] and then select the top-ranked concepts as the relevant concepts for event detection. However, these approaches might not be applicable to our EventNet concept library because the involved concepts are event specific and depend on their associative events. For example, the concept "dog" under "feed a dog" and "groom a dog" is treated as two different concepts because of the different event context. Therefore, concept matching in EventNet needs to consider event contextual information.

To this end, we propose a multistep concept-matching approach that first finds relevant events and then chooses those from the concepts associated with the matched events. In particular, given an event query e_q and an event e in the EventNet library, we use the textual phrase similarity calculation function developed in Reference 19 to estimate their semantic similarity. The reason for adopting such a semantic similarity function is that both event query and candidate events in the EventNet library are textual phrases that need a sophisticated phrase-level similarity calculation that supports the word sequence alignment and strong generalization ability achieved by machine learning. However, these properties cannot be achieved using the standard similarity computation methods based on WordNet or ConceptNet alone. Our empirical studies confirm that the phrase-based semantic similarity can obtain better event-matching results.

However, because of word sense ambiguity and the limited amount of text information in event names, the phrase-similarity-based matching approach can also generate wrong matching results. For example, given the query "wedding shower," the event "take a shower" in EventNet receives a high similarity value because "shower" has an ambiguous meaning, and it is mistakenly matched as a relevant event. Likewise, the best matching results for the query "landing a fish" are "landing an airplane" and "cook fish" rather than "fishing," which is the most relevant. To address these problems, we propose exploiting the structure of the EventNet ontology to find relevant events for such difficult query events. In particular, given the query event, users can manually specify the suitable categories in the top level of the EventNet structure. For instance, users can easily specify that the suitable category for the event "wedding shower" is "Family Life," while choosing "Sports and Fitness" and "Hobbies and Crafts" as suitable categories for "landing a fish." After the user's specification, subsequent event matching only needs to be conducted over the events under the specified high-level categories. This way, the hierarchical structure of EventNet ontology is helpful in relieving the limitations of short text-based semantic matching and helps improve concept-matching accuracy. After we obtain the top matched events, we can further choose concepts based on their semantic similarity to the query event. Quantitative evaluations between the matching methods can be found in Section 1.8.4.

1.8 Experiments

In this section, we evaluate the effectiveness of the EventNet concept library in concept-based event detection. We first introduce the dataset and experiment setup and then report the performance of different methods in the context of various event detection tasks, including zero-shot event retrieval and semantic recounting. After this, we study the efforts of leveraging the EventNet structure for matching concepts in zero-shot event retrieval. Finally, we will treat the 95,000 videos over 500 events in EventNet as a video event benchmark and report the baseline performance of using the CNN model in event detection.

1.8.1 Dataset and Experiment Setup

Dataset. We use two benchmark video event datasets as the test sets of our experiments to verify the effectiveness of the EventNet concept library. (1) The *TRECVID 2013 MED* dataset [1] contains 32,744 videos that span over 20 event classes and the distracting background, whose names are "E1: *birthday party*," "E2: *changing a vehicle tire*," "E3: *flash mob gathering*," "E4: *getting a vehicle unstuck*," "E5: *grooming an animal*," "E6: *making a sandwich*," "E7: *parade*," "E8: *parkour*," "E9: *repairing an appliance*," "E10: *working on a sewing project*," "E11: *attempting a bike trick*," "E12: *cleaning an appliance*," "E13: *dog show*," "E14: *giving directions to a location*," "E15: *marriage proposal*," "E16: *renovating a home*," "E17: *rock climbing*," "E18: *town hall meeting*," "E19: *winning a race without a vehicle*," and "E20: *working on a metal crafts project*." We follow the original partition of this dataset in the TRECVID MED evaluation, which partitions the dataset into a training set with 7,787 videos and a test set with 24,957 videos. (2) The *Columbia Consumer Video (CCV)* dataset [37] contains 9,317 videos that span over 20 classes, which are "E1: *basketball*," "E2: *baseball*," "E3: *soccer*," "E4: *ice skating*," "E5: *skiing*," "E6: *swimming*," "E7: *biking*," "E8: *cat*," "E9: *dog*," "E10: *bird*," "E11: *graduation*," "E12: *birthday*," "E13: *wedding reception*," "E14: *wedding ceremony*," "E15: *wedding dance*," "E16: *music performance*," "E17: *non-music performance*," "E18: *parade*," "E19: *beach*," and "E20: *playground*." The dataset is further divided into 4,659 training videos and 4,658 test videos. Because we focus on zero-shot event detection, we do not use the training videos in these two datasets, but only test the performance on the test set. For supervised visual recognition, features from deep learning models, for example, the last few layers of deep learning models learned over ImageNet 1K or 20K) can be directly used to detect events [25]. However, the focus of this paper is on the semantic description power of the event-specific concepts, especially in recounting the semantic concepts in event detection and finding relevant concepts for retrieving events not been seen before (zero-shot retrieval).

Feature Extraction. On the two evaluation event video datasets, we extract the same features that we did for EventNet videos. In particular, we sample one frame every 2 seconds from a video and extract the 4,096-dimensional deep learning features from the CNN model trained on EventNet video frames. Then we run SVM-based concept models over each frame and aggregate the score vectors in a video as the semantic concept feature of the video.

Comparison Methods and Evaluation Metric. We compare different concept-based video representations produced by the following methods. (1) **Classemes** [21] is a 2,659-dimensional concept representation whose concepts are defined based on LSCOM concept ontology. We directly extract

Classemes on each frame and then average them across the video as video-level concept representation. (2) In Flickr Concept Representation (**FCR**) [34], for each event, the concepts are automatically discovered from the tags of Flickr images in the search results of the event query and organized based on WikiHow ontology. The concept detection models are based on the binary multiple kernel linear SVM classifiers trained with the Flickr images associated with each concept. Five types of low-level features are adopted to represent Flickr images and event video frames. (3) For ImageNet-1K CNN Concept Representation (**ICR-1K**), we directly apply the network architecture in Reference 6 to train a CNN model over 1.2 million high-resolution images in the ImageNet LSVRC-2010 contest that covers 1,000 different classes [13]. After model training, we apply the CNN model on the frames from both the TRECVID MED and CCV datasets. Concept scores of the individual frames in a video are averaged to form the concept scores of the video. We treat the 1,000 output scores as the concept-based video representation from ImageNet-1K. (4) For the ImageNet-20K CNN Concept Representation (**ICR-20K**), we apply the same network architecture as ICR-1K to train a CNN model using over 20 million images that span over 20,574 classes from the latest release of ImageNet [13]. We treat the 20,574 concept scores output from the CNN model as the concept representation. Notably, ICR-1K and ICR-20K represent the most successful visual recognition achievements in the computer vision area, which can be applied to justify the superiority of our EventNet concept library over the state of the art. (5) In our proposed EventNet-CNN Concept Representation (**ECR**), we use our EventNet concept library to generate concept-based video representations. (6) Finally, we note some state-of-the-art results reported in the literature. Regarding the evaluation metric, we adopt AP, which approximates the area under the precision/recall curve, to measure the performance on each event in our evaluation datasets. Finally, we calculate mAP over all event classes as the overall evaluation metric.

1.8.2 Task I: Zero-Shot Event Retrieval

Our first experiment evaluates the performance of zero-shot event retrieval, where we do not use any training videos, but completely depend on the concept scores on test videos. To this end, we use each event name in the two video datasets as a query to match the two most relevant events. We choose the 15 most relevant EventNet concepts based on semantic similarity, and then we average the scores of these 15 concepts as the zero-shot event detection score of the video, through which a video ranking list can be generated. Notably, the two most relevant events mentioned above are automatically selected based on the semantic similarity matching method described in Section 1.7. For Classemes and FCR, we follow the setting in Reference 34 to choose 100 relevant concepts based on semantic similarity using ConceptNet and the concept-matching method described in Reference 34. For ICR-1K and ICR-20K, we choose 15 concepts using the same concept-matching method.

Figure 1.6 [9] shows the performance of different methods on two datasets. From the results, we obtain the following observations: (1) Event-specific concept representations, including FCR and ECR, outperform the event-independent concept representation Classemes. This is because the former not only discovers semantically relevant concepts of the event, but also leverages the contextual information about the event in the training samples of each concept. In contrast, the latter only borrows concepts that are not specifically designed for events, and the training images for concept classifiers do not contain the event-related contextual information. (2) Concept representations trained with deep CNN features, including ICR-20K and ECR, produce much higher performance than the concept representations learned from low-level features, including Classemes and FCR, for most of the events. This is reasonable because the CNN model can extract learning-based

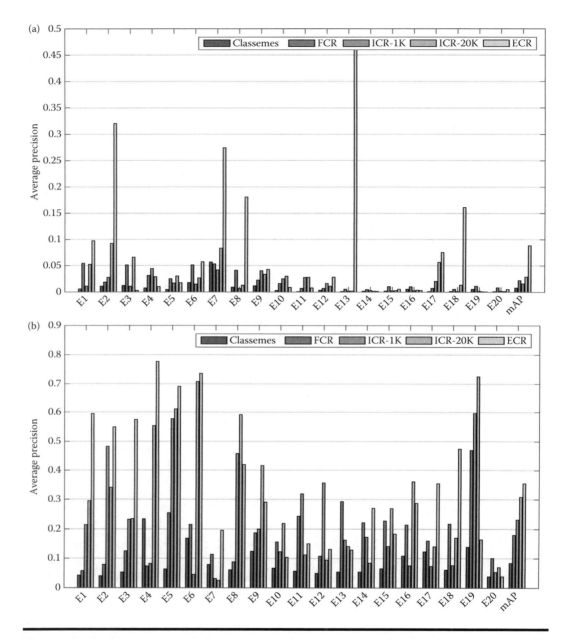

Figure 1.6 Performance comparisons on zero-shot event retrieval task (a: MED; b: CCV). This figure is best viewed in color.

features that have been shown to achieve strong performance. (3) Although all are trained with deep learning features, ECR generated by our proposed EventNet concept library performs significantly better than ICR-1K and ICR-20K, which are generated by deep learning models trained on ImageNet images. The reason is that concepts in EventNet are more relevant to events than the concepts in ImageNet, which are mostly objects independent of events. From this result, we can see that our EventNet concepts even outperformed the concepts from the state-of-the-art visual recognition system, and it is believed to be a powerful concept library for the task of zero-shot event retrieval.

Notably, our ECR achieves significant performance gains over the best baseline ICR-20K, where the mAP on TRECVID MED increases from 2.89% to 8.86% with 207% relative improvement. Similarly, the mAP on CCV increases from 30.82% to 35.58% (15.4% relative improvement). Moreover, our ECR achieves the best performance on most event categories on each dataset. For instance, on the event "E02: *changing a vehicle tire*" from the TRECVID MED dataset, our method outperforms the best baseline ICR-20K by 246% relative improvement. On the TRECVID MED dataset, the reason for the large improvement on "E13: *dog show*" is that the matched events contain exactly the same event "dog show" as the event query. The performance on E10 and E11 is not so good because the automatic event-matching method matched them to the wrong events. When we use the EventNet structure to correct the matching errors as described in Section 1.8.4, we achieve higher performance on these events.

In Figure 1.7 [9], we show the impact on zero-shot event retrieval performance when the number of concepts changes using the concept-matching method described in Section 1.7; that is, we first find the matched events and then select the top-ranked concepts that belong to these events. We select the number of events until the desired number of concepts is reached. On TRECVID MED, we can see consistent and significant performance gains for our proposed ECR method over others. However, on the CCV dataset, ICR-20K achieves similar or even better performance when several concepts are adopted. We conjecture that this occurs because the CCV dataset contains a number of object categories, such as "E8: *cat*" and "E9: *dog*," which might be better described by the visual objects contained in the ImageNet dataset. Alternatively, all the events in TRECVID MED are highly complicated, and they might be better described by EventNet. It is worth mentioning that mAP first increases and then decreases as we choose more concepts from EventNet. This is because our concept-matching method always ranks the most relevant concepts on top of the concept list. Therefore, involving many less relevant concepts ranked at lower positions (after the tenth position in this experiment) in the concept list might decrease performance. In Table 1.2, we compare our results with the state-of-the-art results reported on the TRECVID MED 2013 test set with the same experiment setting. We can see that our ECR method outperforms these results by a large margin.

1.8.3 Task II: Semantic Recounting in Videos

Given a video, semantic recounting aims to annotate the video with the semantic concepts detected in the video. Because we have the concept-based representation generated for the videos using the concept classifiers described earlier, we can directly use it to produce recounting. In particular, we rank the 4,490 event-specific concept scores on a given video in descending order, and then we choose the top-ranked ones as the most salient concepts that occur in the video. Figure 1.8 shows the recounting results for some sample videos from the TRECVID MED and CCV datasets. As can be seen, the concepts generated by our method precisely reveal the semantics presented in the videos.

It is worth noting that the EventNet ontology also provides great benefits for developing a real-time semantic recounting system that requires high efficiency and accuracy. Compared with other concept libraries that use generic concepts, EventNet allows selected execution of a small set of concepts specific to an event. Given a video to be recounted, it first predicts the most relevant events and then applies only those concepts that are specific to these events. This unique two-step

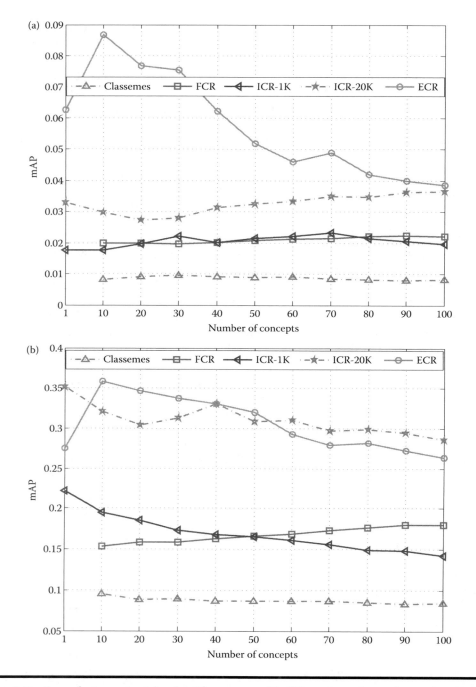

Figure 1.7   Zero-shot event retrieval performance with different numbers of concepts (a: MED; b: CCV). The results of Classemes and FCR are from the literature, in which the results when the concept number is 1 are not reported.

Table 1.2   Comparisons between our ECR with Other State-of-the-Art Concept-Based Video Representation Methods Built on Visual Content

Method	mAP (%)
Bi-concept [5,27]	3.45
Weak concept [31]	3.48
Selective concept [5,26]	4.39
Composite concept [5]	5.97
Annotated concept [14]	6.50
Our EventNet concept	8.86

Note: All results are obtained in the task of zero-shot event retrieval on TRECVID MED 2013 test set.

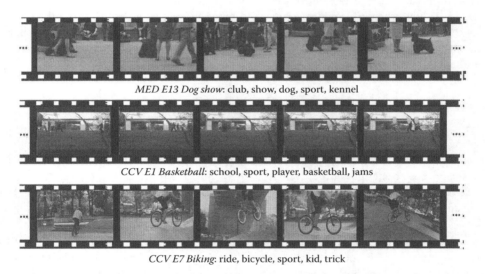

MED E13 Dog show: club, show, dog, sport, kennel

CCV E1 Basketball: school, sport, player, basketball, jams

CCV E7 Biking: ride, bicycle, sport, kid, trick

Figure 1.8   Event video recounting results: Each row shows evenly subsampled frames of a video and the top 5 concepts detected in the video.

approach can greatly improve the efficiency and accuracy of multimedia event recounting because only a small number of event-specific concept classifiers need to be started after event detection.

1.8.4 Task III: Effects of EventNet Structure for Concept Matching

As discussed in Section 1.7, because of the limitations of text-based similarity matching, the matching result of an event query might not be relevant. In this case, the EventNet structure can

Table 1.3 Comparison of Zero-Shot Event Retrieval Using the Concepts Matched without and with Leveraging EventNet Structure

Method (mAP %)	MED	CCV
Without EventNet structure	8.86	35.58
With EventNet structure	8.99	36.07

help users find relevant events and their associated concepts from the EventNet concept library. Here we first perform quantitative empirical studies to verify this. In particular, for each event query, we manually specify two suitable categories from the top 19 nodes of the EventNet tree structure, and then we match events under these categories based on semantic similarity. We compare the results obtained by matching all events in EventNet (i.e., without leveraging the Event-Net structure) with the results obtained by the method we described above (i.e., with leveraging the EventNet structure). For each query, we apply each method to 15 select concepts from the EventNet library and then use them to perform zero-shot event retrieval.

Table 1.3 shows the performance comparison between the two methods. From the results, we can see that event retrieval performance can be improved if we apply the concepts matched with the help of EventNet structure, which proves the usefulness of EventNet structure for the task of concept matching.

1.8.5 Task IV: Multiclass Event Classification

The 95,321 videos over 500 event categories in EventNet can also be seen as a benchmark video dataset to study large-scale event detection. To facilitate direct comparison, we provide standard data partitions and some baseline results over these partitions. It is worth noting that one important purpose of designing the EventNet video dataset is to use it as a testbed for large-scale event detection models, such as a deep convolutional neutral network. Therefore, in the following, we summarize a baseline implementation using the state-of-the-art CNN models, as done in Reference 13.

Data Division. Recall that each of the 500 events in EventNet has approximately 190 videos. In our experiment, we divide the videos and adopt 70% of the videos as the training set, 10% as the validation set, and 20% as the test set. In all, there are approximately 70,000 (2.8 million frames), 10,000 (0.4 million frames), and 20,000 (0.8 million frames) training, validation, and test videos, respectively.

Deep Learning Model. We adopt the same network architecture and learning settings as the CNN model described in Section 1.6.1 as our multiclass event classification model. In the training process, for each event, we treat the frames sampled from the training videos of an event as positive training samples and feed them into the CNN model for model training. Seven days are required to finish 450,000 iterations of training. In the test stage, to produce predictions for a test video, we take the average of the frame-level probabilities over sampled frames in a video and use it as the video-level prediction result.

Evaluation Metric. Regarding the evaluation metric, we adopt the most popular top-1 and top-5 accuracies commonly used in large-scale visual recognition, where the top-1 (top-5) accuracy is a

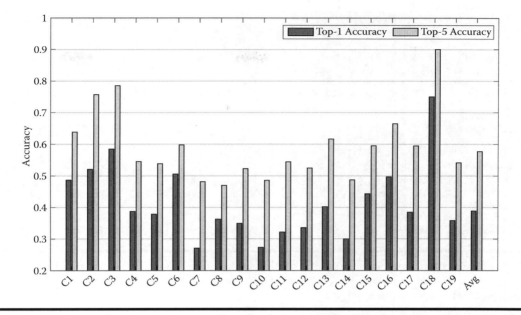

Figure 1.9 **Top-1 and top-5 event classification accuracies over 19 high-level event categories of EventNet structure, in which the average top-1 and top-5 accuracy are 38.91% and 57.67%.**

fraction of the test videos for which the correct label is among the top-1 (top-5) labels predicted to be most probable by the model.

Results. We report the multiclass classification performance by 19 high-level categories of events in the top layer of the EventNet ontology. To achieve this, we collect all events under each of the 19 high-level categories in EventNet (e.g., 68 events under "home and garden"); calculate the accuracy of each event; and then calculate their mean value over the events within this high-level category. As seen in Figure 1.9 [9], most high-level categories show impressive classification performance. To illustrate the results, we choose four event video frames and show their top-5 prediction results in Figure 1.10.

1.9 Large-Scale Video Event and Concept Ontology Applications

In this section, we present several applications using our large-scale video event and concept ontology. In particular, the novel functions of our EventNet system include interactive browser, semantic search, and live tagging of user-uploaded videos. In each of the modules, we emphasize the unique ontological structure embedded in EventNet and utilize it to achieve a novel experience. For example, the event browser leverages the hierarchical event structure discovered from the crowdsourced forum WikiHow to facilitate intuitive exploration of events, the search engine focuses on retrieval of hierarchical paths that contain events of interest rather than events as independent entities, and finally the live detection module applies the event models and associated concept models to explain why a specific event is detected in an uploaded video. To the best of our knowledge, this is the first interactive system that allows users to explore high-level events and associated concepts in videos in a systematic structured manner.

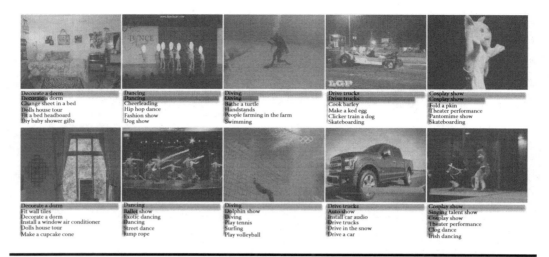

Figure 1.10 Event detection results of some sample videos. The five events with the highest detection scores are shown in descending order. The bar length indicates the score of each event. The event with the red bar is the ground truth.

1.9.1 Application I: Event Ontology Browser

Our system allows users to browse the EventNet tree ontology in an interactive and intuitive manner. When a user clicks a non-leaf category node, the child category nodes are expanded along with any event attached to this category (the event node is filled in red, whereas the category node is in green). When the user clicks an event, the exemplary videos for this event are shown with a dynamic GIF animation of the keyframes extracted from a sample video. Concepts specific to the event are also shown with representative keyframes of the concept. We specifically adopt the expandable, rotatable tree as the visualization tool because it maintains a nice balance between the depth and breadth of the scope when the user navigates through layers and siblings in the tree.

1.9.2 Application II: Semantic Search of Events in the Ontology

We adopt a unique search interface that is different from the conventional ones by allowing users to find hierarchical paths that match user interest, instead of treating events as independent units. This design is important for fully leveraging the ontology structure information in EventNet. For each event in EventNet, we generate its text representation by combining all words of the category names from the root node to the current category that contains the event, plus the name of the event. Such texts are used to set up search indexes in Java Lucene [4]. When the user searches for keywords, the system returns all the paths in the index that contain the query keywords. If the query contains more than one word, the path with more matched keywords is ranked higher in the search result. After the search, the users can click each returned event. Then our system dynamically expands the corresponding path of this event and visualizes it using the tree browser described in the previous section. This not only helps users quickly find target events, but also helps suggest additional events to the user by showing events that could exist in the sibling categories in the EventNet hierarchy.

1.9.3 Application III: Automatic Video Tagging

EventNet includes an upload function that allows users to upload any video and use pretrained detection models to predict the events and concepts present in the video. For each uploaded video, EventNet extracts one frame every 10 seconds. Each frame is then resized to 256 by 256 pixels and fed to the deep learning model described earlier. We average the 500-dimensional detection scores across all extracted frames and use the average score vector as the event detection scores of the video. To present the final detection result, we only show the top event with the highest score as the event prediction of the video. For concept detection, we use the feature in the second-to-last layer of the deep learning model computed over each frame, and then we apply the binary SVM classifiers to compute the concept scores on each frame. We show the top-ranked predicted concepts under each sampled frame of the uploaded video. It is worth mentioning that our tagging system is very fast and satisfies real-time requirements. For example, when we upload a 10 MB video, the tagging system can generate tagging results in 5 seconds on a single regular workstation, demonstrating the high efficiency of the system.

1.10 Summary and Discussion

We introduced EventNet, a large-scale, structured, event-driven concept library, for representing complex events in video. The library contains 500 events mined from WikiHow and 4,490 event-specific concepts discovered from YouTube video tags, for which large margin classifiers are trained with deep learning features over 95,321 YouTube videos. The events and concepts are further organized into a tree structure based on the WikiHow ontology. Extensive experiments on two benchmark event datasets showed major performance improvement of the proposed concept library over zero-shot event retrieval task. We also showed that the tree structure of EventNet helps match the event queries to semantically relevant concepts. Lastly, we demonstrated novel applications on EventNet, the largest event ontology existing today (to the best of our knowledge) with a hierarchical structure extracted from the popular crowdsourced forum WikiHow. The system provides efficient event browsing and search interfaces and supports live video tagging with high accuracy. It also provides a flexible framework for future scaling up by allowing users to add new event nodes to the ontology structure.

References

1. http://www.nist.gov/itl/iad/mig/med.cfm, 2010.
2. http://caffe.berkeleyvision.org, 2013.
3. http://www.wikihow.com/Main-Page, 2015.
4. https://lucene.apache.org/core/, 2015.
5. T. Mensink, A. Habibian, and C. Snoek: Composite concept discovery for zero-shot video event detection. In *ICMR*, 2014.
6. I. Sutskever, A. Krizhevsky, and G. Hinton: ImageNet classification with deep convolutional neural networks. In *NIPS*, 2012.
7. S. Canu, A. Rakotomamonjy, F.R. Bach, and Y. Grandvalet: Simplemkl. *Journal of Machine Learning Research*, 2009.
8. O. Etzioni, A. Ritter, Mausam, and S. Clark: Open domain event extraction from Twitter. In *KDD*, 2012.

9. H. X.-D. Liu, G. Ye, Y. Li, and S.-F. Chang. Eventnet: A large scale structured concept library for complex event etection in video. In *MM*, 2015.

10. I.-H. Jhuo, G. Ye, D. Liu, and S.-F. Chang: Robust late fusion with rank minimization. In *CVPR*, 2012.

11. Y. Li, D. Liu, H. Xu, G. Ye, and S.-F. Chang: Large video event ontology browsing, search and tagging (eventnet demo). In *MM*, 2015.

12. G. Ye, D. Liu, J. Chen, Y. Cui, and S.-F. Chang: Event-driven semantic concept discovery by exploiting weakly tagged internet images. In *ICMR*, 2014.

13. R. Socher, L.-J. Li, K. Li, J. Deng, W. Dong, and L. Fei-Fei: ImageNet: A large-scale hierarchical image database. In *CVPR*, 2009.

14. O. Javed, Q. Yu, I. Chakraborty, W. Zhang, A. Divakaran, H. Sawhney, J. Allan et al.: Sri-Sarnoff aurora system at Trecvid 2013 multimedia event detection and recounting. *NIST TRECVID Workshop*, 2013.

15. O. Javed, S. Ali, A. Tamrakar, A. Divakaran, H. Cheng, J. Liu, Q. Yu, and H. Sawhney: Video event recognition using concept attributes. In *WACV*, 2012.

16. M. Fritz, K. Saenko, B. Kulis, and T. Darrell: Adapting visual category models to new domains. In *ECCV*, 2010.

17. A. Zamir, K. Soomro, and M. Shah: Ucf101: A dataset of 101 human action classes from videos in the wild. *CRCV-TR*, 2012.

18. M.-S. Chen, K.-T. Lai, D. Liu, and S.-F. Chang: Recognizing complex events in videos by learning key static-dynamic evidences. In *ECCV*, 2014.

19. T. Finin, J. Mayfield, L. Han, A. Kashyap, and J. Weese: Umbc ebiquity-core: Semantic textual similarity systems. In *ACL*, 2013.

20. C. Schmid, L. Laptev, M. Marszaek, and B. Rozenfeld: Learning realistic human actions from movies. In *CVPR*, 2008.

21. M. Szummer, L. Torresani, and A. Fitzgibbon: Efficient object category recognition using Classemes. In *ECCV*, 2010.

22. I. Laptev and T. Lindeberg: Space-time interest points. In *ICCV*, 2003.

23. H. Liu and P. Singh: Conceptnet: A pratical commonsense reasoning toolkit. *BT Technology Journal*, 2004.

24. D. Lowe: Distinctive image features from scale-invariant keypoints. *IJCV*, 2004.

25. J. Gemert, M. Jain, and C. Snoek: University of Amsterdam at Thumos Challenge 2014. In *Thumos Challenge*, 2014.

26. K. Sande, M. Mazloom, E. Gavves, and C. Snoek: Searching informative concept banks for video event detection. In *ICMR*, 2013.

27. D. Parikh, M. Rastegari, A. Diba, and A. Farhadi: Multi-attribute queries: To merge or not to merge? In *CVPR*, 2013.

28. G. Miller: Wordnet: A lexical database for English. *Communications of the ACM*, 1995.

29. G. Patterson and J. Hays: Sun attribute database: Discovering, annotating, and recognizing scene attributes. In *CVPR*, 2012.

30. L. Pols: Spectral analysis and identification of dutch vowels in monosyllabic words. Doctoral dissertion, Free University, Amsterdam, 1966.

31. F. Luisier, X. Zhuang, S. Wu, S. Bondugula, and P. Natarajan: Zero-shot event detection using multi-modal fusion of weakly supervised concepts. In *CVPR*, 2014.

32. S. Sadanand and J. Corso: Action bank: A high-level representation of activity in video. In *CVPR*, 2012.

33. A. Berg, T. Berg, and J. Sxhih: Automatic attribute discovery and characterization from noisy web data. In *ECCV*, 2010.

34. J. Chen, Y. Cui, D. Liu, and S.-F. Chang: Building a large concept bank for representing events in video. *arXiv:1403.7591*, 2014.

35. G. Ye, S. Bhattacharya, D. Ellis, M. Shah, Y.-G. Jiang, X. Zeng, and S.-F. Chang: Columbia-UCF TRECVID2010 multimedia event detection: Combining multiple modalities, contextual concepts, and temporal matching. In *NIST TRECVID Workshop*, 2010.
36. J. Wang, X. Xue, Y.-G. Jiang, Z. Wu, and S.-F. Chang: Exploiting feature and class relationships in video categorization with regularized deep neural networks. *arXiv:1502.07209*, 2015.
37. S.-F. Chang, D. Ellis, Y.-G. Jiang, G. Ye, and A. C. Loui: Consumer video understanding: A benchmark database and an evaluation of human and machine performance. In *ICMR*, 2011.

Chapter 2

Leveraging Selectional Preferences for Anomaly Detection in Newswire Events

Pradeep Dasigi and Eduard Hovy

Contents

2.1 Understanding Events

Events are fundamental linguistic elements in human speech. Thus, understanding events is a fundamental prerequisite for deeper semantic analysis of language, and any computational system of human language should have a model of events. One can view an event as an occurrence of a certain action caused by an agent, affecting a patient at a certain time and place and so on. It is the combination of the entities filling said roles that defines an event. Furthermore, certain combinations of these role fillers agree with the general state of the world, and others do not. For example, consider the events described by the following statements:

■ *Man recovering after being bitten by his dog*
■ *Man recovering after being shot by cops*

The *agent* of the *biting* action is *dog* in the first statement, and that of the *shooting* action in the second statement is *cops*. The patient in both statements is *man*. Both combinations of role fillers result in events that agree with most people's worldview. That is not the case with the event in the following statement:

■ *Man recovering after being shot by his dog*

This combination does not agree with our expectations about the general state of affairs, and consequently one might find this event strange. While all three statements above are equally valid syntactically, it is our knowledge about the role fillers—both individually and specifically in combination—that enables us to differentiate between normal and anomalous events. Hence, we hypothesize that an *anomaly is a result of an unexpected or unusual combination of semantic role fillers*.

In this chapter, we introduce the problem of automatic anomalous event detection and propose a novel event model that can learn to differentiate between normal and anomalous events. We generally define anomalous events as those that are unusual compared to the general state of affairs and might invoke surprise when reported. An automatic anomaly detection algorithm has to encode the goodness of semantic role-filler coherence. This is a hard problem since determining what a good combination of role fillers is requires deep semantic and pragmatic knowledge. Moreover, manual judgment of an anomaly itself may be difficult and people often may not agree with each other in this regard. We describe the difficulty in human judgment in greater detail in Section 2.3.1. Automatic detection of anomalies requires encoding complex information, which poses the challenge of sparsity due to the discrete representations of meaning that are words. These problems range from polysemy and synonymy at the lexical semantic level to entity and event coreference at the discourse level.

We define an event as the pair $(V, \mathbf{A})$, where V is the predicate or a semantic verb,* and $\mathbf{A}$ is the set of its semantic arguments like agent, patient, time, location, and so on. Our aim is to obtain a vector representation of the event that is composed from representations of individual words, while explicitly guided by the semantic role structure. This representation can be understood as an embedding of the event in an event space.

2.2 Linguistic Background

Selectional preference, a notion introduced by Wilks [1], refers to the paradigm of modeling semantics of natural language in terms of the restrictions a verb places on its arguments. For example, the knowledge required to identify one of the following sentences as meaningless can be encoded as preferences (or restrictions) of the verb:

---

* By "semantic verb," we mean an action word whose syntactic category is not necessarily a verb. For example, in *coastal attacks killed dozens as tensions rise, attacks* is not a verb but is still an action word.

- *Man eats pasta*
- *Poetry eats computers*

The restrictions include *eat*, requiring its subject to be animate, its object to be edible, and so on. Though the notion was originally proposed for a verb and its dependents in the context of dependency grammar, it is equally applicable to other kinds of semantic relations. In this work, we use this idea in the context of verbs and their semantic role fillers.

The idea is that identifying the right sense of the word can be guided by the preferences of the other words it is related to. Resnik [2] illustrates this through the example of disambiguating the sense of the word *letter* in the phrase *write a letter*. While *letter* has multiple senses, as an object, the verb *write* "prefers" the sense closer to *reading matter* more than others. At the phrasal level, selectional preferences are useful in encoding complex phenomena like metaphors. Metaphorical usage of words usually involves violating selectional restrictions. For example the phrase *kill an idea* is a metaphor, because *kill* does not usually take abstract concepts as objects. The phrase itself is common and one can easily attribute a metaphorical sense to the verb *kill* and resolve the violation. Wilks [3,4], Krishnakumaran and Zhu [5], and Shutova et al. [6], among others, have discussed the selectional preference view of metaphor identification. Automatic acquisition of selectional preferences from text is a well-studied problem. Resnik [7] proposed the first broad coverage computational model of selectional preferences. The approach is based on using Word-Net's hierarchy to generalize across words. It measures the selectional association strength of a triple (v, r, c) with verb v, relation r, and an argument class c as the Kullback-Leibler divergence between the distributions $P(c|v, r)$ and $P(c|r)$ normalized over all classes of arguments that occur with the (v, r) pair. Abe and Li [8] also used WordNet. They modeled selectional preferences by minimizing the length tree cut through the noun hierarchy. Ciaramita and Johnson [9] encoded the hierarchy as a Bayesian network and learn selectional preferences using probabilistic graphical methods. Rooth et al. [10] took a distributional approach and used latent variable models to induce classes of noun-verb pairs, thus learning their preferences. Methods by Erk [11] and Erk et al. [12] are also distributional and have been described earlier in this chapter. Séaghdha [13] proposed the use of latent Dirichlet allocation (LDA) to model preferences as topics. Van de Cruys [14] used nonnegative tensor factorization, and modeled subject-verb-object triples as a three-way tensor. The tensor is populated with co-occurrence frequencies, and the selectional preferences are measured from decomposed representations of the three words in the triple. Van de Cruys [15] also trained neural networks to score felicitous triples higher than infelicitous ones.

Erk et al. [12] also modeled selectional preferences using vector spaces. They measured the goodness of the fit of a noun with a verb in terms of the similarity between the vector of the noun and some "exemplar" nouns taken by the verb in the same argument role. Baroni and Lenci [16] also measured selectional preference similarly, but instead of exemplar nouns, they calculated a prototype vector for that role based on the vectors of the most common nouns occurring in that role for the given verb. Lenci [17] built on this work and modeled the phenomenon that the expectations of the verb or its role fillers change dynamically given other role fillers.

2.3 Data

We crawl 3684 "weird news" headlines available publicly on the website of NBC news,* such as the following:

---

* http://www.nbcnews.com/news/weird-news

- *India weaponizes world's hottest chili*
- *Man recovering after being shot by his dog*
- *Thai snake charmer puckers up to 19 cobras*

We assume that the events extracted from this source, called NBC Weird Events (NWE) henceforth, are anomalous for training. NWE contains 4271 events extracted using SENNA's SRL. We use 3771 of those events as our negative training data. Similarly, we extract events also from headlines in the AFE section of Gigaword, called Gigaword Events (GWE) henceforth. We assume these events are normal. To use as positive examples for training event composition, we sample roughly the same number of events from GWE as our negative examples from NWE. From the two sets, we uniformly sample 1003 events as the test set and validate the labels by getting crowd-sourced annotations.

2.3.1 Annotation

We post the annotation of the test set containing 1003 events as human intelligence tasks (HITs) on Amazon Mechanical Turk (AMT). We break the task into 20 HITs and ask the workers to select one of the four options (*highly unusual*, *strange*, *normal*, and *cannot say*) for each event. We ask them to select *highly unusual* when the event seems too strange to be true, *strange* if it seems unusual but still plausible, and *cannot say* only if the information present in the event is not sufficient to make a decision. We publicly release this set of 1003 annotated events for evaluating future research.

Table 2.1 shows some statistics of the annotation task. We compute the inter-annotator agreement (IAA) in terms of Kripendorff's alpha [18]. The advantage of using this measure instead of the more popular Kappa is that the former can deal with missing information, which is the case with our task since annotators work on different overlapping subsets of the test set. The four-way IAA shown in the table corresponds to agreement over the original four-way decision (including *cannot say*), while the three-way IAA is measured after merging the *highly unusual* and *strange* decisions.

Additionally we use MACE [19] to assess the quality of annotation. MACE models the annotation task as a generative process of producing the observed labels conditioned on the true labels and the competence of the annotators. Then it predicts both the latent variables. The average competence of the annotators, a value that ranges from 0 to 1, for our task is 0.49 for the four-way decision and 0.59 for the three-way decision.

Table 2.1   Annotation Statistics

Total Number of Annotators	22
Normal annotations	56.3%
Strange annotations	28.6%
Highly unusual annotations	10.3%
Cannot say annotations	4.8%
Avg. events annotated per worker	344
Four-way inter-annotator agreement (α)	0.34
Three-way inter-annotator agreement (α)	0.56

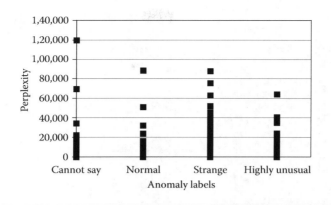

Figure 2.1   Comparison of perplexity scores for different labels.

We generate true label predictions produced by MACE, discard the events for which the prediction remains *cannot say*, and use the rest as the final labeled test set. This leaves 949 events as our test dataset, of which only 41% of the labels are *strange* or *highly unusual*. It has to be noted that even though our test set has equal size samples from both NWE and GWE, the true distribution is not uniform.

2.3.2 Language Model Separability

Given the annotations, we test to see if the sentences corresponding to anomalous events can be separated from normal events by simpler features. We build an n-gram language model from the training data set used for argument composition and measure the perplexity of the sentences in the test set. Figure 2.1 shows a comparison of the perplexity scores for different labels. If the n-gram features are enough to separate different classes of sentences, one would expect the sentences corresponding to the *strange* and *highly unusual* labels to have higher perplexity ranges than *normal* sentences, because the language model is built from a dataset that is expected to have a distribution of sentences where a majority of them contain normal events. As Figure 2.1 shows, except for a few outliers, most data points in all the categories are in similar perplexity ranges. Hence, sentences with different labels cannot be separated based on n-gram language model features.

2.4 Model for Semantic Anomaly Detection

A neural event model (NEM) is a supervised model that learns to differentiate between anomalous and normal events by classifying dense representations of events, otherwise known as "event embeddings." We treat the problem as a binary classification problem, with *normal* and *anomalous* being the two classes. The event embeddings are computed using a structured composition model that represents an event as the composition of the five slot fillers: **action**, **agent**, **patient**, **time**, and **location**. Figure 2.2 shows the pipeline for anomalous event detection using NEM. We first identify the fillers for the five slots mentioned above, by running a PropBank-style [20] semantic role labeler (SRL). We use the following mapping of roles to obtain the event structure:

- ■ V → action
- ■ A0 → agent

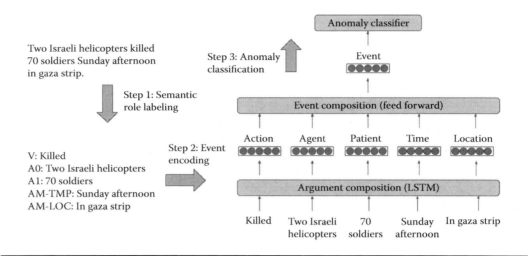

Figure 2.2 Anomaly classification pipeline with neural event model.

- A1 → patient
- AM-TMP → time
- AM-LOC → location

This structured input is then passed to NEM. The model has three components.

2.4.1 Argument Composition

This component encodes all the role fillers as vectors in the same space. This is accomplished by embedding the words in each role filler and then passing them through a recurrent neural network (RNN) with long short-term memory (LSTM) [21] cells. Note that the same LSTM is used for all the slots. Concretely,

$$a_s = \text{LSTM}(I_s) \tag{2.1}$$

where I_s denotes the ordered set of word vector representations in the filler of slot s, and a_s represents the vector representation of that slot filler.

2.4.2 Event Composition

The slot filler representations are then composed using slot-specific projection weights to obtain a single event representation. Concretely,

$$\bar{a}_s = \tanh(W_s^{\mathsf{T}} a_s + b_s) \quad \text{where } s \in \{c, g, p, t, l\} \tag{2.2}$$

$$e = \bar{a}_c + \bar{a}_g + \bar{a}_p + \bar{a}_t + \bar{a}_l \tag{2.3}$$

$W_s \in \mathbb{R}^{d \times d}$ and $b_s \in \mathbb{R}^d$ are slot-specific projection weights and biases, respectively, with s denoting one of action, agent, patient, time and location. d is the dimensionality of the word embeddings. Event composition involves performing non-linear projections of all slot-filler representations and finally obtaining an event representation e.

2.4.3 Anomaly Classification

The event representation is finally passed through a softmax layer to obtain the predicted probabilities for the two classes.

$$p_e = \text{softmax}(W_e^\mathsf{T} e + b_e) \tag{2.4}$$

$W_e \in \mathbb{R}^{d \times 2}$ and $b_e \in \mathbb{R}^2$ are the weight and bias values of the softmax layer, respectively. As it can be seen, the layer projects the event representation into a two-dimensional space before applying the softmax non-linearity.

2.4.4 Training

Given the output from NEM, we define

$$p_e^1(\theta) = P(\text{anomalous}|e; \theta) \tag{2.5}$$

$$p_e^0(\theta) = P(\text{normal}|e; \theta) \tag{2.6}$$

where θ are the parameters in the model, and we compute the label loss based on the prediction at the end of the anomaly classification as a cross entropy loss as follows:

$$J(\theta) = -l \log p_e^1(\theta) + (1 - l) \log p_e^0(\theta) \tag{2.7}$$

where l is the reference binary label indicating whether the event is normal or anomalous. The three components of the model described above (argument composition, event composition, and anomaly classification) are all trained jointly. That is, we optimize the following objective:

$$\theta^* = arg \min_{\theta} J(\theta) \tag{2.8}$$

where θ includes all W_s and b_s from all the slots, W_e and b_e from event composition, and also all the LSTM parameters from argument composition. We optimize this objective using ADAM [22]. The model is implemented* using Keras [23]. Note that the model described here is an extension of the one described in our previously published paper [24]. The main improvements here include using an LSTM-RNN as the encoder in argument composition instead of a simple RNN, and jointly training the argument composition, event composition, and anomaly classification, whereas the older model included training the argument composition separately using an unsupervised objective.

2.5 Results

We merged the two anomaly classes (strange and highly unusual) and calculated the accuracy and F-score (for the anomaly class) of the binary classifier. For the sake of comparison, we also define the following two baseline models.

---

* The code is publicly available at https://github.com/pdasigi/neural-event-model.

2.5.1 PMI Baseline

We compare the performance of our model against a baseline that is based on how well the semantic arguments in the event match the selectional preferences of the predicate. We measure selectional preference using point-wise mutual information (PMI) [25] of the head words of each semantic argument with the predicate. The baseline model is built as follows. We perform dependency parsing using MaltParser [26] on the sentences in the training data used in the first phase of training to obtain the head words of the semantic arguments. We then calculate the PMI values of all the pairs $< h_A, p >$, where h is the head word of argument A and p is the predicate of the event. For training our baseline classifier, we use the labeled training data from the event composition phase. The features for this classifier are the PMI measures of the $< h_A, p >$ pairs estimated from the larger dataset. The classifier thus trained to distinguish between anomalous and normal events is applied to the test set.

2.5.2 LSTM Baseline

To investigate the importance of our proposed event representation, we also implemented an LSTM baseline that directly encodes sentences. The following equations describe the model:

$$w = \text{LSTM}(I) \tag{2.9}$$

$$\bar{w} = \tanh(W_w^\mathsf{T} w + b_w) \tag{2.10}$$

$$p_u = \text{softmax}(W_u^\mathsf{T} \bar{w} + b_u) \tag{2.11}$$

Note that this model is comparable in complexity to and has the same number of nonlinear transformations as NEM. $\bar{w}$ represents a word-level composition instead of an argument-level composition in NEM, and p_u is a probability distribution defined over an unstructured composition as features. Training of this baseline model is done in the same way as NEM.

Table 2.2 shows the results and a comparison with the two baselines. The accuracy of the baseline classifier is lower than 50%, which is the expected accuracy of a classifier that assigns labels randomly. As seen in the table, the LSTM model proves to be a strong baseline, but it underperforms in comparison with NEM, showing the value of our proposed event composition model. The difference between the performance of NEM and the LSTM baseline is statistically significant with $p < 0.0001$. Figure 2.3 shows the ROC curves for NEM and the LSTM baseline.

To further compare NEM with human annotators, we give to MACE the binary predictions produced by NEM and those by the LSTM baseline, along with the annotations, and we measure the competence. For the sake of comparison, we also give to MACE a list of random binary labels

Table 2.2   Classification Performance and Comparison with Baselines

	Accuracy	F-Score
PMI baseline	45.2%	45.1%
LSTM baseline	82.5%	77.4%
NEM	84.9%	79.7%

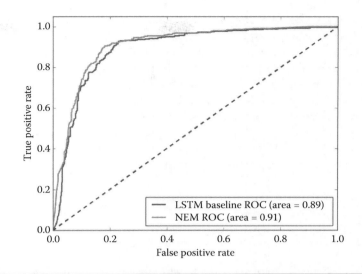

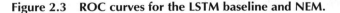

Figure 2.3 **ROC curves for the LSTM baseline and NEM.**

Table 2.3 **Anomaly Detection Competence**

Human highest	0.896
Human average	0.633
Human lowest	0.144
Random	0.054
LSTM baseline	0.743
NEM	0.797

as one of the annotations to measure the competence of a hypothetical worker that made random choices. These results are reported in Table 2.3. Unsurprisingly, the competence of the random classifier is very low, worse than the least competent human. It can be seen that MACE predicts both the LSTM baseline and NEM to be more competent than the human average. This is an encouraging result, especially given that this is a hard problem even for humans.

2.6 Summary and Discussion

In this chapter, we have looked at how selectional preferences can be leveraged to model events and represent them in such a way as to distinguish anomalous events from normal events. Results from our controlled experiments comparing the proposed model with one that directly encodes whole sentences have shown the value of using the proposed structured composition.

One important aspect of anomaly that is currently not handled by NEM is the level of generality of the concepts the events contain. Usually more general concepts cause events to be more normal since they convey lesser information. For example, an American soldier shooting another American soldier may be considered unusual, while a soldier shooting another soldier may not be as unusual, and at the highest level of generalization, a person shooting another person is normal. This information of generality has to be incorporated into the event model. This can be achieved by integrating real-world knowledge from knowledge bases like Wordnet [27] or from corpus statistics like the work by Lin [28] into the event model. Bordes et al. [29] trained continuous representations of entities and relations in knowledge bases. More recently, an alternative approach for doing the same was proposed by Chen et al. [30]. These representations can greatly help with modeling events. Finally, the idea of modeling event composition can help to process event data in general and can be applied to other tasks like finding coreferent events.

References

1. Yorick Wilks. Preference semantics. Technical report, Stanford Univ. CA Dept. of Computer Science, 1973.
2. Philip Resnik. Selectional preference and sense disambiguation. In *Proceedings of the ACL SIGLEX Workshop on Tagging Text with Lexical Semantics: Why, What, and How*, pages 52–57. Washington, DC, 1997.
3. Yorick Wilks. Making preferences more active. In *Words and Intelligence I*, pages 141–166. Springer, 2007.
4. Yorick Wilks. A preferential, pattern-seeking, semantics for natural language inference. In *Words and Intelligence I*, pages 83–102. Springer, 2007.
5. Saisuresh Krishnakumaran and Xiaojin Zhu. Hunting elusive metaphors using lexical resources. In *Proceedings of the Workshop on Computational Approaches to Figurative Language*, pages 13–20. Association for Computational Linguistics, 2007.
6. Ekaterina Shutova, Simone Teufel, and Anna Korhonen. Statistical metaphor processing. *Computational Linguistics*, **39**(2):301–353, 2013.
7. Philip Resnik. Selectional constraints: An information-theoretic model and its computational realization. *Cognition*, **61**(1):127–159, 1996.
8. Naoki Abe and Hang Li. Learning word association norms using tree cut pair models. *arXiv preprint cmp-lg/9605029*, 1996.
9. Massimiliano Ciaramita and Mark Johnson. Explaining away ambiguity: Learning verb selectional preference with Bayesian networks. In *Proceedings of the 18th Conference on Computational Linguistics—Volume 1*, pages 187–193. Association for Computational Linguistics, 2000.
10. Mats Rooth, Stefan Riezler, Detlef Prescher, Glenn Carroll, and Franz Beil. Inducing a semantically annotated lexicon via em-based clustering. In *Proceedings of the 37th Annual Meeting of the Association for Computational Linguistics on Computational Linguistics*, pages 104–111. Association for Computational Linguistics, 1999.
11. Katrin Erk. A simple, similarity-based model for selectional preferences. *Annual Meeting—Association for Computational Linguistics*, **45**(1):216, 2007.
12. Katrin Erk, Sebastian Padó, and Ulrike Padó. A flexible, corpus-driven model of regular and inverse selectional preferences. *Computational Linguistics*, **36**(4):723–763, 2010.
13. Diarmuid O. Séaghdha. Latent variable models of selectional preference. In *Proceedings of the 48th Annual Meeting of the Association for Computational Linguistics*, pages 435–444. Association for Computational Linguistics, 2010.
14. Tim Van de Cruys. A non-negative tensor factorization model for selectional preference induction. *GEMS: GEometrical Models of Natural Language Semantics*, page 83, 2009.
15. Tim Van de Cruys. A neural network approach to selectional preference acquisition. In *Proceedings of the 2014 Conference on Empirical Methods in Natural Language Processing (EMNLP)*, pages 26–35, 2014.

16. Marco Baroni and Alessandro Lenci. Distributional memory: A general framework for corpus-based semantics. *Computational Linguistics*, **36**(4):673–721, 2010.
17. Alessandro Lenci. Composing and updating verb argument expectations: A distributional semantic model. In *Proceedings of the 2nd Workshop on Cognitive Modeling and Computational Linguistics*, pages 58–66. Association for Computational Linguistics, 2011.
18. Klaus Krippendorff. *Content Analysis: An Introduction to Its Methodology*. Sage Publications (Beverly Hills), 1980.
19. Dirk Hovy, Taylor Berg-Kirkpatrick, Ashish Vaswani, and Eduard Hovy. Learning whom to trust with MACE. In *Proceedings of NAACL-HLT*, pages 1120–1130, 2013.
20. Martha Palmer, Daniel Gildea, and Paul Kingsbury. The proposition bank: An annotated corpus of semantic roles. *Computational Linguistics*, **31**(1):71–106, 2005.
21. Sepp Hochreiter and Jürgen Schmidhuber. Long short-term memory. *Neural Computation*, **9**(8):1735–1780, 1997.
22. Diederik Kingma and Jimmy Ba. ADAM: A method for stochastic optimization. *arXiv preprint arXiv:1412.6980*, 2014.
23. Franois Chollet. Keras, 2015.
24. Pradeep Dasigi and Eduard Hovy. Modeling newswire events using neural networks for anomaly detection. In *COLING 2014*, volume **25**, pages 1414–1422. Dublin City University and Association for Computational Linguistics, 2014.
25. Kenneth Ward Church and Patrick Hanks. Word association norms, mutual information, and lexicography. *Computational Linguistics*, **16**(1):22–29, 1990.
26. Joakim Nivre, Johan Hall, Jens Nilsson, Atanas Chanev, Gülsen Eryigit, Sandra Kübler, Svetoslav Marinov, and Erwin Marsi. Maltparser: A language-independent system for data-driven dependency parsing. *Natural Language Engineering*, **13**(02):95–135, 2007.
27. George A. Miller. Wordnet: A lexical database for english. *Communications of the ACM*, **38**(11):39–41, 1995.
28. Dekang Lin. Automatic retrieval and clustering of similar words. In *Proceedings of the 17th International Conference on Computational Linguistics—Volume 2*, pages 768–774. Association for Computational Linguistics, 1998.
29. Antoine Bordes, Jason Weston, Ronan Collobert, Yoshua Bengio et al. Learning structured embeddings of knowledge bases. In *AAAI*, 2011.
30. Danqi Chen, Richard Socher, Christopher D. Manning, and Andrew Y. Ng. Learning new facts from knowledge bases with neural tensor networks and semantic word vectors. *arXiv preprint arXiv:1301.3618*, 2013.

Chapter 3

Abnormal Event Recognition in Crowd Environments

Moin Nabi, Hossein Mousavi, Hamidreza Rabiee,
Mahdyar Ravanbakhsh, Vittorio Murino, and Nicu Sebe

Contents

3.1 Introduction

Recently, there has been a surge of interest in the computer vision community on automated crowd scene analysis; as a result, crowd behavior detection and recognition are topics of many reported works. To understand crowd behavior, a model of crowd behavior needs to be trained using the information extracted from video sequences. Since there are only behavior labels as ground-truth information in most of the proposed crowd-based datasets, traditional approaches for human behavior recognition have relied only on patterns of low-level motion/appearance features to build their behavior models. Despite the huge amount of research on understanding crowd behavior in the visual surveillance community, the lack of publicly available realistic datasets for evaluating crowds' behavioral interactions means there is no fair common test bed for researchers to compare the strength of their methods against real scenarios.

In this chapter, we propose a novel crowd dataset that contains around 45,000 video clips, annotated by one of five different fine-grained abnormal behavior categories. We have also evaluated two state-of-the-art methods with our dataset, showing that our dataset can be effectively used as a benchmark for fine-grained abnormality detection.

Furthermore, we study the problem of crowd behavior classification using not only low-level features but also crowd emotions, called "attributes," as a mid-level representation. We propose an attribute-based strategy to alleviate this problem. While similar strategies have been adopted recently for object and action recognition, as far as we know, this is the first attempt to show that crowd emotions can be used as attributes to understand crowd behavior.

This method has hardly been studied in crowd behavior analysis, but it is worth studying, because there is a huge semantic gap between high-level concepts of crowd behavior and low-level visual features. The main idea of the attribute-based strategy is to train a set of emotion-based classifiers, which can subsequently be used to represent the crowd motion. For this purpose, in the collected dataset each video clip is provided with both annotations of "crowd behaviors" and "crowd emotions." In our model, the crowd emotion attributes are considered latent variables, and we propose a unified attribute-based behavior representation framework, which is built on a latent SVM formulation. In the proposed model, latent variables capture the level of importance of each emotion attribute for each behavior class.

3.1.1 Background

In most of the proposed approaches for behavior recognition in individuals [1–11], behavior frameworks are regularly built on patterns of low-level motion/appearance features, for example, a histogram of oriented gradients (HOG) [40], histogram of optical flow (HOF) [41], or motion boundary histogram (MBH), and are directly related to behavior types (*panic, fight, neutral*, etc.) using modern machine learning techniques, for example, a support vector machine. For instance, in References 2 and 3, optical flow histograms were used to demonstrate the global motion in a crowded scene. They derived the histogram of the optical flow and extracted some statistics from it to model human behaviors. Then, a set of simple heuristic rules was used to detect specific dangerous crowd behaviors. More advanced techniques, on the other hand, introduce models extracted from fluid dynamics or other physics laws to model a crowd as a group of moving particles. Together with social force models (SFM), these techniques are likely to explain the behavior of a crowd as the result of the interactions of individuals [5,6]. In Reference 5, for example, the SFM was applied to detect global abnormalities and estimate local abnormalities by detecting focus regions in the current frame. On the other hand, several approaches cope with the complexity of a dynamic scene analysis by partitioning a given video into spatio-temporal patches. In References 1 and 2, Kratz and Nishino derived spatio-temporal gradients from each pixel of videos. Then, the gradients of a spatio-temporal volume were modeled using spatio-temporal motion pattern models, which are basically 3D Gaussian clusters of gradients. Using dynamic textures, Mahadevan et al. [7] modeled the observed motion in each spatio-temporal volume, which can be considered as an extension of a PCA-based representation. Whereas PCA spaces only model the appearance of a given patch texture, dynamic textures also represent the statistically valid transitions among textures in a patch. Making use of a mixture of dynamic textures (MDT), all the possible dynamic textures were represented, allowing them to estimate the probability of a test patch to be abnormal. In this way, it was shown that not only temporal anomalies but also pure appearance anomalies can be detected. In the same work, the authors also introduced an interesting definition of spatial saliency based on mutual information [4] between features and foreground/background classes. However, in order to achieve a better classification accuracy level, the aforementioned models need a great deal of ground-truth crowd behavior training information for each class, typically hundreds of thousands of sample images for each behavior class to be learned. Therefore, considering high-level semantic concepts such as crowd emotions would be beneficial to represent the crowd behaviors. In different circumstances, emotions belonging to individuals have a significant effect on their behavior. For example, in a pure low-level feature-based behavior recognition framework, individuals who approach each other and shake hands might be considered as a fighting crowd, whereas they behave normally and are happy emotionally (see Figure 3.6b). In other words, in terms of classifying crowd behaviors, two groups of individuals who are very similar in the aspect of their low-level features might be classified in an entirely different way by considering crowd emotions as well (See Figures 3.1 and 3.6).

Despite the relatively vast literature on emotion recognition for face [12–17] and posture [18–20], only a few works have aimed at emotion recognition from crowd motion [21–23]. To the best of our knowledge, there is no work that aims at emotion recognition and detection of behavior types in an integrated framework. Lack of publicly available *realistic* datasets (i.e., with high density crowds, various types of behaviors, etc.) is another constraint. This causes difficulty for researchers to have a reasonable common test bed to compare their works and fairly evaluate the strength and efficiency of their methods in real scenarios.

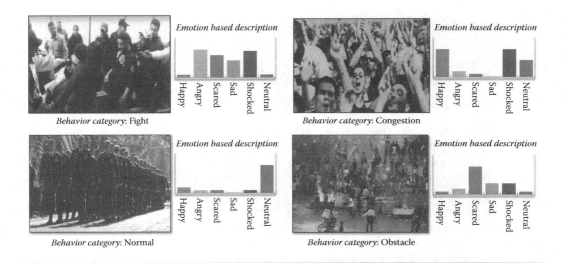

Figure 3.1 We propose to represent human behaviors by a set of emotions as intermediate representations that directly correspond to visual specifications explaining the spatio-temporal evolution of the behavior in a video (e.g., *scared, happy, excited, sad, neutral, angry*). We believe that an emotion-based behavior model is more descriptive and discriminative for behavior recognition than traditional approaches.

Inspired by recent works on attribute-based representation in object/action recognition literature [24–26], we aim to build a framework wherein crowd emotion information is used as a mid-level representation for crowd behavior recognition. The capability of determining behaviors by emotions as attributes in behavior classification is beneficial to recognize not only familiar behaviors but to recognize behavior classes that have never been seen before and that have no available training samples.

3.1.2 Our Contributions

The proposed approach aims at exploring how the crowd emotion attributes can improve the crowd behavior recognition process. As the first contribution, we have created a crowd dataset with both crowd behavior and crowd emotion annotations. Our dataset includes a large set of video clips annotated with both crowd behavior labels (e.g., *panic, fight, congestion,* etc.) and crowd emotion labels (e.g., *happy, excited, angry,* etc.). We have evaluated a set of baseline methods on both behavior class detection and emotion recognition, showing that the proposed dataset can be effectively used as a benchmark in the mentioned communities. As another contribution, we have used ground-truth emotion information provided in our dataset as an intermediate layer to recognize behavior classes. We call this method "emotion-based crowd representation" [27,28].

The rest of the chapter is constructed as follows: a short review on traditional datasets and the characteristics of our proposed dataset are reported in Section 3.2; the emotion-based crowd representation idea for crowd behavior recognition is presented in Section 3.3. In Section 3.4, we test the proposed methods on our dataset and discuss the results achieved. Finally, in Section 3.5, we briefly elaborate on other worthwhile investigation applications and promote further research on the proposed dataset.

3.2 The Crowd Anomaly Detection Dataset

In this section, after a brief review of the well-known datasets for the task of crowd behavior analysis, we introduce our dataset in detail.

3.2.1 Previous Datasets

Despite the significant demand for understanding crowd behaviors, there is still a significant gap between the accuracy and efficiency of typical behavior recognition methods in research labs and the real world. The most important reason for this gap is that the majority of experiments on the proposed algorithms have used non-standard datasets with only a small number of sequences taken under controlled circumstances with limited behavior classes.

Among all the existing datasets, we select a subset of the most cited ones and analyze their characteristics in detail. The datasets that we select are UMN [5], UCSD [29], CUHK [30], PETS2009 [31], Violent Flows [32], Rodriguez's dataset [33], and UCF Behavior [34]. We also select a set of criteria that allow us to compare the datasets. The criteria include number of videos, annotation level, density, types of scenarios, indoor/outdoor, and extra annotation (metadata). In the following, we list the aforementioned existing state-of-the-art crowd datasets along with their important characteristics.

UMN [5] is a publicly available dataset including normal and abnormal crowd videos from the University of Minnesota. Each video consists of an initial part with normal behavior and ends with sequences of abnormal behavior. Despite the huge amount of abnormal behavior scenarios, only the *panic* one is included in this dataset, which is not realistic in the real world.

The UCSD [29] dataset was generated from a stationary camera mounted at an elevation, overlooking pedestrian walkways. The crowd density in the walkways ranges from sparse to very crowded. Abnormal events occurred because of either (i) the circulation of non-pedestrian objects in the walkways or (ii) abnormal pedestrian motion patterns. As mentioned, the UCSD dataset considers only two definitions for abnormal events, which cannot be fully responsible for abnormal behavior detection in a crowded scene.

PETS2009 [31] consists of multi-sensor subsets with various crowd activities. The aim of this dataset is to use new or existing systems for (i) crowd count and density estimation, (ii) tracking of individual(s) within a crowd, and (iii) detection of separate flows and specific crowd events in a real-world environment. For instance, the event recognition subset consists of scenarios such as "walking," "running," "evacuation," and "local dispersion." Lack of some other realistic scenarios including *fight, scared, abnormal object,* etc. is a deficiency for this dataset.

Violent Flows [32] is a dataset of real-world videos downloaded from the web consisting of crowd violence, along with standard benchmark protocols designed to test both violent/nonviolent classification and violence outbreak detection. The problem here is that the average length of the video clips is 3.60 seconds, which is a limiting parameter for analyzing the scene properly. Also the types of violent behaviors are related to just fighting most of the time in video clips.

Rodriguez's dataset [33] was gathered by crawling and downloading videos from search engines and stock footage websites (e.g., Getty Images and YouTube). In addition to the large number of crowd videos, the dataset consists of ground-truth trajectories for 100 individuals, which were selected randomly from the set of all moving people. This dataset is not open to the public yet.

UCF [34] was acquired from the web (Getty Images, BBC Motion Gallery, YouTube, Thought Equity) and PETS2009, representing crowd and traffic scenes. It is publicly available in the form of image sequences. Unlike [12], it is mainly designed for crowd behavior recognition with ground-truth labels.

This dataset only focused on a few crowd flow behaviors such as merging, splitting, circulating, and blocking, which cannot fully cover all the abnormal crowd behaviors. None of the aforementioned datasets are able to reflect abnormal human behavior in real crowd conditions. In Figure 3.2, a few sample frames for state-of-the-art crowd datasets are presented.

3.2.2 Importance of Dataset Characteristics

The number of videos is an important characteristic of a dataset, because having a sufficient number of recorded videos can be very helpful, not only for training with more samples, but also for being more efficient in evaluation time.

Annotation level is another important criteria of the dataset. It can be specified as pixel level, frame level, or video level, which technically reflects the richness of a dataset.

Crowd density is an important factor has to be considered. Crowded scenes result in more occlusion, clutter, etc., and make it harder to detect different types of behaviors.

Types of scenarios is another critical characteristic of a dataset that reflects the types of events happening in all the video sequences. Datasets with more scenario types are more challenging, since the proposed algorithms should work with larger variations in conditions (i.e., real-world setup).

The indoor/outdoor criterion is the location in which the video sequences have been recorded, and it has a peculiar effect on illumination conditions, background clutters, occlusions, etc.

Figure 3.2 (a) Normal and abnormal frames of the UCSD dataset. (b) Normal and abnormal frames from the three scenarios of the UMN dataset. (c) Normal and violent crowd from the violence-in-crowds dataset. Videos are from different scenes. (d) Normal and abnormal frames of the PETS2009 dataset. (e) Frames of crowded scenes from the Rodriguez dataset. (f) Normal and abnormal frames of the UCF dataset.

Last but not least, including extra annotation is another important feature of a dataset, which we insist on in this work. It is also one of the features that makes our dataset unique and provides the possibility for researchers to move toward higher-level interpretations of the video sequences. In our dataset, we specifically introduced "crowd emotion" as an extra annotation.

In Table 3.1, we describe all aforementioned crowd behavior datasets in terms of their explained features. A common demerit for all of them is the lack of any extra annotation, so these datasets rely only on low-level features to discriminate between types of behavior classes. Lack of diverse subjects and scenarios, low-volume crowd density, and a limited number of video sequences are other limitations of the previous datasets.

3.2.3 The Proposed Dataset

The proposed dataset includes 31 video clips or 44,000 individual frames with the resolution of 554 × 235. The video clips and frames were recorded at 30 frames per second using a fixed video

Table 3.1   Existing Datasets for Crowd Behavior Analysis in Terms of Their Characteristics

Dataset	Video Samples	Annotation Level	Crowd Density	Scenario Types	Indoor/Outdoor	Metadata
UMN [5]	11	Frame	Medium	Panic	Both	No
UCSD [29]	98	Frame/pixel	High/medium	Abnormal object	Outdoor	No
PETS2009 [31]	59	Frame	Medium	Panic	Outdoor	No
Violent Flows [32]	246	Video	Dense	Fight	Outdoor	No
Rodriguez [33]	520	Video	Dense	Pedestrian	Outdoor	No
UCF [34]	61	Video	Dense	Crowd	Outdoor	No
Our dataset	31	Frame	Dense	Multi-category	Outdoor	Crowd emotion

recorder elevated at a height, viewing individuals moving. The crowd density was regarded as variable, ranging from sparse to very crowded. In each scenario, the pedestrian locations and direction of walking were randomly selected. In order to make scenarios more realistic and applicable, we used some fixed and passing abnormal objects as threats to individuals in several scenes. Those scenarios are video clips with a suspicious backpack left by an unknown person in the crowd, a motorcycle passing the crowded scene, and a motorcycle without a rider that is left between individuals. In our dataset, we have introduced five distinct basic types of crowd behavior classes. Each scenario configuration was sketched in accordance with circumstances typically met in crowding issues. They can be explained as, namely, the normal movements of individuals in a crowded scenes (*neutral*), a crowded scene including abnormal objects (*obstacle* or *abnormal object*), individuals evacuating the scene (*panic*), physical conflict between individuals (*fight*), and two or more individuals gathering together closely (*congestion*). In order to obtain a crowd dataset with a pool of various behavior scenarios, we tried to have at least two video clips relating to each behavior class from different fields of view and with diverse crowd density. In psychology, *emotion* is defined as "a feeling evoked by environmental stimuli or by internal body states" [35]. This can characterize human behavior in terms of the actions in the environment or changes in the internal status of the body. Considering basic emotions, we introduce six types of basic crowd emotions in our dataset, namely, *angry, happy, excited, scared, sad,* and *neutral,* as behavior class attributes. As mentioned earlier, the state-of-the-art techniques for emotion recognition mainly rely on the appearance of face/posture and usually fail in the case of a high-density crowd. However, we target the emotion recognition from a totally different perspective and utilize crowd motion instead of the appearance of individuals. This is specifically useful in low-resolution videos and high-density crowd scenes wherein there is more occlusion and clutter (which is typically the case for video surveillance systems).

To alleviate the subjectivity of emotion and elevate the reliability of the emotion labels in the dataset, a group of five workers independently annotated the dataset and the final labels have been selected via majority voting (e.g., picking the label with more votes). To ensure consistency among workers, we conducted an agreement study. We found that the overall agreement among workers in selecting the same crowd emotion attributes was about 92% with a Kappa value of 0.81, and the maximum inconsistency was between two emotion attributes, namely, *happy* and *excited*, which were confused with each other almost 4% of the time. In Table 3.2, some beneficial information from recorded video clips is presented, including the total number of frames and the number of frames associated with each predefined behavior and emotion class.

Our specified emotion labels as attributes can assist behavior class recognition because they present high-level semantic information that is much richer than pure low-level visual features. These labels can be applied to improve the characterization of behavior classes and provide a more descriptive and discriminative framework for the task of crowd behavior classification. In Figure 3.3, we demonstrate some frames of two sample video clips in our dataset, along with both emotion and behavior ground-truth labels. As can be seen, the crowded videos might contain

Table 3.2   Number of Frames Corresponding to Each Behavior and Emotion Label

Emotion labels No. of frames	Sad 1140	Happy 1977	Excited 3804	Scared 1975	Angry 5915	Neutral 28815	Total 43626
Behavior labels No. of frames	Panic 2002	Obstacle 5120	Congestion 2368	Fight 4423	Neutral 29713		Total 43626

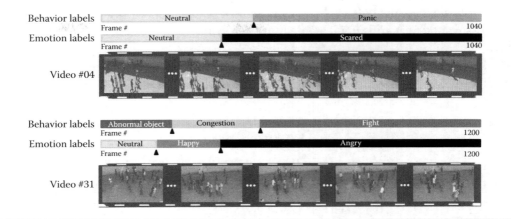

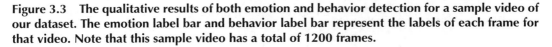

Figure 3.3 **The qualitative results of both emotion and behavior detection for a sample video of our dataset. The emotion label bar and behavior label bar represent the labels of each frame for that video. Note that this sample video has a total of 1200 frames.**

several behavior and emotion labels depending on the temper and feeling of individuals in the scene. For instance, in Video 04, the frames begin normally and individuals have neutral behaviors and feelings, but after a while (about 800 frames) a gang of hoodlums attacks the individuals and makes them panicked and scared, such that all of them disperse.

In Table 3.3, we annotate each crowd behavior type with its associated scenarios, which was performed during dataset recording. Note that despite the presence of other scenarios, we tried to select more possible and realistic ones in our dataset.

Some sample frames of our dataset along with their behavior type annotations are presented in Figure 3.4. For each crowd emotion type, some sample scenarios used in our dataset are presented in Table 3.4.

The videos, ground-truth annotations, and baseline codes are available to the public. We believe this dataset can be used as a benchmark for future research in both abnormal behavior detection and emotion recognition tasks.

3.3 Emotion-Based Crowd Representation

We strongly believe that crowd behaviors are better explained by crowd attributes such as crowd emotion. So, instead of extracting low-level features and solving the classification problem by introducing a classifier that maps the feature vector to a specific class label, we explain how we indicate behavior classes with a set of crowd emotions.

If we consider ground-truth emotion information available during both training and testing, we can simply regard them as part of the input data and cope with a standard classification problem (see *Emotion-Aware Baseline* for evaluation, Section 3.4.2). However, if we don't have emotion information during testing and only take emotions into account in the training data, the procedure becomes rather tricky and the emotion information is not fully reliable. In this section, we assume that we have access to emotion information only during training time.

Given a set of N video clips in the dataset $\{(x^{(n)}, e^{(n)}, y^{(n)})\}_{n=1}^{N}$, we aim to train a model wherein emotion labels e are used to assign a behavior label y to an unseen test video clip x. In the

Table 3.3 Crowd Behavior Types Introduced in Our Dataset along with Associated Scenarios Implemented for Each Type

Type of Behavior	Scenarios
Panic	Suspicious backpack Hoodlum attack Earthquake Sniper attack Terrorist firework
Fight	Previous personal issues between individuals that suddenly meet each other within the crowd Intentional or unintentional bad physical contact between two or more people in the crowd
Congestion	Demonstration Helping out an individual facing a health problem Breaking up a fight between two or more individuals
Obstacle or abnormal object	Suspicious backpack Motorcycle crossing the crowd Motorcycle left in the crowd Bag theft with motorcycle An individual that fell to the ground for some reason
Neutral	Individuals moving with almost fixed velocities in random directions Two or more people meeting one another

training phase, each example is represented as a tuple $(\mathbf{f}, \mathbf{e}, y)$, where $\mathbf{f} \in \mathbb{F}^d$ is the d-dimensional low-level feature extracted from video clip x. The behavior class label of the image is represented by $y \in \mathbb{Y}$. The crowd emotions of a video clip x are denoted by a K-dimensional vector $\mathbf{e} = (e_1, e_2, \ldots, e_K)$, where $e_k \in \mathbb{E}_k$ $(k = 1, 2, \ldots, K)$ indicates the kth emotion of the video clip. For example, if the kth emotion attribute is *angry*, we will have $\mathbb{E}_k = \{0, 1\}$, where $e_k = 1$ means the crowd is angry, while $e_k = 0$ means it is not. Since our dataset is designed to be applied also for a standard multi-class emotion recognition setup, here we describe each video clip with a binary-valued emotion attribute with a single non-zero value, that is, $\mathbb{E}_k = \{0, 1\}$ $(e = 1, 2, \ldots, K)$, s.t. $\|\mathbf{e}\|_0 = 1$. But we emphasize that our proposed method is not limited to binary-valued attributes with a single emotion. It can be extended to multi-emotion and continuous-valued attributes. Discarding the emotion information, we can simply train a classifier $\mathcal{C} \colon \mathbb{F}^d \rightarrow \mathbb{Y}$ that maps the feature vector f to a behavior class label y (see *Low-level visual feature baseline* for evaluation, Section 3.4.1). On the contrary, by introducing the emotion-attribute layer between the low-level features and behavior classes, the classifier C that maps f to a behavior class label is decomposed into

$$\mathcal{H} = \mathcal{B}(\mathcal{E}(f))$$
$$\mathcal{E} \colon \mathbb{F}^d \rightarrow \mathbb{E}_k \quad \text{and} \quad \mathcal{B} \colon \mathbb{E}_k \rightarrow \mathbb{Y} \tag{3.1}$$

Figure 3.4 **Examples of different scenario clips. (a) Three sample clips of a *neutral* scenario. (b) Three sample clips of a *congestion* scenario. (c) Sample clips of a *fight* scenario. (d) Three sample clips of a *panic* scenario.**

where $\mathcal{E}$ includes K individual emotion classifiers $\{\mathcal{C}_{e_i}(f)\}_{i=1}^{n}$, each classifier maps f to the corresponding ith emotion of $\mathbb{E}^n$, and $\mathcal{B}$ maps an emotion attribute $\mathbf{e} \in \mathbb{E}^n$ to a behavior class label $\mathbf{y} \in \mathbb{Y}$. The emotion classifiers are learned during training using the emotion annotations provided by our dataset. Particularly, the classifier $\mathcal{C}_{e_i}(f)$ is a binary linear SVM trained by labeling the examples of all behavior classes whose emotion value $e_i = 1$ as positive examples and others as negative.

Assuming no emotion ground-truth information is available during test time, we represent each video clip x by $\phi(x) \in \mathbb{E}_k$:

$$\phi(x) = [s_1(x), s_2(x), \ldots, s_K(x)] \tag{3.2}$$

where $s_k(x)$ is the confidence score of the kth emotion classifier $\mathcal{C}_{e_k}$ in $\mathcal{E}$. This emotion-based crowd representation vector has an entry for each emotion attribute and is used to show the degree of presence of an emotion attribute in a video clip (see *Emotion-Based Representation Experiments*, Section 3.4.2). The mapping $\mathcal{B}$ is finally obtained by training a multi-class linear SVM for behavior classes on emotion-based crowd representation vectors. The fact that abnormal behavior classes and behavior instances share the same semantic space and the capability to manually define $\mathcal{B}$ makes it possible to recognize a novel abnormal behavior class with no training samples available, which is beyond the scope of the current work (see Figure 3.5f). As can be seen, a set of emotions forms a semantic space form $\mathbb{E}^n$, in which each behavior class or behavior instance is shown by a dataset frame. A "frame" represents a behavior instance; a "star" represents a known behavior class y that has training examples (the surrounding frames). In this space, an unknown behavior b_x that belongs to one of the behavior classes can be recognized by attaching its closest behavior class to it.

Table 3.4 Some Examples of Emotions Applied to Videos to Characterize Mentioned Scenarios

Type of Basic Emotions	Scenarios	No. of Videos
Angry	Previous personal issues between individuals who suddenly meet each other Intentional or unintentional bad physical contact between people Demonstration Motorcycle left in the crowd Motorcycle crossing the crowd	11
Happy	One or more individuals greeting in the crowd	5
Excited	Demonstration Bag theft with motorcycle Two or more friends suddenly visit each other in the crowd	9
Scared	Sniper attack Terrorist firework Hoodlum attack Motorcycle crossing the crowd Bag theft in the crowd with motorcycle	12
Sad	An individual facing a health problem in the crowd Demonstration	4
Neutral	All videos begin with neutral frames	All

3.3.1 Emotions as Latent Variables

Given a set of N training instances $\{(x^{(n)}, y^{(n)})\}_{n=1}^{N}$, we need to train a classification model to recognize an unseen video clip x. As mentioned earlier, we select crowd emotions as attributes, which are discriminative and yet able to extract the intra-class changing of each behavior. Note that intra-class changing may cause video clips to correspond to different sets of emotion information, despite belonging to the same behavior class. For instance, the behavior class *congestion* in some video clips of our dataset has the *angry* emotion attribute, while in other samples it contains the *happy* emotion attribute (see Figure 3.6). The same situation may happen for other behavior classes. To address this problem, emotion attributes are treated as latent variables and we learn the model using the latent SVM [36,37]. Regarding emotion attributes as an abstract part of a behavior class, we introduce a semantic space $\mathbb{E}^n$, wherein location of an emotion attribute is defined as a latent variable, $e_i \in \mathbb{E}^n$. The probability of a video clip possessing this emotion-attribute is higher when we have larger values of e_i. Considering W as a parameter vector, we aim to train a classifier f_W to predict the behavior class of an unknown video clip x during testing, $y^* = arg\max_{y \in \mathbb{Y}} f_W(x,y)$. It is note worthy that we cannot characterize this prediction only by the video–label pair (x,y); its corresponding emotion-attribute values $e \in \mathbb{E}^n$ are also needed. Specifically, a video-label pair (x,y) is scored by the function of the

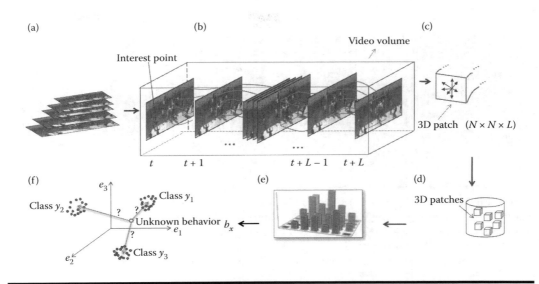

Figure 3.5 **Mixture of low-level features, namely, HOG, HOF, and MBH, with high-level semantic concepts (emotion labels) for the task of crowd behavior classification. (a) Dense sampling. (b) Tracking of dense points in *L* frames. (c) Computing HOG, MBH, and HOF. (d) Code book extraction. (e) Introducing emotions as mid-level representation. (f) Behavior emotion space E^n.**

following form:

$$f_W(x, y) = arg \max_{e \in \mathbb{E}} \phi(x, y, e) \qquad (3.3)$$

where $\phi(x, y, e)$ is a feature vector relating to the raw feature x, a parameter vector preparing a weight for each feature w, and y is the raw behavior class label for each feature. The linear model is defined as:

$$W^T \phi(x, y, e) = W_x \varphi_1(x) + \sum_{l \in \mathbb{E}} W_{e_l}^T \varphi_2(x, e_l) + \sum_{l, m \in \mathbb{E}} W_{e_l, e_m}^T \varphi_3(e_l, e_m) \qquad (3.4)$$

where parameter vector W is $W = \{W_x; W_{e_l}; W_{e_l, e_m}\}$, and $\mathbb{E}$ is an emotion-attribute set. In Equation 3.4, if we only keep the potential function $W_x \varphi_1(x)$ and discard others, we can train W_x using a binary linear SVM. By providing the score, the potential function $W_x \varphi_1(x)$ evaluates how well the raw feature $\varphi_1(x)$ of a video clip matches the model vector W_x, which is a set of coefficients learned from the raw feature x. In our implementation, we use this observation and represent $\varphi(x)$ as the score output of the pretrained linear SVM instead of keeping it as a high-dimensional feature vector. In this way, W_x is a scalar value providing SVM score weights. For a specific emotion attribute, like e_l, the potential function $W_{e_l}^T \varphi_2(x, e_l)$ prepares the score of an individual emotion attribute, which is used to show the presence of an attribute in the video clip x. As we mentioned in Section 3.3, the initial value of a specific emotion attribute e_l is extracted from its class label during training and is provided by a pretrained emotion-attribute classifier during testing. The simultaneous occurrence of a pair of emotion attributes (e_l, e_m) is captured by the edge function $W_{e_l, e_m}^T \varphi_3(e_l, e_m)$, wherein the feature vector $\varphi_3(e_l, e_m)$ is an $\mathbb{E} \times \mathbb{E}$ dimensional indicator for edge function configurations and the corresponding W_{e_l, e_m}^T has weights of all configurations. From a set of training instances, the model vector W is learned by solving the following formulation as a

(a)   (b)

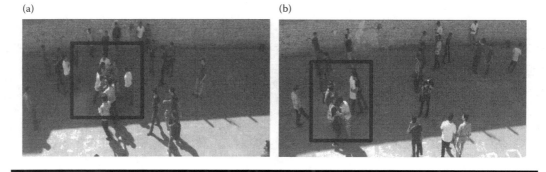

Figure 3.6 **Two sample frames of our dataset. In frame (a), individuals are fighting, while in frame (b) people are greeting each other. Considering only visual low-level features, (a) and (b) are similar; however, they are completely different when also considering crowd emotion as a high-level semantic representation. In spite of having the *congestion* behavior class in both frames, in frame (a) individuals are *angry*, while in frame (b) individuals are *happy* emotionally.**

learning objective function:

$$W^* = \min_{W} \lambda ||W||^2 + \sum_{j=1}^{n} \max(0, 1 - y_j \cdot f_w(x_j)) \qquad (3.5)$$

where λ is the trade-off parameter controlling the amount of regularization, and the second term performs a soft margin. Due to the existence of an inner max in f_W, the objective function in Equation 3.5 is semi-convex. In our implementation, the optimization problem is solved by adopting the coordinate descent [36], as follows:

■ Holding W fixed, we find the best emotion-attribute configuration e^* that maximizes $W \cdot \phi(x, y, e)$
■ Holding e^* fixed, we find a parameter W that optimizes the convex objective in Equation 3.5

In our current process, we use training data to create the emotion-attribute relation graph. For the sake of computational efficiency, we dedicate two statues, namely {0} and {1}, to emotion attributes. Finally, we apply belief propagation [36] to find the best emotion-attribute configuration e^* for $f_W(x, y) = \max_{e \in \mathbb{E}} W^T \phi(x, y, e)$ (see *Latent-Emotion Crowd Representation Experiment*, Section 3.4.2).

3.4 Experiments

The broad variety of crowd emotion attributes needs a low-level feature representation to explain several visual aspects. In this section, we first apply the state-of-the-art dense trajectories [38,39] approach for behavior recognition as a baseline. Figure 3.7 shows the dense trajectories computed for different crowded scenarios in our dataset. Following that, we propose emotion-based crowd representation by introducing crowd emotions as intermediate representations for the type of behavior classification. We believe that by applying an emotion layer as a bridge between low-level features and crowd behavior labels, it is possible to construct a more efficient learning behavior

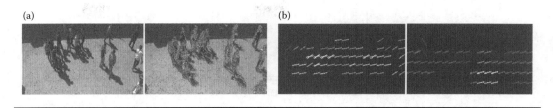

Figure 3.7 (a) Dense trajectories computed for different crowded scenarios in our dataset. (b) Histogram of oriented tracklets computed for two sample crowded scenarios in our dataset.

classification framework. In Figure 3.5, the schematic form of the applied baseline is demonstrated. Note that we fixed the evaluation protocol during all the experiments. Furthermore, we divided the train and test data in a leave-one-sequence-out fashion. More precisely, for 31 iterations (equal to the number of video sequences) we leave out all the video clips of a sequence to test and train on all the video clips of the 30 remaining sequences. In the evaluation process, we used the average accuracy criterion both in tables and confusion matrices. We use dense trajectory features for all the confusion matrices.

3.4.1 Baseline Methods

Low-level visual feature baseline: We adopt the well-known dense trajectories [38,39] to represent each video clip of our dataset. For this purpose, the state-of-the-art trajectory-aligned descriptors, namely, the HOG [40], HOF [41], MBH [42], and dense trajectories [39], are computed within a space-time volume around the trajectory to encode the motion information. The size of the volume is 32×32 pixels and it is 15 frames long (see Figure 3.5). In order to evaluate our dense trajectory features, we use a standard bag-of-features approach. More specifically, we first construct a code-book for each descriptor (HOG, HOF, MBH, and trajectory) separately. The number of visual words per descriptor is fixed to $d = 1000$, which has shown empirically to yield good results over a wide range of datasets. For the sake of time and simplicity, we cluster a subset of 150,000 randomly selected training features using k-means. In order to increase precision, k-means is initialized ten times and the result with the lowest error is kept. Descriptors are assigned to their closest vocabulary word using Euclidean distance. The resulting histograms of visual word occurrences are used as video descriptors. For classification, a standard one-vs-all multi-class SVM classifier is used. For this purpose, we separately evaluate computed low-level feature descriptors using only the crowd behavior ground-truth label information. The average precision for each of them is reported in the first column of Table 3.5. Results show that the dense trajectory feature achieved 38.71% precision in crowd-behavior-type detection and has better performance compared to the other four feature descriptors. Figure 3.8 shows the confusion matrix for five different crowd behavior classes with varied performance. Some interesting observations can be made from the confusion tables. For example, the *panic* crowd behavior class has the best average precision of 74.82% compared to the other classes, probably because of being a simpler visual task. Also, some *panic* crowd behavior classes are misclassified as *fight* with the most average precision since both classes share similar motion patterns (very sharp movements).

3.4.2 Emotion-Based Representation Experiments

In this part we present a series of experiments with respect to our emotion-based proposed method described in Section 3.3. For this purpose, we first assume that we have access to the ground-truth

Table 3.5 Comparison of Different Feature Descriptors (Trajectory, HOG, HOF, MBH, and Dense Trajectory) on Low-Level Visual Feature, Emotion-Based and Latent-Emotion Categories in Our Dataset

	Our Dataset		
	Low-Level Visual Feature	Emotion-Based	Latent-Emotion
Trajectory	35.30	40.05	40.04
HOG	38.80	38.77	42.18
HOF	37.69	41.50	41.51
MBH	38.53	42.72	42.92
Dense trajectory	38.71	43.64	43.90

Note: We report average accuracy over all classes for our dataset.

		Prediction				
		Panic	Fight	Congestion	Obstacle	Neutral
Truth	Panic	74.82%	15.18%	5.64%	3.39%	0.97%
	Fight	24.48%	30.47%	17.18%	18.24%	9.63%
	Congestion	32.17%	18.11%	23.43%	18.91%	7.38%
	Obstacle	9.25%	25.54%	19.02%	27.94%	18.25%
	Neutral	9.40%	16.80%	17.65%	19.27%	36.88%

Figure 3.8 Confusion matrix for the low-level visual feature class.

emotion labels during both testing and training. Unlike in the second experiment, it is assumed that we have access to them only during training.

3.4.2.1 Emotion-Aware Baseline

In this part we use the basic ground-truth crowd emotion information, namely, *angry, happy, excited, scared, sad,* and *neutral,* to create attribute features. We first simply build a six-dimensional binary feature vector for all the test and training data. As an example, if the crowd possesses the *happy* emotion class, the feature vector can be represented as $\{0, 1, 0, 0, 0, 0\} \in \mathbb{E}^6$, with each dimension indicating the presence or absence of a crowd emotion-attribute class. As the next process, considering created features, we train a multi-class SVM classifier using crowd behavior labels. During testing we evaluate the pretrained classifier with test examples. The average precision result for this experiment over all crowd behavior classes is shown in the second column of Table 3.6.

It is obvious that the average precision achieved using a binary feature created with an emotion ground-truth label is 83.79%, which is almost 50% higher than the one achieved using low-level visual features. Such significant margins suggest that having a precise emotion recognition method can be very helpful for crowd behavior understanding. Motivated by these results, in the following experiments we apply the crowd emotion information as a mid-level representation for the task of understanding crowd behavior.

Table 3.6   Comparison of Dense Trajectory Descriptor on Low-Level Visual Features, Emotion-Aware and Emotion-Based Categories in Our Dataset

	Our Dataset		
	Low-Level Visual Feature	*Emotion-Aware*	*Emotion-Based*
Trajectory	38.71	83.79	43.64

Note: We report average accuracy over all classes for our dataset.

3.4.2.2 Emotion-Based Crowd Representation Experiment

In this part, we first simply use the ground-truth emotion information to separately evaluate the aforementioned low-level feature descriptors. Figure 3.9 shows the performance comparison between varied combinations of different types of emotion information in a confusion matrix based on dense trajectory feature descriptors with an average accuracy of 34.13%. The results reported in the confusion matrix of Figure 3.9 can be fairly used for abnormality behavior detection procedures. As the second part of this experiment, we assume that no emotion information is available for the test data, so we teach a set of binary linear SVMs using the emotion labels of training data. As we mentioned in Section 3.3, we know $C_{e_i}(f)$ as emotion classifiers. The output of an emotion classifier is a vector wherein each dimension shows the confidence score of each emotion-attribute prediction. We consider this vector as an emotion-based crowd representation vector for behavior classification. We extract this vector for all the training and test data and, following that, we train multi-class SVMs with behavior labels. This behavior classifier is finally evaluated on test data to report the final accuracy of behavior classification.

We applied this method separately to HOG, HOF, MBH, trajectory, and dense trajectory low-level feature descriptors. The average accuracy resulting for each of them is presented in the second column of Table 3.5. As can be seen, the dense trajectory feature descriptor achieved the best precision among the other low level feature descriptors with 43.64%. This experiment has the highest accuracy compared to the two other baselines, increasing them by almost 7%. Also, in the confusion matrix in Figure 3.10, the best detection result belongs to the *panic* behavior class with 71.87% and the most conflict belongs to the *fight* behavior category with 11.88%. On the other hand, the worst detection result belongs to the *congestion* behavior class with the most conflict of 21.92% into the *panic* crowd behavior class. These results are in line with the average

	Prediction					
Truth	Angry	Happy	Excited	Scared	Sad	Neutral
Angry	25.42%	15.40%	16.12%	26.45%	11.14%	5.47%
Happy	17.60%	18.10%	23.92%	15.05%	19.06%	6.27%
Excited	20.39%	11.90%	32.22%	5.91%	16.11%	13.47%
Scared	14.02%	10.22%	6.58%	65.92%	2.86%	0.40%
Sad	26.92%	6.75%	6.31%	27.66%	29.56%	2.80%
Neutral	9.59%	17.88%	17.51%	7.54%	13.90%	33.58%

Figure 3.9   Confusion matrix for the emotion class.

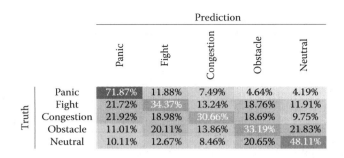

		Prediction				
		Panic	Fight	Congestion	Obstacle	Neutral
	Panic	71.87%	11.88%	7.49%	4.64%	4.19%
	Fight	21.72%	34.37%	13.24%	18.76%	11.91%
Truth	Congestion	21.92%	18.98%	30.66%	18.69%	9.75%
	Obstacle	11.01%	20.11%	13.86%	33.19%	21.83%
	Neutral	10.11%	12.67%	8.46%	20.65%	48.11%

Figure 3.10   Confusion matrix for the emotion-score-based class.

accuracies achieved in emotion-based classifiers and the emotion-aware baseline. They also support the idea of having better emotion recognition classifiers and more precise emotion labels to boost the performance of crowd behavior category recognition.

3.4.2.3 Latent-Emotion Crowd Representation Experiment

In this part we treat emotion labels as latent variables and train the model using the latent SVM. In the third column of Table 3.5, the best result of this experiment is reported as 43.90% for the dense trajectory descriptor. Considering Table 3.5, it is obvious that the result for the latent-emotion experiment is much better compared to the low-level visual feature experiment and is also better compared to the emotion-based experiment.

3.5 Conclusions

In this chapter, we have proposed a novel crowd dataset with both annotations of abnormal crowd behavior and crowd emotion. We believe this dataset not only can be used as a benchmark in the computer vision community, but can also open up doors toward understanding the correlations between the two tasks of crowd behavior understanding and emotion recognition. As the second contribution, we present a method that exploits jointly the complementary information of these two tasks, outperforming all baselines of both tasks significantly. In particular, future work will be directed toward recognizing a novel abnormal behavior class with no training samples available, by manually defining the emotion-to-behavior mapping function.

References

1. Louis Kratz and Ko Nishino. Anomaly detection in extremely crowded scenes using spatio-temporal motion pattern models. In *Computer Vision and Pattern Recognition, 2009. CVPR 2009. IEEE Conference on*, pages 1446–1453. IEEE, 2009.
2. Louis Kratz and Ko Nishino. Tracking with local spatio-temporal motion patterns in extremely crowded scenes. In *Computer Vision and Pattern Recognition (CVPR), 2010 IEEE Conference on*, pages 693–700. IEEE, 2010.
3. Barbara Krausz and Christian Bauckhage. Analyzing pedestrian behavior in crowds for automatic detection of congestions. In *Computer Vision Workshops (ICCV Workshops), 2011 IEEE International Conference on*, pages 144–149. IEEE, 2011.

4. Weixin Li, Vijay Mahadevan, and Nuno Vasconcelos. Anomaly detection and localization in crowded scenes. *Pattern Analysis and Machine Intelligence, IEEE Transactions on*, **36**(1):18–32, 2014.

5. Ramin Mehran, Akira Oyama, and Mubarak Shah. Abnormal crowd behavior detection using social force model. In *Computer Vision and Pattern Recognition, 2009. CVPR 2009. IEEE Conference on*, pages 935–942. IEEE, 2009.

6. Raghavendra Ramachandra, Alessio Del Bue, Marco Cristani, and Vittorio Murino. Optimizing interaction force for global anomaly detection in crowded scenes. In *Computer Vision Workshops (ICCV Workshops), 2011 IEEE International Conference on*, pages 136–143. IEEE, 2011.

7. Vikas Reddy, Conrad Sanderson, and Brian C. Lovell. Improved anomaly detection in crowded scenes via cell-based analysis of foreground speed, size and texture. In *Computer Vision and Pattern Recognition Workshops (CVPRW), 2011 IEEE Computer Society Conference on*, pages 55–61. IEEE, 2011.

8. Hamidreza Rabiee, Hossein Mousavi, Moin Nabi, and Mahdyar Ravanbakhsh. Detection and localization of crowd behavior using a novel tracklet-based model. *International Journal of Machine Learning and Cybernetics*, 2017. https://doi.org/10.1007/s13042-017-0682-8.

9. Hossein Mousavi, Moin Nabi, Hamed Kiani Galoogahi, Alessandro Perina, and Vittorio Murino. Abnormality detection with improved histogram of oriented tracklets. In Vittorio Murino and Enrico Puppo (Eds.). *Image Analysis and Processing—ICIAP 2015*. ICIAP 2015. Lecture Notes in Computer Science, vol 9280. Springer, Cham, Switzerland.

10. Hossein Mousavi, Moin Nabi, Hamed Kiani Galoogahi, Alessandro Perina, and Vittorio Murino. Crowd motion monitoring using tracklet-based commotion measure. In *2015 IEEE International Conference on Image Processing (ICIP)*, pages 2354–2358, September 27–30, 2015, Quebec City, QC, Canada. doi:10.1109/ICIP.2015.7351223.

11. Mahdyar Ravanbakhsh, Moin Nabi, Hossein Mousavi, Enver Sangineto, and Nicu Sebe. Plug-and-play {CNN} for crowd motion analysis: An application in abnormal event detection. *CoRR*, arXiv preprint arXiv:1610.00307.

12. Roddy Cowie, Ellen Douglas-Cowie, Nicolas Tsapatsoulis, George Votsis, Stefanos Kollias, Winfried Fellenz, and John G. Taylor. Emotion recognition in human-computer interaction. *Signal Processing Magazine, IEEE*, **18**(1):32–80, 2001.

13. Paul Ekman. An argument for basic emotions. *Cognition & Emotion*, **6**(3–4):169–200, 1992.

14. Paul Ekman and Wallace V. Friesen. Facial action coding system. 1977.

15. Paul Ekman and Klaus Scherer. Expression and the nature of emotion. *Approaches to Emotion*, **3**:19–344, 1984.

16. Alvin I. Goldman and Chandra Sekhar Sripada. Simulationist models of face-based emotion recognition. *Cognition*, **94**(3):193–213, 2005.

17. Björn Schuller, Gerhard Rigoll, and Manfred Lang. Hidden Markov model-based speech emotion recognition. In *Acoustics, Speech, and Signal Processing, 2003. Proceedings (ICASSP'03). 2003 IEEE International Conference on*, volume **2**, pages II–1. IEEE, 2003.

18. Mark Coulson. Attributing emotion to static body postures: Recognition accuracy, confusions, and viewpoint dependence. *Journal of Nonverbal Behavior*, **28**(2):117–139, 2004.

19. Sidney K. Dmello, Scotty D. Craig, Amy Witherspoon, Bethany Mcdaniel, and Arthur Graesser. Automatic detection of learners affect from conversational cues. *User Modeling and User-Adapted Interaction*, **18**(1–2):45–80, 2008.

20. Selene Mota and Rosalind W. Picard. Automated posture analysis for detecting learner's interest level. In *Computer Vision and Pattern Recognition Workshop, 2003. CVPRW'03. Conference on*, volume **5**, pages 49–49. IEEE, 2003.

21. Mirza Waqar Baig, Emilia I. Barakova, Lucio Marcenaro, Matthias Rauterberg, and Carlo S. Regazzoni. Crowd emotion detection using dynamic probabilistic models. In *From Animals to Animats 13*, pages 328–337. Springer, 2014.

22. Mirza Waqar Baig, Mirza Sulman Baig, Vahid Bastani, Emilia I. Barakova, Lucio Marcenaro, Carlo S. Regazzoni, and Matthias Rauterberg. Perception of emotions from crowd dynamics. In *Digital Signal Processing (DSP), 2015 IEEE International Conference on*, pages 703–707. IEEE, 2015.

23. Joanna Edel McHugh, Rachel McDonnell, Carol OSullivan, and Fiona N. Newell. Perceiving emotion in crowds: The role of dynamic body postures on the perception of emotion in crowded scenes. *Experimental Brain Research*, **204**(3):361–372, 2010.

24. Ali Farhadi, Ian Endres, and Derek Hoiem. Attribute-centric recognition for cross-category generalization. In *Computer Vision and Pattern Recognition (CVPR), 2010 IEEE Conference on*, pages 2352–2359. IEEE, 2010.

25. Christoph H. Lampert, Hannes Nickisch, and Stefan Harmeling. Learning to detect unseen object classes by between-class attribute transfer. In *Computer Vision and Pattern Recognition, 2009. CVPR 2009. IEEE Conference on*, pages 951–958. IEEE, 2009.

26. Jingen Liu, Benjamin Kuipers, and Silvio Savarese. Recognizing human actions by attributes. In *Computer Vision and Pattern Recognition (CVPR), 2011 IEEE Conference on*, pages 3337–3344. IEEE, 2011.

27. Hamidreza Rabiee, Javad Haddadnia, and Hossein Mousavi. Crowd behavior representation: An attribute-based approach. *SpringerPlus*, **5**:1179, 2016. doi:10.1186/s40064-016-2786-0.

28. Hamidreza Rabiee, Javad Haddadnia, Hossein Mousavi, M. Kalantarzadeh, Moin Nabi, and Vittorio Murino. Novel dataset for fine-grained abnormal behavior understanding in crowd. In *13th IEEE International Conference on Advanced Video and Signal Based Surveillance (AVSS)*. IEEE, August 23–26, 2016, doi:10.1109/AVSS.2016.7738074.

29. Vijay Mahadevan, Weixin Li, Viral Bhalodia, and Nuno Vasconcelos. Anomaly detection in crowded scenes. In *Computer Vision and Pattern Recognition (CVPR), 2010 IEEE Conference on*, pages 1975–1981. IEEE, 2010.

30. Xiaogang Wang, Xiaoxu Ma, and William Eric Leifur Grimson. Unsupervised activity perception in crowded and complicated scenes using hierarchical Bayesian models. *Pattern Analysis and Machine Intelligence, IEEE Transactions on*, **31**(3):539–555, 2009.

31. J. Ferryman, A. Shahrokni et al. An overview of the PETS 2009 challenge. 2009.

32. Tal Hassner, Yossi Itcher, and Orit Kliper-Gross. Violent flows: Real-time detection of violent crowd behavior. In *Computer Vision and Pattern Recognition Workshops (CVPRW), 2012 IEEE Computer Society Conference on*, pages 1–6. IEEE, 2012.

33. Mikel Rodriguez, Josef Sivic, Ivan Laptev, and Jean-Yves Audibert. Data-driven crowd analysis in videos. In *Computer Vision (ICCV), 2011 IEEE International Conference on*, pages 1235–1242. IEEE, 2011.

34. Berkan Solmaz, Brian E. Moore, and Mubarak Shah. Identifying behaviors in crowd scenes using stability analysis for dynamical systems. *Pattern Analysis and Machine Intelligence, IEEE Transactions on*, **34**(10):2064–2070, 2012.

35. Gordon H. Bower and Paul R. Cohen. Emotional influences in memory and thinking: Data and theory. Affect and cognition, pages 291–331, 2014.

36. Pedro Felzenszwalb, David McAllester, and Ramanan Deva. A discriminatively trained, multiscale, deformable part model. In *Computer Vision and Pattern Recognition, 2008. CVPR 2008. IEEE Conference on*, pages 1–8. IEEE, 2008.

37. Yang Wang and Greg Mori. Max-margin hidden conditional random fields for human action recognition. In *Computer Vision and Pattern Recognition, 2009. CVPR 2009. IEEE Conference on*, pages 872–879. IEEE, 2009.

38. Bo Wang, Mao Ye, Xue Li, Fengjuan Zhao, and Jian Ding. Abnormal crowd behavior detection using high-frequency and spatio-temporal features. *Machine Vision and Applications*, **23**(3):501–511, 2012.

39. Heng Wang, Alexander Kläser, Cordelia Schmid, and Cheng-Lin Liu. Action recognition by dense trajectories. In *Computer Vision and Pattern Recognition (CVPR), 2011 IEEE Conference on*, pages 3169–3176. IEEE, 2011.

40. Navneet Dalal and Bill Triggs. Histograms of oriented gradients for human detection. In *Computer Vision and Pattern Recognition, 2005. CVPR 2005. IEEE Computer Society Conference on*, volume **1**, pages 886–893. IEEE, 2005.

41. Ivan Laptev, Marcin Marszałek, Cordelia Schmid, and Benjamin Rozenfeld. Learning realistic human actions from movies. In *Computer Vision and Pattern Recognition, 2008. CVPR 2008. IEEE Conference on*, pages 1–8. IEEE, 2008.

42. Navneet Dalal, Bill Triggs, and Cordelia Schmid. Human detection using oriented histograms of flow and appearance. In *Computer Vision–ECCV 2006*, pages 428–441. Springer, 2006.

Chapter 4

Cognitive Sensing: Adaptive Anomalies Detection with Deep Networks

Chao Wu and Yike Guo

Contents

4.1 Introduction

A world that is purely predictable and deterministic requires less intelligence [1]. But in real cases, the world is always dynamic, unpredictable, ambiguous, and noisy [2]. From a cognitive point of view, the intelligence of any intelligent agent (like an animal) is a kind of ability to achieve equilibrium with its uncertain environment. It can sense or act (to fit or intervene with its environment) to minimize its free energy, which is essentially the divergence between its internal model about the environment and the real environment [3].

Such intelligence is under some constraints. Facing a dynamic and high-dimensional world, even for the most complex systems as human brains, neural computation resources are limited [4]. Our action and intervention capabilities within the environment (like motion capability) are also limited. To handle an uncertain world with constrained resources, intelligent agents developed several crucial cognitive mechanisms: We use attention [5] and surprise [6] to select information that deserves to be processed and allocate neural resources for feature binding [7]. We have long-term and short-term working memory [8] to organize the information hierarchically. Our brain is constituted of deep networks [9], each of which acts as a universal model and supports the "one learning algorithm" [10]. Such deep networks are considered to be very useful to organize and process our knowledge.

Current sensing methods often ignore the fact that their sensing targets are dynamic and can change over time. The authors of [11] provided a survey of current model-based sensing systems, which belong to four basic categories: model-based data acquisition, data cleaning, query processing, and data compression. However, to build an accurate model should not always be the goal. What we need is to establish an adaptive modeling framework. (Related research to the work here is data assimilation [12,13], which incorporates observations into numerical models to calibrate it and optimize sensor placement. It has been widely used in applications like numerical weather prediction. However, compared to the method described in this paper, data assimilation is more specific to certain numerical models, while our method is more generic and can be integrated with machine learning methods like deep learning.) Lack of adaptability hinders us from building more intelligent sensing systems. Can cognitive mechanisms, or at least some of them, be adopted in a sensing system to make it more intelligent? This idea motivated the work in this chapter: we tried to get inspirations from biological intelligence and designed an adaptive computational framework for sensing and modeling a dynamic target under system resource constraints. The emphasis here is to detect target's anomalies, or surprises, which indicate events or new behaviors of the target. Examples of anomalies include accidents (*events*) in traffic (*target*), seizures (*events*) for human brains (*target*), and progression (*new behavior*) of a disease (*target*).

Specifically, in this chapter, we will (1) set a different system goal for building a sensing system, which is to minimize the free energy between the model and its target; (2) adopt an attention-based mechanism to detect anomalies and control the model update; (3) use a training data window as the working memory mechanism; (4) utilize a deep network for model representation; and (5) use partial input, based on surprise minimization sensor selection, to reduce the sensing dimension.

In Section 4.2, a detailed methodology of our framework is given. Section 3 provides both simulated evaluation and evaluation through an application. Section 4 provides some discussion and concludes the chapter with a future research plan.

In summary, we will present an active sensing framework that is motivated by approaches in computational neuroscience based on active inference. Formally, this corresponds to the minimization of variational free energy or, more simply, surprise. The key thing that we bring to the table is that surprise can also be used to select informative data points that enable efficient model inversion and learning. Furthermore, the detection of anomalies or surprising observations may, in itself, be very useful. We will demonstrate these points using simulated time series from a volatility model, in which the distribution of variables changes over time. This simulation is used to illustrate the utility of sampling data based on its surprise. In the second example, surprise is not used to select data channels but to detect anomalies that may be interesting in their own right; namely, the emergence of pathological seizure activity in EEG traces.

4.2 Methods

4.2.1 Notations and Problem Definition

Here we firstly define the notations used in this paper.

Target: As shown in Figure 4.1, we represent the target that we want to understand as $x = (x_1, x_2, \ldots, x_i, \ldots, x_n) \in R^n$ with dimension n, which is the size of spatial-temporal resolution of the target (e.g., if the target is the hourly temperature in one day, then $n = 24$. x can have infinite dimensions and $n = \infty$. x is a time series: at time t, we have $x^t = (x_1, x_2, \ldots, x_n)^t$, and we denote the collection of x as $X = \{x^1, x^2, \ldots, x^m\}$.

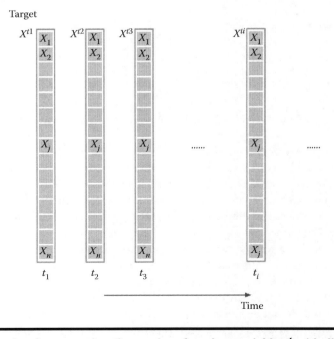

Figure 4.1   Target: Sensing target is a time series of random variable x^t with dimension n.

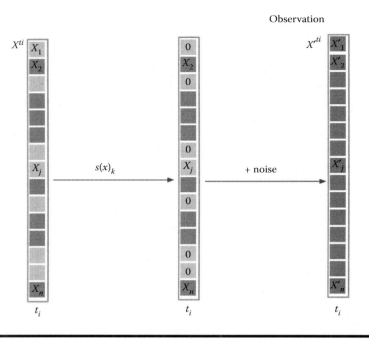

Figure 4.2   Observation: Observation is a corrupted and noised version of the target.

Observation: In most cases, we cannot observe x directly, but only observe partial x' (in lower dimension k) with noise ϵ, as shown in Figure 4.2. We define these noisy and partial observations from sensors as $X' = \{x'^1, x'^2, \dots, x'^m\}$, where $|x'|_0 = k$ and $k < n$. We assume $x' = s(x)_k + \epsilon$, where function $s(x)_k$ selects k elements in x, keeps their values, and sets the other elements to 0:

$$s(x)_k \begin{cases} x'_j = x_j, \, j \in \{m\}_k \\ x'_j = 0, \, j \notin \{m\}_k \end{cases}$$

$s(x)$ is the sensor selection method and $\{m\}_k$ are selected k elements from index set $\{m\} = \{1, 2, \dots, m\}$.

Model: The model y can be considered as generating the causes of hidden states x that are inferred on the basis of observations x'. The model (and its hidden states) can therefore be viewed as a representation of how observations x' were generated. This is known as a generative model and usually entails some parameters θ. This is the same framework used in models of human perception that can be viewed as some higher representation of its input [9]. y can be a distribution, a learned dictionary, or a stacked autoencoder as used in this chapter.

Problem definition: For a sensing system, the goal is to infer the posterior distribution of hidden states given observations, which is difficult when the generative model changes over time. Therefore, we try to approximate the posterior, with a proposal density $q(x|y)$. Given this approximation, there are two challenges: First, the mapping from y to x implicit in $q(x|y)$ should not only approximate the posterior but should be able to adapt to changes in the generative model. Second, when only partial observations are available, we want them to be informative. In other words, we design the function $s(x)_k$ optimally. This then becomes the well-known sensor selection problem.

With adaptive mapping from y to x, we then evaluate the new observations with the established model to check whether the model fails. If so, we say there are *anomalies* (or *outliers*, *surprises*). Anomalies in data can then be translated to significant (and often critical) actionable information in a wide variety of application domains [14].

4.2.2 Cognitive Approach

According to the free energy principle [3], any intelligent agent will sense or act to minimize its free energy $F(x,y)$, which is the KL (Kullback-Leibler) divergence between its internal approximation with the model and the real environment.

Based on the Infomax principle [15], the best mapping from y to x maximizes the mutual information between x and y, which can be represented as the difference between the entropy of x and conditional entropy of x given y [16]:

$$\mathrm{MI}(x; y) = H(x) - H(x|y)$$

As described in [16], if we assume that the entropy $H(X)$ is constant, the objective is then to minimize the conditional entropy, which, by definition, is

$$arg \min_{y} - H(x|y) = arg \max_{y} E_{p(x,y)} \log p(x|y)$$

With the approximation $q(x|y)$, we have

$$E_{p(x,y)}[\log q(x|y)] \le E_{p(x,y)}[\log p(x|y)]$$

which is a lower bound of $H(x|y)$. Assume we transform x to y with a deterministic or stochastic mapping $y = f_\theta(x)$, reconstruct x from y by $x = g\theta'(y)$, and use an empirical average over the observations as an unbiased estimation.

From the point of view of variational Bayesian inference, the function $y = f_\theta(x)$ is effectively a recognition function, while the corresponding mapping from hidden causes y to hidden states x, namely, $g\theta'(y)$, is the process of generation observations (or their hidden states).

We end up maximizing the mutual information in the following form:

$$arg \max_{\theta,\theta'} E_{p(x)}[\log q(x|y = f_\theta(x), \theta')]$$

This corresponds to the reconstruction error criterion for autoencoders, as we will see later.

Before describing the details in our methodology, let's give an overall workflow of the methodology, as shown in Figure 4.3. We use some sensor selection algorithm $s(x)_k$ upon target x to get observation x' and use a working memory to store the data required for model training and updates. The model training component trains and updates y (its parameter θ) with data in memory. The established model is tested with a new observation to detect anomalies. An anomaly happens when the target demonstrates new behavior or the model is rough. An anomaly triggers actions including a memory update and model update, and thus it causes a computational cost. Such a model update optimizes the free energy, and sensor selection keeps trying to find new bounds of free energy for further optimization.

We will discuss the details of these components in the remainder of this section.

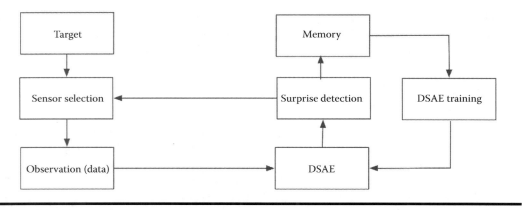

Figure 4.3 Overall work flow: The logical work flow of the methodology.

4.2.3 Model Representation

We utilize a variation of stacked autoencoders [17] as the model representation. An autoencoder neural network is (unsupervised) trained with back-propagation, setting the output values to be equal to the inputs, as shown in Figure 4.4. The result network takes an input x and transforms it into a hidden representation $y \in R^d$ through a deterministic function $y = f_\theta(x) = s(Wx + b)$ (with sigmoid activation function s), parameterized by $\theta = \{W, b\}$. W is a $d \times n$ weight matrix. b is the bias vector. The resulting y is then mapped back to a reconstructed vector $z \in R^n$ in input space $z = g_{\theta'}(y) = g_{\theta'}(f_\theta(x^i)) = s(W'y + b')$, with $\theta' = \{W', b'\}$. The weight matrix W' of the reverse mapping is constrained by $W' = W^T$.

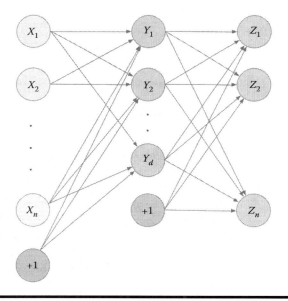

Figure 4.4 A basic autoencoder: Reconstruction of input with an autoencoder.

We get the optimized parameters θ^* and θ'^* by minimizing the reconstruction error (with loss function L) between x^i and z^i:

$$\theta^*, \theta'^* = arg \min_{\theta, \theta'} E_{p(x)}[L(x, z)]$$

Since $L(x,z) \propto - \log p(x|z)$ [and thus $L(x,z) \propto - \log q(x|z)$], we have

$$\theta^*, \theta'^* = arg \max_{\theta, \theta'} \log q(x|z = g_{\theta'}(f_\theta(x)))$$

$$= arg \max_{\theta, \theta'} \log q(x|y = f_\theta(x), \ \theta')$$

which is the same form of optimization described above.

With the m training set, we will try to optimize:

$$\theta^*, \theta'^* = arg \max_{\theta, \theta'} \frac{1}{m} \sum_{i=1}^{m} L(x^i, z^i)$$

$$= arg \max_{\theta, \theta'} \frac{1}{m} \sum_{i=1}^{m} L(x^i, g_{\theta'}(f_\theta(x^i)))$$

By placing constraints on the network, we are able to discover structure about the data. Instead of limiting the size for each hidden layer $||y||_0$, we impose sparsity constraints [18]. We add an extra penalty term to the optimization objective.

Let $\hat{\rho}_j$ be the average activation of hidden unit j, averaged over the m training examples,

$$\hat{\rho}_j = \frac{1}{m} \sum_{i=1}^{m} [a_j(x^i)]$$

where a_j denotes the activation of this hidden unit when the network is given a specific input x. ρ corresponds to a sparsity parameter and is the parameter of a categorical probability distribution. This is typically chosen to have a small value close to zero (e.g., 0.05). Therefore, the penalty term is the KL divergence between these two distributions (s_l is the size of the lth hidden layer)

$$\sum_{j=1}^{s_l} KL(\rho||\hat{\rho}_j) = \rho \log \frac{\rho}{\hat{\rho}_j} + (1 - \rho) \log \frac{1 - \rho}{1 - \hat{\rho}_j}$$

The cost function becomes

$$\frac{1}{m} \sum_{i=1}^{m} L(x^i, z^i) = \frac{1}{2m} \sum_{i=1}^{m} \sum_{j=1}^{n} \left(z_j^{(i)} - x_j^{(i)} \right)^2 + \frac{\lambda}{2} \sum_{l=1}^{n_l-1} \sum_{i=1}^{s_l} \sum_{j=1}^{s_l+1} \left(W_{ij}^l \right)^2 + \beta \sum_{l=2}^{n_l-1} \sum_{j=1}^{s_l} KL(\rho||\hat{\rho}_j)$$

Such an autoencoder is used as a building block to train deep networks, with the learned representation of the kth layer used as input for the $(k + 1)$th layer to learn a second-level representation. We train the $(k + 1)$th layer after the kth has been trained. These layers are "stacked" in

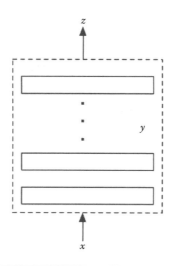

Figure 4.5   Stacked autoencoder: A stack of autoencoders are trained in a greedy layer-wise approach.

a greedy layer-wise approach as in [19]. This greedy layer-wise procedure has been shown to yield significantly better performance than random initialization [20].

Once a stack of encoders has been built (Figure 4.5), in addition to input reconstruction, its highest-level representation can also be used as input to a stand-alone supervised learning algorithm, such as SVM or another layer of encoder as a classifier (Figure 4.6).

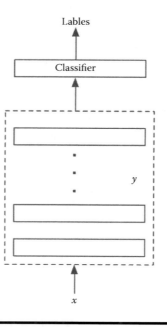

Figure 4.6   Stacked autoencoder with classifier: The highest level of autoencoders is used as input for a classifier.

We utilize such a deep network as the model representation. After the network is trained with historical observations, the model's output should be consistent with its input. The inconsistency between the input and the reconstructed output will be treated as a surprise or anomaly, as described later.

The advantage of using a deep network is its ability to model complex data. It has been a long-held belief that several layers of nonlinearity achieve better generalization performance on a difficult modeling problem. It is not a coincidence, considering the similar hierarchical architecture of regions of human brains, like the visual cortex [9]. Recent topological network analyses of brain circuits suggest that modular and hierarchical structural networks are particularly suited for the functional integration of local (functionally specialized) neuronal operations that underlie cognition [21]. Such hierarchical network architecture provides our brain with the ability to correct errors in a cascade of cortical processing events [9,22,23].

4.2.4 Memory

Inspired by human short-term working memory, we designed a simple memory for the data modeling. A memory is defined as $M = \{x^{*1}, x^{*2}, \ldots, x^{*k}\}$. k is the size of memory M (k is normally fixed, but can vary for specific system requirements). x^{*k} is the observation. The model described above will be trained or updated only with the data within this memory.

The same historical observation x can have multiple copies in this memory, which are partially sorted so that for any $x^{*i} = x^p$ and $x^{*j} = x^q$, if $i > j$, then $p \geq q$. Therefore, in the front of the memory, we have the oldest observations, while at the end of the memory, we have the most recent observations. We design a memory update strategy, so that the model values new observations more than those old observations, and it even forgets old observations (Figure 4.7 demonstrates the procedure for memory updates): when a new observation arrives, we apply a forget function $M = \Phi(x^*)$ to pick out and remove old data, and then we append the memory with a new observation (with multiple copies). We can use some naive approach for the forget function (e.g., randomly picking old observations) or a probabilistic function, so the older the data, the greater the chance that it will be removed. For data at index i in M, we define its probability of being forgotten as

$$\psi(i) = e^{-\delta i}$$

For all i, when $\Psi(i) \geq \eta$, we remove the $M(i)$ and append with the new observation x^* to $M(k)$.

The decay rate δ and threshold η control the speed of the memory update. If δ is small or η is small, it means that the old memory will be removed quickly, and the model changes fast.

Such a memory is crucial if the target is dynamic: if the target's behaviors are consistent (as in a normal machine-learning setting), all observations can reflect the target's state; however, when the target is changing, the model should have the ability to forget what it learned before and to adapt to the new state of the target.

For different model training methods, memory can play different roles. For point estimation method like the stacked autoencoder, the memory provides the data for model training and retraining. For Bayesian estimations like Gaussian process regression [24], the memory provides the data for calculating likelihood and thus influences the model update.

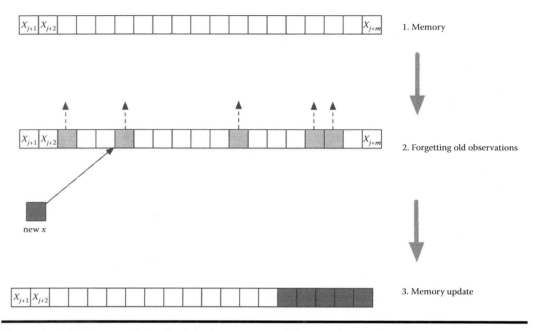

Figure 4.7   Memory update: Update the memory with new observation.

4.2.5 Surprise and Anomaly Detection

Attentional surprise [6] can exist only in the presence of uncertainty and is defined in a relative and subjective manner. It is related to the expectations of the observer: even derived from identical observations, the same data may carry different amounts of surprise at different times [25]. Therefore, it can be seen as the subjective measurement of information (we call it "subjective entropy").

In this paper, surprise is defined as the KL divergence between $q(x|y)$ and $p(x|x',y)$, as described above:

$$\text{surprise} = D_{\text{KL}}(q(x|y)||p(x|y))$$

Generally, this measure of surprise will correspond to a root-mean-squared error that scores the discrepancy between the observed input and the input predicted on the basis of the generative model. This is also known as prediction error in predictive coding. Under some simplifying assumptions, the sum of squared prediction errors corresponds to free energy.

Such surprise is the trigger for the model update (or retraining). If the surprise is larger than the surprise threshold ξ: $surprise > \xi$, it indicates the failure of the current model, and we need to update the model; also we need to update the memory to include this new significant observation.

In model representations like the stacked autoencoder, such a calculation of surprise cannot be conducted straightforwardly. We then use some other methods, like surprise computation with KL divergence defined in [6], to determine whether the model prediction has large variance of real observations, or we simply define the surprise for the autoencoder network as the loss value between the reconstructed output and observed input:

$$\text{surprise}(x) = L(x, g_{\theta'}(f_\theta(x')))$$

When this loss function (root-mean-squared error) output is greater than the surprise threshold ξ, it means the autoencoders cannot represent the input well at the moment. Then it's necessary to update the model to fit the current input, with the data from updated memory (however, we should notice that for the stacked autoencoders used in this chapter, an incremental model update is not applicable, and the update is actually done by retraining).

This attentional surprise also enables a new method of anomaly detection. Examples include seizure detection in EEG, which will be shown later in this paper. An anomaly, in our context, is either caused by the new behavior of the target (e.g., change of its distribution) or the roughness of the model (e.g., an under-fitted model). We expect more anomalies in the early time of the system and fewer later.

This kind of surprise simulates the human attention mechanism to some extent, acting as an information-processing bottleneck that allows only a small part of incoming sensory information to reach working memory and trigger a model update, instead of attempting to fully process the massive sensory input.

Humans maintain a certain level of alertness. When it's high, more resources are prepared for attention, and even subtle signs can be detected (e.g., when we are driving in an unknown area, we would like to pay more attention and allocate more computational resources). A similar idea is adopted here. We can find several parameters (and hyper-parameters) that provide us the chance to control the surprise and model update, including (1) surprise threshold (for model update frequency); (2) memory size (for the adaptive level of the model); and (3) sensor selection parameters (to predefine the region of sensing and change the frequency of surprise, as shown later). These top-down settings control the overall alertness of the sensing system, as well as the resource consumption. Top-down settings can be changed according to different system objectives and tasks.

4.2.6 Surprise Minimization Sensor Selection and Denoising Stacked Autoencoder (SAE)

When we only observe partial input x', the KL divergence (or detected surprise) is not greater than that with actual x (because some data are missing):

$$D'_{KL} \leq D_{KL}$$

In other words, there exists some space between D'_{KL} and D_{KL}: when we update the model and minimize surprise, we actually partially optimize D_{KL}. Therefore, to minimize the actual KL divergence, it's necessary for sensor selection schema to keep selecting new x' to find a new optimization bound. Two different strategies can be used: random and non-random sensor selections.

Although random selection can reduce the space (according to our experiment shown later), it requires a large amount of iterations, especially when the sensor number is limited. We tried to design some non-random sensor selection algorithm $s(x)_k$ that can reduce the space between D'_{KL} and D_{KL} more efficiently.

Specifically, we designed a surprise minimization sensor selection. We define the target's sensing space as $\Omega = \{0,1\}^n$ with dimension n. n is the number of available sensor placements or space/time resolution. The value 1 presents a sensed placement, while 0 presents a place not sensed. Assume with the current sensor selection that $s \in \Omega$ at the previous observation (an example is shown in Figure 4.8), we have data x', and we update the model to y. We search for a subset of sensory space $s' \subset s$, where surprise$_{s'} > \xi$. In other words, it's the region that the updated model cannot well fit.

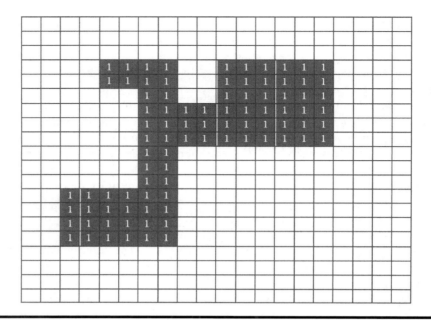

Figure 4.8 Placement: Current placement *s* with *n* = 400, dark (1) cells are selected for sensing.

We define the next sensing space s^*:

$$s^* = s' \cup B \cup \omega$$

$B \in \Omega$ is the predefined attentional area, which is a "spotlight" region (subset of sensory space), indicating where we are interested in [4]. With this predefined region, we can locally refine the approximation, focusing computational resources to suit the task and context at hand. ω generates the randomness of sensory selection. We create ω with random sampling method χ on Ω:

$$\omega \sim \chi(\Omega)$$

The creation of s^* is illustrated in Figure 4.9. When there is a constraint of the size of s^*, $|s^*| = p$, we randomly select p elements from s^*. This s^* will then be used as $\{m\}_k$ for selecting observations.

For a stacked autoencoder, we lower the dimension of sensing by using x' as a corrupted version of x (denoising stacked autoencoders (DSAE) [16]). Within s, $x' = x$, and outside this region $x' = 0$.

x' is mapped, as with the ordinary autoencoders, to a hidden representation $y = f_\theta(x') = s(Wx' + b)$, from which we reconstruct $z = g_{\theta'}(y) = s(Wy' + b')$. z is now a deterministic function of x' rather than x. The objective function minimized by the stochastic gradient descent becomes

$$arg \min_{\theta,\theta'} E_{p(z,x')}[L(x', g_{\theta'}(f_\theta(x')))]$$

where L is the loss function. It's also used to compute the surprise to detect the anomaly, as described above. Figure 4.10 shows the schematic representation of the training and anomaly detection procedure. With $J_{train}(\theta) = \frac{1}{m}L(x', g_{\theta'}(f_\theta(x')))$ for m observations in current memory, we use stochastic gradient descent to train.

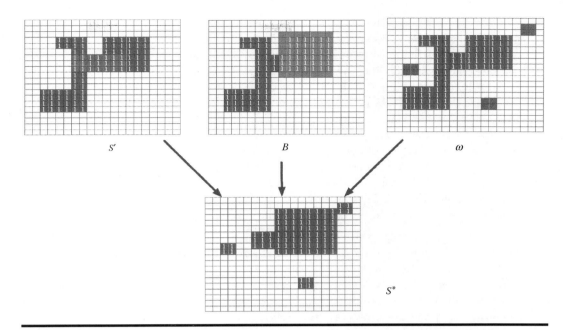

Figure 4.9   Placement update: Creation of s* with s′, B, and Ω.

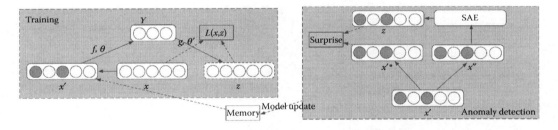

Figure 4.10   Denoising SAE: Training and anomaly detection with denoising SAE.

For $i = 1, \ldots, m,$

$$\theta_j = \theta_j - \frac{\alpha \partial}{\partial \theta_j} L(x', g_{\theta'}(f_\theta(x')))$$

By selecting those s': surprise$_{s'} > \xi$, we find those input units with a big contribution to the reconstruction error. We keep sensing them and update the model with their observations to minimize their errors, and thus we minimize the overall surprise.

4.2.7 Summary

Here we summarize the components in the methodology. These components' implementation can vary according to different applications or requirements:

1. *Model representation*: In this chapter, we use deep networks that are capable of modeling non-linear and complex targets. These networks are similar to the neural structure of humans,

and they are adaptive. They are suitable when sensing that the target is dynamic. However, when we have prior knowledge about the target, other model representations can be more suitable. For distributions from known processes like a Gaussian process, we can choose Bayesian-based methods like Gaussian process regression [24] (which also has generic modeling capability). These methods have the advantage of incremental model updates (instead of retraining the model). The problems of model retraining include not only a higher computational cost, but also the difficulty to get sufficient data for model training and updates. One particular model we noted is dictionary learning [26], which has the advantage of Bayesian inference as well as the freedom of model representation.

2. *Working memory*: The evolution of the model can be flexibly controlled by choosing different forget functions, different decay rates, etc. Although we fix the size of memory here, we will try enabling it with a flexible size.

3. *Surprise*: We can also compute surprise with the KL divergence between the model posterior and prior [6]: $\mathrm{KL}(p(y|x), p(y)) = \int p(x|y) \log \frac{p(y|x)}{p(y)} dy$. However, this approach requires estimating the distribution of the whole model space, which is not applicable for many cases. Other approaches can also be considered. For example, with the expectation and standard deviation of x, we can use a confidential interval or Chebyshev's theorem [27] to estimate the possibility of an observation instance, and we use its negative log as surprise. Some other anomaly detection algorithms [14] can also be chosen to detect surprise.

4. *Sensor selection*: Although we chose non-random selection in this paper, random sensor selection is also applicable, which has many good features like computational advantages, potential for compressive sensing [28], etc. For non-random sensor selection, we also have many other choices [29–32].

As a result, although we presented some specific components for implementing the computational framework, we are working on creating a computational pipeline based on this framework with an open architecture, providing multiple choices of components for users to choose for different applications.

4.3 Results

In this section, we evaluate the methodology described in the previous section with both simulated experiments and a real-world application.

4.3.1 Simulation Experiment

The dataset contains a simulated flow count of people entering a building. Each data record gives the (hourly) count of people entering the building for a day:

```
00-12-0908-2014: 110
00-13-0908-2014: 113
00-14-0908-2014: 115
00-15-0908-2014: 122
00-16-0908-2014: 127
00-17-0908-2014: 125
00-18-0908-2014: 123
```

Table 4.1 Distributions Used in Simulation Experiments

Name	Type	Parameters
N_1	Gaussian	$\mu = 20, \lambda = 20$
N_2	Gaussian	$\mu = 100, \lambda = 30$
N_3	Gaussian	$\mu = 20, \lambda = 30$
N_4	Gaussian	$\mu = 40, \lambda = 30$
N_5	Gaussian	$\mu = 60, \lambda = 3$
N_6	Gaussian	$\mu = 80, \lambda = 30$
N_7	Gaussian	$\mu = 100, \lambda = 30$
N_8	Gaussian	$\mu = 120, \lambda = 30$
N_9	Gaussian	$\mu = 140, \lambda = 30$
N_{10}	Gaussian	$\mu = 160, \lambda = 30$
N_{11}	Gaussian	$\mu = 180, \lambda = 30$
N_{12}	Gaussian	$\mu = 200, \lambda = 30$
Pois	Poisson	$\mu_1 = 20, \mu_2 = 50, \mu_3 = 70, \lambda = 30$
M	Mixture of 3 Gaussians	Mixture of N_1, N_2, and N_3

As a result, the simulated data are a 24-dimensional time series.

We generated this data based on certain generative models (Gaussian distributions and Poisson distribution; see Table 4.1 for details). We generated the data by randomly sampling these distributions with some additional noise and got the simulated hourly counts of people entering the building. We then built a sensing system based on the components described above and tried to understand this generative model from observation. The same challenge is posed for a sensing system: the target (its generative model) can change, and the observations are not complete.

We conducted four experiments with this dataset to show the following:

1. When the target changes, we can achieve faster KL divergence convergence with a memory mechanism;
2. Compared to other model representations, our deep network can achieve acceptable performance;
3. With partial observations, we can achieve KL minimization by both random sensor selection and surprise minimization sensor selection, but the latter performs better;
4. With the surprise mechanism, we can control the alertness of the system and find anomalies that we want to detect.

We ran the experiments on an array of 12 dual-core 2.80-GHz Intel Xeon CPUs and 32.0 GB RAM.

4.3.1.1 Change of Target Distribution with/without Memory

In the first experiment, the parameters of generative distribution change during the observation (e.g., the mean and variance of a Gaussian change to some new values, and the data generator generates the new data by sampling the new distribution). All data are normalized using standard deviation to the range between 0 and 1 in data preprocessing. The autoencoder network has five hidden layers with 200-200-500-200-200 hidden units, trained with the approach described above. Here we assume the distribution changes from N_1 to N_2. Surprise is computed as the reconstruction error, as described above. As one can see from Figure 4.11, with a deep network as the model representation, when we enable the memory window, the model can quickly capture the changed distribution and minimize surprise. Using the same model without memory, the minimization takes a much longer time.

We also evaluated the role of δ (memory decay rate). By setting different values of δ, we can show that smaller δ makes the model more adaptive to the target change, as shown in Table 4.2, and the model will "forget" previous data more easily. However, we notice it also increases the chance of over-fitting.

4.3.1.2 Change of Distribution Type and Model Representation

In the second experiment, we make more dramatic changes to the generative model. Instead of changing the parameters of distribution, we change the type of distribution, from Gaussian (N_1) to Poisson (*Pois*). As shown in Figure 4.12, we compared the performance of three different model representations here.

All the modeling methods are implemented within the surprise minimization scheme described above. For deep autoencoders, we used the same five-layer network (200-200-500-200-200 hidden

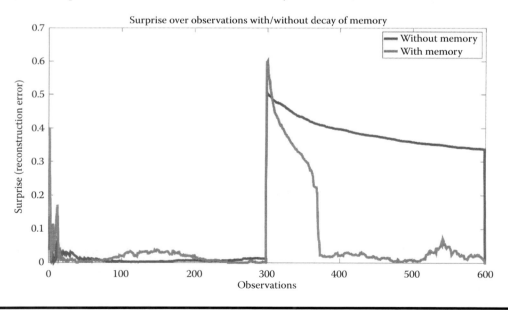

Figure 4.11 **The target's distribution changes during the observations: The *Y* axis shows the surprise value, and the *X* axis shows time (count of observations). It's clear that using a memory mechanism can achieve faster surprise minimization.**

Table 4.2 Model Update Performance with Different Memory Decay Rate δ (with η Set to 0.5)

δ	Iterations before Convergence
0.1	25.8
0.2	58.3
0.8	143.6
2	352.2

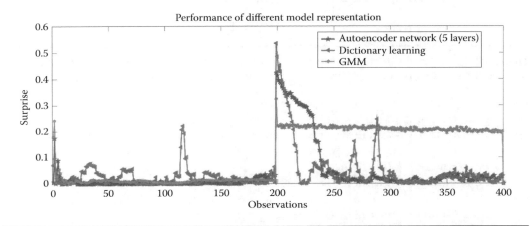

Figure 4.12 The distribution process changed from Gaussian to Poisson: Deep network and dictionary learning behave more adaptively than GMM.

units). Its surprise is calculated as reconstruction error as before. For GMM, we set the number of the mixture to 3 and estimated the model with the *fitgmdist* function (in MATLAB). The resulting model is used for prediction is made by sampling the resulting model. Surprise is then calculated as the error between the prediction value and real observation. For dictionary learning, we used the method in [26] (and the code by the author of [33]). The learned dictionary generates the predictions, which are compared to observations to get surprise.

While the Gaussian model cannot achieve surprise minimization, the others, including dictionary learning and an autoencoder network, work well. We also tried to use an autoencoder network with fewer layers (three layers with 200-500-200 hidden units), but it is not as easy to optimize surprise (with 135.7 average iterations for surprise minimization) as it is for the five-layer deep network (with 24.2 average iterations for surprise minimization). It clearly shows that the deep hierarchical architecture improves the model's capability.

4.3.1.3 Partial Observation and Sensor Selection

In the third experiment, we compare the random sensor selection with surprise minimization sensor selection. We used a mixture Gaussian generative model M_1 to generate 1000 data records for each day (so there are 1000 possible sensor placements in temporal space). We picked 25%, 50%,

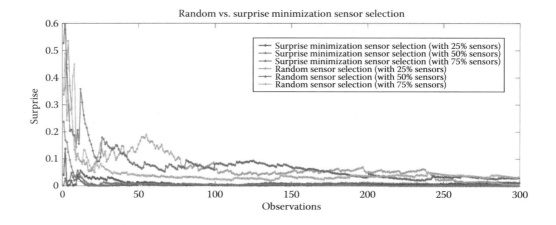

Figure 4.13 Sensor selection: Both random and surprise minimization sensor selection can achieve the real KL distance convergence. However, the latter can achieve better performance.

and 75% of available places for sensing, with both random and non-random sensor selection. For surprise minimization sensor selection, the initial placement is randomly picked, and then selection *s* is iteratively determined by the algorithm describe before, until it meets 25%, 50%, and 75% constraints. For random sensor placement, we select the places for sensing by sampling from a uniform distribution $U(0, 1000)$.

The experiment result is shown in Figure 4.13. As one can see, although the random sensor selection can minimize the KL divergence between estimation and real distribution, the surprise minimization approach can achieve faster convergence.

4.3.1.4 Surprise

For a changing target (from N_3 to N_{12}), we set different surprise thresholds. Table 4.3 shows the impact of different surprise thresholds. It shows that with a lower surprise threshold, we detect more anomalies, while it consumes more computation (iterations for model update).

We can see that while a low surprise threshold can capture most anomalies (the change of distribution), a high surprise threshold misses a large number of them. However, it's not always desired to set a low surprise threshold, not only because of the computational cost, but also because it will generate a large number of false alarms (e.g., treating noise as anomalies). As a result, setting

Table 4.3 Different Surprise Thresholds (ξ) and Their Impact on Anomaly Detection and Model Updates

ξ	Count of Anomalies	Iterations for Model Update	True Positive Rate
0.1	64	563	100%
0.3	51	476	91.67%
0.5	25	322	83.33%
0.7	17	135	75.38%
0.9	9	89	66.67%

an appropriate threshold value can achieve a balance between performance and resource costs. We can select this threshold by cross-validating with historical data.

4.3.1.5 Summary

From these simulation experiments, we can see that the cognitive mechanisms we adopted bring desired features when we want to model a dynamic sensing target. From the result, we also find that other than the target's changes, surprise value can also be high at the beginning of the system, because at that stage, without sufficient observations, the model is not well trained.

4.3.2 Application

The shift from the familiar, centralized, expert-driven health-care model to the personalized, informal, and decentralized health-care model encourages the usage of wireless sensor networks to provide capabilities of continuous, remote monitoring [34]. These sensor networks are used to measure physiological signals (including heartbeats, brain waves, oxygen saturation, etc.) of patients or health users. We believe that for this kind of monitoring systems, two features are highly required: firstly, it should be able to detect abnormal situations, which normally means something is wrong or even dangerous and action needs to be taken; secondly, it should be based on a personalized model, instead of an average model for a large population. Here we have applied our methodology to an application, which is about seizure detection in EEG.

4.3.2.1 Application Overview

Billions of people live with various types of mental illnesses and mental health problems. Taking epilepsy as an example, almost 60 million people around the world suffer from epilepsy. The research in EEG-based neuro-markers has demonstrated the possibility of monitoring mental disorder non-invasively [35]. A number of researchers have proposed seizure detection techniques (decision trees [36], SVM [37], neural networks [38], KNN [39], etc.) to aid in diagnosis and treatment. However, most of these techniques have high false-positive rates [40], which limits their clinical usefulness. Moreover, it is common in EEG classification tasks to preprocess the raw signal to extract features either directly or algorithmically from a larger pool of candidates. This feature engineering approach (as in [41–43]) requires extensive domain knowledge, intuition, and creativity, so it is application specific, labor intensive, and time consuming, and it cannot scale well to new patterns of seizures. There is also another limitation regarding the amount of labeled data required for training. In order to train the detection algorithms, most of the existing systems require patient-specific seizure data, which are not easy to acquire. This also means that it is difficult to detect seizures in new patients who have had few or no seizures.

Facing these challenges, here we use the methodology described above to carry out patient-specific seizure detection. Our model of a deep network is capable of learning meaningful features from raw, unlabeled data (i.e., unsupervised feature learning), making it less dependent on feature extraction and enabling it to detect seizures without having them encountered before. The surprise mechanism is used to detect anomalies, which are seizures in this case.

4.3.2.2 Method

The workflow is shown in Figure 4.14. The core is an anomaly detector based on stacked autoencoders described above. It determines which period of EEG data has an abnormal pattern. Since

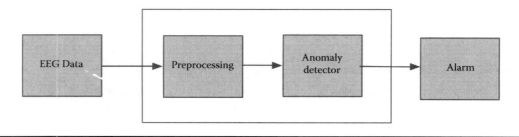

Figure 4.14 Workflow for EEG seizure detection: EEG data are firstly preprocessed, and then an anomaly detector tries to find the anomalies in the data and issue alarms.

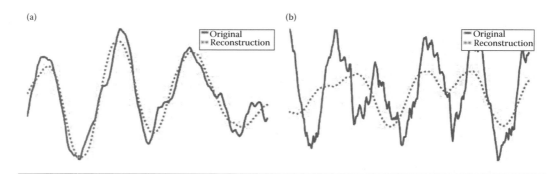

Figure 4.15 Reconstruction of EEG data: For normal EEG data, trained stacked autoencoders can well reconstruct the signal, but for anomaly data, the reconstruction is not accurate. (a) Normal. (b) Anomaly.

the abnormal patterns in EEG data such as seizures are rare and transient, it is better for the detector to detect abnormal patterns by utilizing only the normal EEG data. Therefore, we hypothesize that a stacked autoencoder network trained to reconstruct EEG data will learn to reconstruct well only for the normal EEG data such as background data, which are prevalent in the training set (Figure 4.15). Thus, EEG data that have reconstruction errors with a value higher than a specified threshold are treated as anomalies. While some aspects of even common signals seem harder for the autoencoder network to learn (e.g., higher-frequency, lower-amplitude components), we have found that the autoencoder network generally learns most aspects of the common signals better than those of the uncommon signals.

EEG data were firstly preprocessed using mean normalization. The details of these multi-channel EEG data are provided below and constitute a standard acquisition format. The preprocessed EEG data were further rescaled with standard deviation, so that most of the data lay in the range of values that the autoencoder network is able to reconstruct (i.e., between 0 and 1). After the preprocessing step, these data were used to train the network. The neural network consists of one input layer (with 256 input units), three layers of autoencoders (with 500-500-2000 hidden units), and one output layer. The number of nodes in the input layer was equal to the number of time bins in each EEG data segment, and the number of nodes in the output layer was the same as the input layer. The architecture of the hidden layers was chosen via cross-validation. The output of the anomaly detector was then utilized by the seizure detector to trigger a seizure alarm.

We used mini-batch gradient descent with the following parameters for the cost function: $\lambda = 0.03$, $\beta = 3$, $\rho = 0.1$, and $\alpha = 0.05$ (i.e., learning rate). The batch size was 10, and the number of epochs used in the first and second steps were 10 and 20, respectively. The network produces a reconstructed signal as close as possible to the input signal.

The anomaly detector decides whether each EEG segment is an anomaly by computing the reconstruction error of each EEG segment and comparing it with a threshold. Suppose there are k channels in the ith EEG segment $\{x^{(i,1)}, \ldots, x^{(i,k)}\}$, where $x^{(i,c)} \in R^n$ is the ith EEG segment from the cth channel, and n is the number of data in each EEG segment. The anomaly detector firstly reconstructs the ith EEG segment $\{\hat{x}^{(i,1)}, \ldots, \hat{x}^{(i,k)}\}$ from k channels, where $\hat{x}^{(i,c)}$ is the reconstruction of $x^{(i,c)}$, by feed-forwarding each EEG segment into the network. Then a loss function such as *root-mean-square error* (RMSE) or *dynamic time warping* (DTW [44]) is used to compute the reconstruction error. In our experiment, we found that the errors computed from both RMSE and DTW were very similar, but DTW took a longer time than RMSE. RMSE was therefore employed in this study:

$$E^{(i,c)} = \sqrt{\left[\sum_{j=1}^{n} (\hat{x}_j^{(i,c)} - x_j^{(i,c)}) \right] / n}$$

Each EEG segment, $\hat{x}^{(i,c)}$, will be flagged as anomalous:

$$\phi^{(i,c)} = \begin{cases} 1, & \text{if } E^{(i,c)} > \xi \\ 0, & \text{otherwise} \end{cases}$$

where $\phi^{(i,c)} = 1$ indicates that $x^{(i,c)}$ is labeled as anomalous (or surprise), and ξ is a positive threshold that varies across patients. This threshold can be estimated via cross-validation on the training set of each patient. Figure 4.16 shows an example of a seizure that we detected with this approach.

We keep a working memory with a size of $M = 10000$, which is enough for training the network. Once an anomaly is detected, and we want to include it into our normal pattern (so that we can ignore the known seizure pattern and look for new types of seizures), then we update the memory with the approach described above, where old EEG signals have a greater chance to be replaced. Then we retrain the model with the data in this memory. However, if we just want to detect seizure constantly, we will not update the memory and model when we encounter seizures.

4.3.2.3 Dataset

Our system was evaluated using the CHB-MIT database [45]. This database contains EEG recordings from pediatric patients at Boston Children's Hospital, who were suffering from intractable seizures. These EEG data were recorded by using the international 10–20 system of EEG electrode positions and nomenclature [46], and they were sampled at 256 Hz with 16-bit resolution. Most of these EEG data contain 23 channels, and a few of them contain 24 or 26 channels. We only use those EEG data with 23 channels. The EEG data of each patient are stored in what are called seizure and non-seizure files (the term *seizure files* is used to refer to the files that contain one or more seizure phases, and the term *non-seizure files* for the files that do not contain any seizures). In this study, EEG data were segmented into 1-s EEG data, containing 256 records in each segment, before being used to train and evaluate our system. EEG data from nine patients in the CHB-MIT database were randomly chosen to evaluate our system.

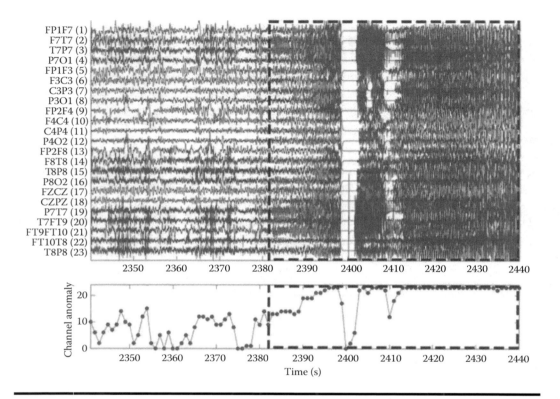

Figure 4.16 Seizure data in EEG: The data in the box are some examples of EEG seizure data.

4.3.2.4 Evaluation

With this dataset, we performed layer-wise training and then fine-tuned the deep network with back-propagation on the unlabeled data. As in the previous experiments, we ran the evaluation on an array of 12 dual-core 2.80-GHz Intel Xeon CPUs and 32.0 GB RAM.

The anomaly detector for each patient was trained by using EEG data from that patient. The trained anomaly detector was used to identify which EEG segment is anomalous. Table 4.4 shows a summary of the performance of the seizure detection. It can be seen that the detection performance of patients F and H was not as high as expected. We found that their seizure patterns were fairly similar to their normal patterns, and this precluded the anomaly detector from discriminating between seizure and normal data. We found the run time for each 1-s EEG data was approximately 10.38 ms, which allows our system to be used in real-time seizure detection. If we evaluated our seizure detectors by not considering these two patients, it shows that our system detected 96.36% of the seizures with a false detection rate of 4.11 h^{-1} (approximately four false detections per hour). Otherwise, the sensitivity decreased to 82.09%, but the false detection rate and the detection time were roughly the same.

Table 4.5 shows a general comparison of seizure detection performance between the proposed system and the existing systems. Some of them were evaluated with the same CHB-MIT database, and some of them were evaluated with their own data. Therefore, our system provides a promising detection performance (with unsupervised learning), which is comparable to other published

Table 4.4 Performance of Seizure Detection Application in the Unsupervised Setting

Patient	Age	Gender	Recording Length (h)	Number of Seizures	Sensitivity (%)	False Detection Rate (h^{-1})	Mean Detection Latency (s)
A	11	F	7	7	100.00	0.14	9.14
B	14	F	7	7	85.71	10.86	13.83
C	7	F	5	5	100.00	6.20	4.20
D	3.5	M	5	5	100.00	2.60	11.00
E	3	M	14	7	85.71	1.71	13.17
F	9	F	7	8	0	0	0
G	6	F	6	8	100.00	10.33	13.13
H	13	F	4	4	50.00	0.25	10.50
I	–	–	12	16	100.00	1.92	8.94
All	–	–	55	67	82.09	3.45	10.38

Table 4.5 Comparison of Seizure Detection Performance

Seizure Detection System	Sensitivity (%)	False Detection Rate (h^{-1})	Mean Detection Latency (sec.)
Saab and Gotman [47]	76	0.34	10
Kuhlmann et al. [48]	81	0.60	16.9
Shoeb and Guttag [49]	96	–	4.6
Ahammad et al. [42]	98.5	–	1.76
Zandi et al. [50]	90.5	0.51	8.37
Proposed System	96.36	4.11	10.38

seizure detection systems. Also, the sensitivity and the false detection of our system are competitive with other systems.

4.3.2.5 Discussion

1. *Classification*: In theory, the anomalies detected here are not just seizures, but all abnormal patterns that the model believes they are. Therefore, it's helpful to build an additional layer for anomaly classification. When sufficient patient-specific seizure data are available, they are used to train the anomaly classifier to determine which period of EEG data is of seizure type, to further reduce the number of false alarms. The workflow is shown in Figure 4.17. After feeding with seizure data and learning the parameters of stacked autoencoders, instead of reconstructing the input, we use the features extracted as the input for an additional neural network layer of classifier, optimize their weights with a smaller amount of labeled data),

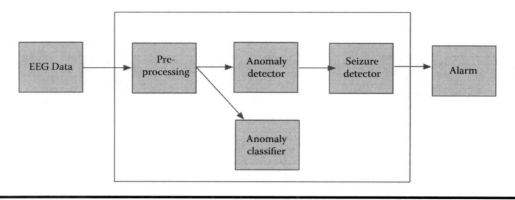

Figure 4.17 Workflow for EEG seizure classification: Our system can be extended for seizure classification.

and finally fine-tune the whole hierarchy. The average sensitivity was improved to 85.07% (with a false detection rate of 0.31 and mean detection latency of 11.02 s), according to our evaluation. Other methods such as logistic/softmax regression or a SVM can also be used for the predictor at the final layer. According to our experiment, when there were sufficient seizure data, our system detected all of the seizures with a false detection rate of 0.34 h^{-1} and a mean latency of 11.18 s.

2. *Top-down setting*: As described above, some top-down setting allows us to control the alertness of the EEG detection system. We can adjust ξ to detect anomalies with different levels of anomalies (but for seizures, if we set the threshold too high, we will miss a large number of them). We can change the size of the memory. We can even set the prior of which channels are believed to be more informative by setting the initial weight of the first layer of the deep network, instead of random initialization.

3. *Sensor selection*: There is no sensor selection problem in this application, since the channels of EEG devices are fixed and cannot be removed or added during the run time. However, one possible action is selecting more relevant channels from the learning deep networks and reducing the necessary channels for seizure detection.

4.3.2.6 Summary

To the best of our knowledge, our seizure detection system is the first system that utilizes the capability of a deep network to learn discriminating features from raw unlabeled EEG data for seizure detection in an unsupervised setting. Some researchers have employed other deep learning techniques, like deep belief nets (DBNs), to extract features for anomaly detection [51] and EEG classification [52]. However, they have not applied this technique in the context of seizure detection. Also, our system was implemented using SAE, which learns direct encoding (i.e., non-probabilistic) models, while DBN learns probabilistic models, which could be more computationally expensive and could lead to approximate inference problems when networks become larger [53].

From a clinical perspective, such a system coupled with a visualization tool will be extremely useful for data visualization of "abnormal" activity for nurses and neurophysiologists during continuous real-time monitoring of patient EEG signals. High levels of anomalies will alert physicians to take care of the patient. In addition, when the same deep network (the first layer) is trained and fine-tuned with labeled data from ordinary preseizure and seizure periods, with an additional supervised learning stage, the resulting deep network becomes a predictor that can anticipate a preictal seizure in real time and trigger an alarm for intervention. We envisage that a similar approach can be applied in a wide spectrum of applications for personal mental health monitoring.

4.4 Discussion

Historically, designing a computing system by learning human cognition is not new. Cognitive science discoveries had inspired a great deal of research on unsupervised learning (e.g., the analysis by synthesis approach [54]). Another example is the formation of the Infomax principle and independent component analysis [55,56] from the inspiration of efficient coding [57,58]. However, it was not until recent years that the advance of cognitive science and neuroscience (through projects like Human Connectome [59]) made it possible to build a clearer picture of how our brain works. Based on these findings, we believe the meeting of brain informatics (BI) [60,61] and AI will be the next drive for both developments. From the application demonstrated before, we can see the potential of our methodology in sensing and modeling dynamic targets, especially in healthcare. Although because of the limitation of computation ability, the performance (or its adaptive capability) is not comparable with intelligent agents like a human, such work shows the effort to take inspiration from cognitive science and neuroscience and apply them to sensing systems.

This cognitive perspective has also inspired new insights into anomalies. We use an unsupervised method to train our model, and this model can reconstruct the input (with low loss function output) when the input has been seen before (within the range of the model's representation capability). Only once the observation is new to the model and cannot be reconstructed do we detect an anomaly. This new observation will later become normal data once we update the model. Therefore, the system can continuously learn and tolerate new anomalies and only detect those it has never seen before or those that have been forgotten by the system (due to the memory update and model retraining). This anomaly is also seen as an attentional surprise, induced by a mismatch between the sensory signals encountered and those predicted. Such a surprise plays a role similar to surprise for humans and acts as a kind of proxy for sensory information [62] (to select an input for the process). A similar principle has been applied in methods like predictive coding [63].

To conclude, the main contribution of our work is to provide a new perspective on how to build an intelligent sensing system, which has the following features:

1. *New objective of sensing*: Compared to previous works, we set a different objective for a sensing system, which is the intelligence to adapt to a dynamic target. Instead of acquiring as much data as accurately as possible and then processing it (causing the so-called "big data problem" [64]), we proposed to build a computational framework to drive efficient data acquisition based on cognitive mechanisms. This new objective for a sensing system brought a new workflow of sensing.

2. *Cognition inspired components*: To achieve this objective, we adopted several components, including memory, surprise, etc. Although these components only mimic human cognition in a relatively rough way, they still bring many desired features. Within these components, we can find several parameters or hyper-parameters for adjusting the performance and resource consumption, and thus the system has the characteristic of elasticity: if required, the system can be set with higher alertness, consuming more resources.

3. *Model representation*: Among various model representations, we chose an autoencoder-based deep network, because of its "universal and non-linear" capability of modeling data. This

model representation has inherent advantages over many other models. Also, we don't target building a perfect model, but instead concentrate on the ability to adjust the model with target evolution. With such an ability, the model can optimize its long-term performance (average surprise) when the target keeps changing its behavior.

4. *Anomaly detection*: Here, an anomaly is another name for a surprise, which represents the occurrence of model failure, because of either the target's new behavior or model roughness. Therefore, compared with some context in which anomaly detection is mainly about sensor fault detection, here anomaly is not something to avoid: it's the stimulus for a model update. It also reflects the dynamics of the target or some significant change that we should notice. For example, when modeling an EEG signal, an anomaly can mean a new type of mental disorder. Such a goal is slightly different from ordinary anomaly detection, which excludes the outliers from the model, but is instead related to novelty detection [65,66], which tries to detect emergent and novel patterns in the data, and incorporates them into the normal model.

5. *Sensor selection*: We proposed a novel sensor selection algorithm, which fits the whole computational framework. It integrates the prior knowledge of attention area, the minimization of surprise, and a certain degree of randomness. It finds new bounds for free energy minimization, given only partial observations. Such a goal has some link with traditional informative criteria: finding new observations that can cause significant surprise is related to finding observations that are informative. Many traditional sensor selection algorithms can also be used in our methodology. Another important feature of our sensor selection is the role of the predefined attention area, so that events that happen within this area will be better captured. This idea has an analogy with human attentional area (for focusing computational resources for local refinement [4]). However, in order to avoid being trapped in this area, we also include some randomness, so that the event outside the attention area has the chance to be noticed.

6. *Balance between adaptivity and resource constraints*: To balance between resource consumption and performance, the key mechanism is attention. In this work, we use top-down settings to achieve this balance: although surprise is triggered in a bottom-down manner, the overall alertness is controlled by these top-down settings. Therefore we can control the model update and sensor placement and thus the computational and sensing cost.

We need to mention that the main limitation of our work is about the computational cost: training or retraining a deep network can cost over an hour on a powerful server cluster, which means we cannot update the model in real time. Although we can control the surprise threshold to limit the anomalies' frequency, such latency limits the application of the framework. Another limitation is the availability of the data, since the training of a deep network needs a large amount of data. We also drop old observations in working memory, which might still be valuable for modeling (we are trying to use some layered memory to solve this issue). Also, for current model representation, it's difficult to integrate some prior knowledge into it.

A large amount of work is planned. First of all, we will try to elaborate the components in the framework to make it more suitable for sensing intelligence. A layered or network-structured working memory will be designed to organize the data or knowledge hierarchically; model representation will be fused with external knowledge like ontology and support reasoning. Also, we are investigating conducting a Bayesian inference within our framework to include the prior, as well as the Bayesian model update and full estimation of surprise. Another work is to develop a generic sensing control interface, so that the framework can drive the actions in sensor networks directly from the model and achieve sensor selection. We can extend this interface to support certain decision-making systems to achieve intervention. Therefore, we can not only change the recognition density, but also change the sensory input by acting on the world. Last but not least, we are working on developing a computational pipeline with different options for components in the framework, integrating this pipeline with our existing WikiSensing and WikiModelling platform [67], and accelerating the computation of deep learning with the cluster.

References

1. Caron, S. J. C. Brains don't play dice—Or do they? *Science*. 2013; **342**(6158): 574–574.
2. Hutchins, E. Cognition in the Wild. Cambridge, MA: MIT press. 1995; 262082314.
3. Friston, K. The free-energy principle: A unified brain theory? *Nature Reviews Neuroscience*. 2010; **11**(2): 127–138.
4. Whiteley, L. and M. Sahani. Attention in a Bayesian framework. *Frontiers in Human Neuroscience*. 2012; **6**: 100.
5. Moran, J. and R. Desimone. Selective attention gates visual processing in the extrastriate cortex. *Science*. 1985; **229**(4715): 782–784.
6. Itti, L. and P. F. Baldi. Bayesian surprise attracts human attention. Advances in Neural Information Processing Systems. 2005; 547–554.
7. Treisman, A. M. and G. Gelade. A feature-integration theory of attention. *Cognitive Psychology*. 1980; **12**(1): 97–136.
8. Baddeley, A. Working memory. *Science*. 1992; **255**(5044): 556–559.
9. Clark, A. Whatever next? Predictive brains, situated agents, and the future of cognitive science. *The Behavioral and Brain Sciences*. 2013; **36**(3): 181–204. doi:10.1017/S0140525X12000477.
10. Von Melchner, L., S. L. Pallas, and M. Sur. Visual behaviour mediated by retinal projections directed to the auditory pathway. *Nature*. 2000; **404**(6780): 871–876.
11. Sathe, S., T. G. Papaioannou, H. Jeung, and K. Aberer. A survey of model-based sensor data acquisition and management. In *Managing and Mining Sensor Data*. Springer, US. 2013; 9–50.
12. Evensen, G. Sequential data assimilation with a nonlinear quasi-geostrophic model using Monte Carlo methods to forecast error statistics. *Journal of Geophysical Research: Oceans*. 1994; **99–C5**: 10143–10162.
13. Kalnay, E. *Atmospheric Modeling, Data Assimilation, and Predictability*. Cambridge University Press, Cambridge, UK. 2003.
14. Chandola, V., A. Banerjee, and V. Kumar. Anomaly detection: A survey. *ACM Computing Surveys (CSUR)*. 2009; **41**(3): 15.
15. Linsker, R. An application of the principle of maximum information preservation to linear systems. *Advances in Neural Information Processing Systems*. pp. 186–194, NIPS in Denver, Colorado. 1989.
16. Vincent, P., H. Larochelle, I. Lajoie, Y. Bengio, and P-A. Manzagol. Stacked denoising autoencoders: Learning useful representations in a deep network with a local denoising criterion. *The Journal of Machine Learning Research*. 2010; **11**: 3371–3408.
17. Vincent, P., H. Larochelle, Y. Bengio, and P-A. Manzagol. Extracting and composing robust features with denoising autoencoders. In *Proceedings of the 25th International Conference on Machine Learning*, Helsinki, Finland. ACM. 2008; 1096–1103.
18. UFLDL Tutorial: Autoencoders and Sparsity. Available: http://ufldl.stanford.edu/wiki/index.php/Autoencoders_and_Sparsity.
19. Bengio, Y., P. Lamblin, D. Popovici, and H. Larochelle. Greedy layer-wise training of deep networks. *Advances in Neural Information Processing Systems*. 2007; **19**: 153.
20. Salakhutdinov, R. and G. E. Hinton. Deep Boltzmann machines. In *International Conference on Artificial Intelligence and Statistics*, Florida, USA. 2009; 448–455.
21. Park, H-J. and K. Friston. Structural and functional brain networks: From connections to cognition. *Science*. 2013; **342**(6158):1238411.

22. Rao, R. P. N. and D. H. Ballard. Predictive coding in the visual cortex: A functional interpretation of some extra-classical receptive-field effects. *Nature Neuroscience*. 1999; **2**(1): 79–87.

23. Murray, S. O., D. Kersten, B. A. Olshausen, P. Schrater, and D. L. Woods. Shape perception reduces activity in human primary visual cortex. *Proceedings of the National Academy of Sciences 99*. 2002; **23**: 15164–15169.

24. Rasmussen, C. E. and C. KI Williams. *Gaussian Processes for Machine Learning*. Vol. I. MIT Press, Cambridge. 2006.

25. Itti, L. and P. Baldi. Bayesian surprise attracts human attention. *Vision Res*. 2009; **49**: 1295–1306.

26. Zhou, M., H. Chen, L. Ren, G. Sapiro, L. Carin, and J. W. Paisley. Non-parametric Bayesian dictionary learning for sparse image representations. In *Advances in Neural Information Processing Systems*, Vancouver, Canada. 2009; 2295–2303.

27. Amidan, B. G., T. A. Ferryman, and S. K. Cooley. Data outlier detection using the Chebyshev theorem. *IEEE Aerospace Conference*, Big Sky, USA. 2005.

28. Baraniuk, R. G. Compressive sensing. *IEEE Signal Processing Magazine*. 2007; **24**(4): 118–121.

29. Rowaihy, H., S. Eswaran, M. Johnson, D. Verma, A. Bar-Noy, T. Brown, and T. La Porta. A survey of sensor selection schemes in wireless sensor networks. In *Defense and Security Symposium, International Society for Optics and Photonics*, Cardiff, Wales, United Kingdom. 2007; 65621A–65621A.

30. Wang, H., K. Yao, G. Pottie, and D. Estrin. Entropy-based sensor selection heuristic for target localization. In *Proceedings of the 3rd International Symposium on Information Processing in Sensor Networks*, Berkeley, USA. ACM. 2004; 36–45.

31. Joshi, S. and S. Boyd. Sensor selection via convex optimization. *Signal Processing, IEEE Transactions on*. 2009; **57**(2): 451–462.

32. Lin, F. Y. S. and P-L. Chiu. A near-optimal sensor placement algorithm to achieve complete coverage-discrimination in sensor networks. *Communications Letters, IEEE*. 2005; **9**(1): 43–45.

33. Mingyuan Z. BPFA Denoising Inpainting. Available: http://people.ee.duke.edu/~mz1/Softwares/BPFA_Denoising_Inpainting_codes_Inference_10292009.zip.

34. Wood, A., G. Virone, T. Doan, Q. Cao, L. Selavo, Y. Wu, L. Fang, Z. He, S. Lin, and J. Stankovic. ALARM-NET: Wireless sensor networks for assisted-living and residential monitoring. University of Virginia Computer Science Department Technical Report 2. 2006.

35. Pauri, F., F. Pierelli, G-E. Chatrian, and W. William. Erdly. Long-term EEG-video-audio monitoring: Computer detection of focal EEG seizure patterns. *Electroencephalography and Clinical Neurophysiology*. 1992; **82–1**: 1–9.

36. Polat, K. and S. Gunes. Classification of epileptiform EEG using a hybrid system based on decision tree classifier and fast Fourier transform. *Applied Mathematics and Computation*. 2007; **187**: 1017–26.

37. Gardner, A. B., A. M., Krieger, G, Vachtsevanos, and B, Litt. One-class novelty detection for seizure analysis from intracranial EEG. *Journal of Machine Learning Research*. 2006; **7**: 1044.

38. Webber, W. R. S., R. P. Lesser, R. T. Richardson, and K. Wilson. An approach to seizure detection using an artificial neural network (ANN). *Electroencephalography and Clinical Neurophysiology*. 1996; **98–4**: 250–272.

39. Chaovalitwongse, W. A., Y-J. Fan, and R. C. Sachdeo. On the time series k-nearest neighbor classification of abnormal brain activity. *Systems, Man and Cybernetics, Part A: Systems and Humans, IEEE Transactions on*. 2007; **37**(6): 1005–1016.

40. Flanagan, D., R., Agarwal, Y. H. Wang, and J. Gotman. Improvement in the performance of automated spike detection using dipole source features for artefact rejection. *Clinical Neurophysiology*. 2003; **114**: 38–49.

41. Adeli, H., S. Ghosh-Dastidar, and N. Dadmehr. A wavelet-chaos methodology for analysis of EEGs and EEG subbands to detect seizure and epilepsy. *IEEE Transctions on Biomedical Engineering*. 2007; **54–2**: 205–11.

42. Ahammad, N., T. Fathima, and P. Joseph, Detection of epileptic seizure event and onset using EEG. *BioMedical Research International*. 2014; **2014**: 7.

43. Polat, K. and S. Gunes. Classification of epileptic for EEG using a hybrid system based on decision tree classifier and fast Fourier transform. *Applied Mathematics and Computation*. 2007; **187–2**: 1017–1026.

44. Müller, M. Dynamic time warping. *Information Retrieval for Music and Motion*. 2007; **2**:69–84.

45. Goldberger, A. L., L. A. Amaral, L. Glass, J. M. Hausdorff, P. C. Ivanov, R. G. Mark, J. E. Mietus, G. B. Moody, C. K. Peng, and H. E. Stanley. PhysioBank, PhysioToolkit, and PhysioNet: Components of a new research resource for complex physiologic signals. *Circulation*. 2000; **101–23**: e215–e220.

46. Schölkopf, B., R. C. Williamson, A. J. Smola, J. Shawe-Taylor, and J. C. Platt. Support vector method for novelty detection. *In NIPS*. 1999; **12**: 582–588.

47. Saab M. E. and J. Gotman. A system to detect the onset of epileptic seizures in scalp EEG. *Clinical Neurophysiology*. 2005; **116–2**: 427–442.

48. Kuhlmann, L., A. N. Burkitt, M. J. Cook, K. Fuller, D. B. Grayden, L. Seiderer, and I. M. Mareels. Seizure detection using seizure probability estimation: Comparison of features used to detect seizures. *Annals of Biomedical Engineering*. 2009; **37–10**: 2129–2145.

49. Shoeb, A. H. and J. V. Guttag. Application of machine learning to epileptic seizure detection. *Proceedings of the 27th International Conference on Machine Learning (ICML-10)*, St. Louis, USA. 2010; 975–982.

50. Zandi, A. S., M. Javidan, G. A. Dumont, and R. Tafreshi. Automated real-time epileptic seizure detection in scalp EEG recordings using an algorithm based on wavelet packet transform. *Biomedical Engineering, IEEE Transactions on*. 2010; **57–7**: 1639–1651.

51. Wulsin, D., J. Blanco, R. Mani, and B. Litt. Semi-supervised anomaly detection for EEG waveforms using deep belief nets. *2010 Ninth International Conference on Machine Learning and Applications (ICMLA)*, Washington DC, USA. 2010; 436–441.

52. Wulsin, D. F., J. R. Gupta, R. Mani, J. A. Blanco, and B. Litt. Modeling electroencephalography waveforms with semi-supervised deep belief nets: Fast classification and anomaly measurement. *Journal of Neural Engineering*. 2011; **8–3**: 036015.

53. Bengio, Y., A. Courville, and P. Vincent. Representation learning: A review and new perspectives. *Pattern Analysis and Machine Intelligence, IEEE Transactions on*. 2013; **35–8**: 1798–1828.

54. Yuille, A. and D. Kersten. Vision as Bayesian inference: Analysis by synthesis? *Trends in Cognitive Sciences*. 2006; **10**(7): 301–308.

55. Bell, A. J. and T. J. Sejnowski. An information-maximization approach to blind separation and blind deconvolution. *Neural Computation*. 1995; **7**(6): 1129–1159.

56. Hyvärinen, A., J. Karhunen, and E. Oja. *Independent Component Analysis*. John Wiley & Sons, New York. 2004; 46.

57. Barlow, H. B. Possible principles underlying the transformations of sensory messages. In *Sensory Communication* (ed. Rosenblith, W. A.). MIT Press, Cambridge, Massachusetts, 1961; pp. 217–234.

58. Olshausen, B. A. and D. J. Field. Natural image statistics and efficient coding. *Network: Computation in Neural Systems*. 1996; **7**(2): 333–339.

59. Human Connectome project. Available: http://www.humanconnectome.org.

60. Zhong, N., J. Liu, Y. Yao, J. Wu, S. Lu, Y. Qin, K. Li, and B. Wah. Web intelligence meets brain informatics. In *Web Intelligence Meets Brain Informatics*. Springer Berlin Heidelberg. 2007; 1–31.

61. Ma, J., J. Wen, R. Huang, and B. Huang. Cyber-individual meets brain informatics. *IEEE Intelligent Systems*. 2011; **5**: 30–37.

62. Feldman, H. and K. J. Friston. Attention, uncertainty, and free-energy. *Frontiers in Human Neuroscience*. 2010; 4.

63. Shi, Y. Q. and H. Sun. *Image and Video Compression for Multimedia Engineering. Fundamentals, Algorithms, and Standards*. CRC Press. 1999.

64. Manyika, J., M., Chui, B., Brown, J., Bughin, R., Dobbs, and C. Roxburgh. *Big Data: The Next Frontier for Innovation, Competition, and Productivity*. McKinsey Global Institute, New York. 2011.

65. Markou, M. and S. Singh. Novelty detection: A review—Part 1: Neural network based approaches. *Signal Processing*. 2003; **83–12**: 2481–2497.

66. Markou, M. and S. Singh. Novelty detection: A review—Part 2: Neural network based approaches. *Signal Processing*. 2003; **83–12**: 2499–2521.

67. Wu, C., D., Birch, D., Silva, C. H., Lee, O., Tsinalis, and Y. Guo, Concinnity: A generic platform for big sensor data applications. Cloud computing. *IEEE*. 2014; **1**(2): 42–50.

Chapter 5

Language-Guided Visual Recognition

Mohamed Elhoseiny, Yizhe (Ethan) Zhu, and Ahmed Elgammal

Contents

Visual recognition uses machine learning methods to analyze images that can give you insights into your visual content. This is often associated with example images to learn about different visual categories like "cats" and "dogs." However, people have the capability to learn through exposure to visual categories associated with linguistic descriptions. For instance, teaching visual concepts

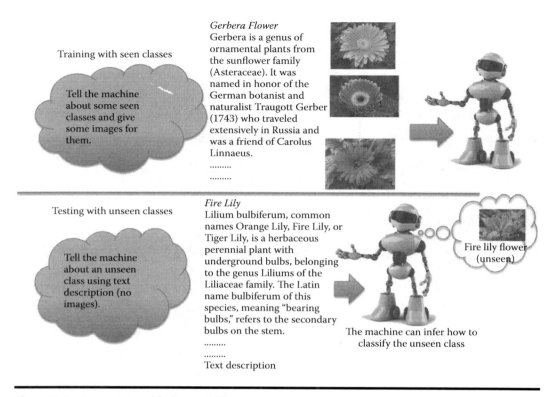

Figure 5.1   Language-guided recognition.

to children is often accompanied by descriptions in text or speech. In a machine learning context, these observations motivate exploring how this learning process could be computationally modeled to learn visual facts. We aim at recognizing a visual category (e.g., parakeet auklet/*Gerbera* flower) from language description without any images (also known as *zero-shot learning*); see Figure 5.1. Zero-shot learning in simple terms is a form of extending supervised learning to a setting of solving, for example, a classification problem when not enough labeled examples are available for all classes.

We use Wikipedia articles of visual categories as the language descriptions (i.e., recognize "parakeet auklet" using only its Wikipedia article). We denote this capability as "language-guided visual recognition (LGVR)." In this chapter, we formally define LGVR, its benchmarks, and performance metrics. We also discuss the challenges in the zero-shot learning setting and illustrate differences between the two learning settings that we denote as the "super-category-shared" setting and harder yet understudied setting that we denote as "super-category exclusive" (discussed next).

5.1 Challenges in Language-Guided Visual Recognition

5.1.1 Language-Guided Visual Recognition vs Attribute-Based Zero-Shot Learning

LGVR is a zero-shot learning setting, and it is rather more challenging compared to attribute-based zero-shot learning that we elaborate next. Attributes [1,2] are manually defined by humans to describe shape, color, and surface material (for example, furry, striped, etc.). Therefore, an unseen category has to be specified in terms of the used vocabulary of attributes. If there are hundreds of these attributes, their existence has to be defined for each unseen class. In contrast, for LVGR zero-shot learning, only one text description for each visual class needs to be provided, which can be found in Wikipedia for instance.

5.1.2 Super-Category-Shared vs Super-Category-Exclusive Zero-Shot Learning

To split a dataset into training and testing classes, we highlight that there are two kinds of splitting schemes, in terms of how close the seen classes are to the unseen classes: super-category-shared splitting (SCS) and super-category-exclusive (SCE) splitting. In the dataset, some classes often are the further division of one category. For example, both "black-footed albatross" and "Laysan albatross" belong to the category "albatross" in CUB2011, and both "Cooper's hawk" and "Harris's hawk" are under the category "hawks" in NABirds. For SCS, unseen classes are deliberately picked in the condition that there exist seen classes with the same super-category. In this scheme, the relevance between seen classes and unseen classes is very high. On the contrary, in SCE, all classes under the same category as unseen classes would either belong to the seen or the unseen classes. For instance, if "black-footed albatross" is an unseen class, then all other albatrosses are unseen classes as well, and so no albatrosses are seen during training. It is not hard to see that the relevance between seen and unseen classes is minimal in the SCE split. Intuitively, the SCE split is much harder compared to the SCS split. Most of the existing works have mainly studied the SCS split, which is the easier split. In this chapter, we illustrate the difference in performance of the state-of-the-art methods for the SCS and SCE splits.

5.2 Modeling LGVR

Figure 5.2 illustrates the learning setting. The information in our problem comes from two different domains: the visual domain and the textual domain, denoted by $\mathcal{V}$ and $\mathcal{T}$, respectively. Similar to traditional visual learning problems, we are given training data in the form $V = \{(x_i, l_i)\}_N$, where x_i is an image and $l_i \in \{1 \ldots N_{sc}\}$ is its class label. We denote the number of classes available at training as N_{sc}, where sc indicates "seen classes." As is typically done in a visual classification setting, we can learn N_{sc} binary one-vs-all classifiers, one for each of these classes.

Our goal is to be able to predict a classifier for a new category based only on the learned classes and textual description(s) of that category. In order to achieve that, the learning process also has to include textual description of the seen classes (as shown in Figure 5.2). Depending on the domain, we might find a few, a couple, or as little as one textual description for each class. We denote the textual training data for class j by $\{t_i \in \mathcal{T}\}^j$. We assume we are dealing with the extreme case of having only one textual description available per class, which makes the problem even more challenging. For simplicity, the text description of class j is denoted by t_j. However, the formulation we propose in this paper directly applies to the case of multiple textual descriptions per class.

The rest of this chapter is organized as follows. Section 5.3 formally defines the problem. We discuss the development of the task of predicting visual classifier $\Phi(t_*)$ from an unseen text description t_* in Section 5.3.1. We start by predicting $\Phi(t_*)$ in three ways.

The Bobolink (Dolichonyx oryzivorus) is a small New World blackbird and the only member of genus Dolichonyx.

Description: Adults are 16–18 cm (6–8 in) long with short finch-like bills. They weigh about 1 oz. Adult males are mostly black, although they do display creamy napes, and white scapulars, lower backs and rumps. Adult females are mostly light brown, although their coloring includes black streaks on the back and flanks, and dark stripes on the head; their wings and tails are darker. The collective name for a group of bobolinks is a chain.

Distribution and movement: These birds migrate to Argentina, Bolivia and Paraguay. One bird was tracked flying 12,000 mi over the course of the year, and up to 1,100 mi in one day. They often migrate in flocks, feeding on cultivated grains and rice, which leads to them being considered a pest by farmers in some areas. Although Bobolinks migrate long distances, they have rarely been sighted in Europe-like many vagrants from the Americas, the overwhelming majority of records are from the British Isles. Each fall, Bobolinks gather in large numbers in South American rice fields, where they are inclined to eat grain. This has earned them the name "ricebird" in these parts. However, they are called something entirely different in Jamaica (Butterbirds) where they are collected as food, being that they are very fat as they pass through on migration.

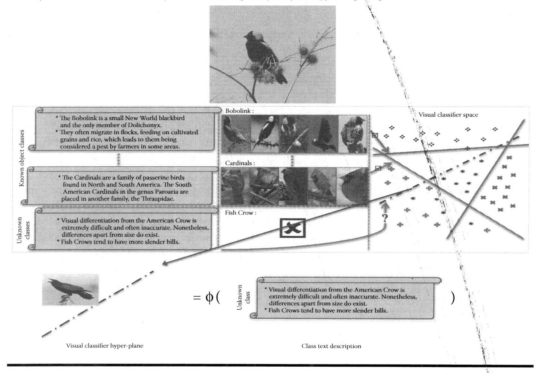

Figure 5.2   Top: Example Wikipedia article about the painted bunting, with an example image. Bottom: The proposed learning setting. For each category we are give one (or more) textual description(s) (only a synopsis of a larger text is shown) and a set of training images. Our goal is to be able to predict a classifier for a category based only on the narrative (zero-shot learning).

We discuss the task of predicting visual classifier $\Phi(t_*)$ from an unseen text description t_* using multiple methods; see Table 5.1.

1. Linear prediction model (Section 5.4.1): A linear classifier is predicted given a text description.
2. Kernel prediction model (Section 5.4.2): Introduces non-linearity to the classifier prediction model in both the text and visual modalities and hence captures the non-linearity of the transfer between the two modalities and improves on the linear model.
3. Part-based model with deep convolutional neural network (Section 5.4.3): A part-based CNN model that uses multiple layers for non-linearities and shows the value of using parts for predicting visual classifiers from text. The model is able to connect text terms to their relevant bird parts (e.g., wing, tail) and suppress connections to non-visual text terms without any part-text annotation.

Table 5.1   Classifier Prediction Functions (Linear, Kernel, and with Part-Based CNN)

Linear Prediction	Kernel Prediction	Part-Based CNN Prediction
$\Phi(t_*) = c(\mathbf{t}_*)$	$\Phi(t_*) = \beta(t_*)$	$\Phi(t_*) = \boldsymbol{\rho}(t_*)$

5.3 Problem Definition

Figure 5.2 illustrates the learning setting. The information in our problem comes from two different domains: the visual domain and the textual domain, denoted by $\mathcal{V}$ and $\mathcal{T}$, respectively. Similar to traditional visual learning problems, we are given training data in the form $V = \{(x_i, l_i)\}_N$, where x_i is an image and $l_i \in \{1 \ldots N_{sc}\}$ is its class label. We denote the number of classes available at training as N_{sc}, where sc indicates "seen classes." As typically done in the visual classification setting, we can learn N_{sc} binary one-vs-all classifiers, one for each of these classes.

Our goal is to be able to predict a classifier for a new category based only on the learned classes and textual description(s) of that category. In order to achieve that, the learning process also has to include textual description of the seen classes (as shown in Figure 5.2). Depending on the domain, we might find a few, a couple, or as little as one textual description for each class. We denote the textual training data for class j by $\{t_i \in \mathcal{T}\}^j$. We assume we are dealing with the extreme case of having only one textual description available per class, which makes the problem even more challenging. For simplicity, the text description of class j is denoted by t_j. However, the formulation we propose in this paper directly applies to the case of multiple textual descriptions per class. We present next the notations that we used for both linear and kernel classifiers, respectively.

5.3.1 Linear Classifier

Let us consider a typical linear classifier in the feature space in the form

$$f_j(\mathbf{x}) = \mathbf{c}_j^\top \cdot \mathbf{x}$$

where $\mathbf{x}$ (bold) is the visual feature r of an image x (not bold) amended with 1 and $\mathbf{c}_j \in \mathbb{R}^{d_v}$ is the linear classifier parameters for class j. Given a test image, its class is determined by

$$l^* = \arg \max_j f_j(\mathbf{x}) \tag{5.1}$$

Similar to the visual domain, the raw textual descriptions have to go through a feature extraction process. Let us denote the linear extracted textual feature by $T = \{\mathbf{t}_j \in \mathbb{R}^{d_t}\}_{j=1 \ldots N_{sc}}$, where $\mathbf{t}_j$ is the features of text description t_j (not bold). Given a textual description t_* of a new unseen category $\mathcal{U}$ with linear feature vector representation $\mathbf{t}_*$, the problem can now be defined as predicting linear classifier parameters $\Phi(t_*) = c(\mathbf{t}_*) \in \mathbb{R}^{d_v}$, such that it can be directly used to classify any test image $\mathbf{x}$ as

$$l^* = \arg \max_j c(\mathbf{t}_j)(\mathbf{x}) \tag{5.2}$$

where $\{\mathbf{t}_j\}$ is the set of the text description of the classes (one description per class).

5.3.2 Kernel Classifier

On way to introduce non-linearity into the previous model is to use kernels to measure similarity between text description and images instead of linear models. We assume that each of the texts and the visual domains is equipped with a kernel function corresponding to a reproducing kernel Hilbert space (RKHS). Let us denote the kernel for the visual domain $\mathcal{V}$ by $k(\cdot, \cdot)$ and the kernel for the text domain $\mathcal{T}$ by $g(\cdot, \cdot)$.

According to the generalized representer theorem [3], a minimizer of a regularized empirical risk function over an RKHS could be represented as a linear combination of kernels, evaluated on the training set. Adopting the representer theorem on classification risk function, we define a kernel classifier of a visual class j as follows:

$$f_j(x) = \sum_{i=1}^{N} \beta_j^i k(x, x_i) + b$$

$$f_j(x) = \beta_j^\mathsf{T} \cdot \mathbf{k}(x) = \mathbf{c}_j^\mathsf{T} \cdot [\varphi(x); 1]$$

(5.3)

where $x \in \mathcal{V}$ is the test image, x_i is the ith image in the training data V, $\mathbf{k}(x) = [k(x, x_1), \ldots, k(x, x_N), 1]^\mathsf{T}$, and $\beta_j = [\beta_j^1 \ldots \beta_j^N, b]^\mathsf{T}$. Having learned $f_j(x^*)$ for each class j (e.g., using the SVM classifier), the class label of the test image x can be predicted by Equation 5.1, similar to the linear case. Equation 5.3 also shows how β_j is related to $\mathbf{c}_j$ in the linear classifier, where $k(x, x') = \varphi(x)^\mathsf{T} \cdot \varphi(x')$ and $\varphi(\cdot)$ is a feature map that does not have to be explicitly defined given the definition of $k(\cdot, \cdot)$ on $\mathcal{V}$. Hence, our goal in the kernel classifier prediction is to predict $\beta(t_*)$ instead of $\mathbf{c}(t_*)$ since it is sufficient to define $f_{t_*}(x)$ for a text description t_* of an unseen class given $\mathbf{k}(x)$.

Similar to the linear classifier prediction, the idea is to use the text description t_*, associated with an unseen class, and the training images to directly predict the unseen kernel-classifier parameters. In other words, the kernel classifier parameters of the unseen class are a function of its text description t_*, the image training data V, and the text training data $\{t_j\}, j \in 1 \ldots N_{sc}$; that is,

$$f_{t_*}(x) = \beta(t_*)^\mathsf{T} \cdot \mathbf{k}(x)$$

$f_{t_*}(x)$ could be used to classify new points that belong to an unseen class in a multi-class prediction as in Equation 5.1. In this case, $\Phi(t_*) = \beta(t_*)$; see Table 5.1. In contrast to the linear classifier prediction, there is no need to explicitly represent an image x or a text description t by features, which are denoted by the bold symbols in the previous section. Rather, only $k(\cdot, \cdot)$ and $g(\cdot, \cdot)$ must be defined, which leads to more general classifiers.

5.4 Visual Classifier Prediction

We discuss the task of predicting visual classifier $\Phi(t_*)$ from an unseen text description t_* in multiple methods; see Table 5.1.

1. Linear prediction model; see Section 5.4.1 and Equation 5.7 for the linear $\Phi(t_*)$ definition
2. Kernel prediction model; see Section 5.4.2 and Equation 5.11 for the kernel $\Phi(t_*)$ definition

3. Part-based model with deep convolutional neural network (part-based CNN); see Section 5.4.3 and Equation 5.14 for the part-based CNN $\Phi(t_*)$ definition

5.4.1 Linear Prediction Model

The classifier prediction model could be posed as a domain adaptation from the textual to the visual domain. In the computer vision context, domain adaptation work has focused on transferring categories learned from a source domain, with a given distribution of images, to a target domain with a different distribution, for example, images or videos from different sources [4–7]. What we need is an approach that learns the correlation between the textual domain features and the visual domain features and then uses that correlation to predict a new visual classifier given textual features.

This can be achieved by learning a linear transfer function $\mathbf{W}$ between $\mathcal{T}$ and $\mathcal{V}$. The transformation matrix $\mathbf{W}$ can be learned by optimizing, with a suitable regularizer, over constraints of the form $\mathbf{t}^\mathsf{T}\mathbf{W}\mathbf{x} \geq l$ if $\mathbf{t} \in \mathcal{T}$ and $\mathbf{x} \in \mathcal{V}$ belong to the same class, and $\mathbf{t}^\mathsf{T}\mathbf{W}\mathbf{x} \leq u$ otherwise. Here l and u are model parameters. This transfer function acts as a compatibility function between the textual features and visual features. The function gives high values if the features are from the same class and a low value if they are from different classes.

It is not hard to see that this transfer function can act as a classifier. Given a textual feature $\mathbf{t}^*$ and a test image, represented by $\mathbf{x}$, a classification decision can be obtained by $\mathbf{t}_*^\mathsf{T}\mathbf{W}\mathbf{x} \gtrless b$, where b is a decision boundary that can be set to $(l + u)/2$. Hence, our desired predicted classifier in Table 5.1 can be obtained as

$$c(\mathbf{t}_*) = \mathbf{t}_*^\mathsf{T}\mathbf{W} \tag{5.4}$$

However, since learning $\mathbf{W}$ was done over seen classes only, it is not clear how the predicted classifier $c(\mathbf{t}_*)$ will behave for unseen classes.

5.4.1.1 Optimization

Let $\mathbf{T}$ be the textual feature data matrix and $\mathbf{X}$ be the visual feature data matrix, where each feature vector is amended with a 1. Notice that amending the feature vectors with a 1 is essential in our formulation since we need $\mathbf{t}^\mathsf{T}\mathbf{W}$ to act as a classifier. We need to solve the following optimization problem:

$$\min_{\mathbf{W}} r(\mathbf{W}) + \lambda \sum_i c_i(\mathbf{T}\mathbf{W}\mathbf{X}^\mathsf{T}) \tag{5.5}$$

where c_i's are loss functions over the constraints and $r(\cdot)$ is a matrix regularizer. It was shown in Reference 5, under conditions on the regularizer, that the optimal $\mathbf{W}$ is in the form of $\mathbf{W}^* = \mathbf{T}\mathbf{K}_T^{-(1/2)}\mathbf{L}^*\mathbf{K}_X^{-(1/2)}\mathbf{X}^\mathsf{T}$, where $\mathbf{K}_T = \mathbf{T}\mathbf{T}^\mathsf{T}$, $\mathbf{K}_X = \mathbf{X}\mathbf{X}^\mathsf{T}$. $\mathbf{L}^*$ is computed by minimizing the following minimization problem:

$$\min_{\mathbf{L}}[r(\mathbf{L}) + \lambda \sum_p c_p(\mathbf{K}_T^{1/2}\mathbf{L}\mathbf{K}_X^{1/2})], \tag{5.6}$$

where $c_p(\mathbf{K}_T^{1/2}\mathbf{L}\mathbf{K}_X^{1/2}) = (\max(0, (l - e_i\mathbf{K}_T^{1/2}\mathbf{L}\mathbf{K}_X^{1/2}e_j)))^2$ for the same class pairs of index i,j, or $= (\max(0, (e_i\mathbf{K}_T^{1/2}\mathbf{L}\mathbf{K}_X^{1/2}e_j - u)))^2$ otherwise, where e_k is a one-hot vector of zeros except for one at the kth element, and $u > l$. In our work, we used $l = 2$, $u = -2$ (note that any appropriate l and

u can work). We used a Frobenius norm regularizer. This energy is minimized using a second-order BFGS quasi-Newton optimizer. Once L is computed, $\mathbf{W}^*$ is computed using the transformation above. Finally $\Phi(t_*) = c(\mathbf{t}_*) = \mathbf{t}_*^\mathsf{T}\mathbf{W}$, simplifying $\mathbf{W}^*$ as $\mathbf{W}$.

There is no guarantee that such a classifier will put all the seen data on one side and the new unseen class on the other side of that hyperplane. One suggestion is to force the new classifier to put all the seen instances on one side of the hyperplane and to be consistent with the learned domain transfer function. This leads to the following constrained optimization problem:

$$\Phi(t_*) = \hat{c}(\mathbf{t}_*) = \underset{\mathbf{c},\zeta_i}{\operatorname{argmin}}\Big[\mathbf{c}^\mathsf{T}\mathbf{c} - \alpha \mathbf{t}_*^\mathsf{T}\mathbf{W}\mathbf{c} + C\sum \zeta_i\Big]$$

$$\text{s.t.} : -(\mathbf{c}^\mathsf{T}\mathbf{x}_i) \geq \zeta_i, \quad \zeta_i \geq 0, \quad i = 1 \dots N \tag{5.7}$$

$$\mathbf{t}_*^\mathsf{T}\mathbf{W}\mathbf{c} \geq l$$

$$\alpha, C, l : \text{hyperparameters}$$

The first term is a regularizer over the classifier $\mathbf{c}$. The second term enforces that the predicted classifier has a high correlation with $\mathbf{t}_*^\mathsf{T}\mathbf{W}$; $\mathbf{W}$ is learned by Equation 5.8. The constraints $-\mathbf{c}^\mathsf{T}\mathbf{x}_i \geq \zeta_i$ enforce all the seen data instances to be on the negative side of the predicted classifier hyperplane with some misclassification allowed through the slack variables ζ_i. The constraint $\mathbf{t}_*^\mathsf{T}\mathbf{W}\mathbf{c} \geq l$ enforces that the correlation between the predicted classifier and $\mathbf{t}_*^\mathsf{T}\mathbf{W}$ must be no less than l; this is to enforce a minimum correlation between the text and visual features.

Solving for $\hat{c}$: Equation 5.7 is a quadratic program on $\mathbf{c}$ with linear constraints that can be solved be any existing quadratic optimizer (e.g., IBM CPLEX solver*).

5.4.2 Kernel Prediction Model

Prediction of $\Phi(t_*) = \beta(t_*)$ (Section 5.3.2) is decomposed into training (domain transfer) and prediction phases, detailed as follows.

During training, we learn a kernel domain transfer function to transfer the text description information $t_* \in \mathcal{T}$ to kernel-classifier parameters $\beta \in \mathbb{R}^{N+1}$ in the $\mathcal{V}$ domain. We call this domain transfer function $\beta_{DA}(t_*)$, which has the form of $\Psi^\mathsf{T}\mathbf{g}(t_*)$, where $\mathbf{g}(t_*) = [g(t_*, t_1) \dots g(t_*, t_{N_{sc}})]^\mathsf{T}$; Ψ is an $N_{sc} \times N + 1$ matrix, which transforms t to kernel classifier parameters for the class that t_* represents.

We aim to learn Ψ from V and $\{t_j\}, j = 1 \dots N_{sc}$, such that $\mathbf{g}(t)^\mathsf{T}\Psi\mathbf{k}(x) > l$ if t and x correspond to the same class and $\mathbf{g}(t)^\mathsf{T}\Psi\mathbf{k}(x) < u$ otherwise. Here l controls the similarity lower bound if t and x correspond to the same class, and u controls the similarity upper bound if t and x belong to different classes. We model the kernel domain transfer function as follows:

$$\Psi^* = \arg\min_{\Psi} L(\Psi) = \Big[\frac{1}{2}r(\Psi) + \lambda_1 \sum_k c_k(\mathbf{G}\,\Psi\,\mathbf{K})\Big] \tag{5.8}$$

where $\mathbf{G}$ is an $N_{sc} \times N_{sc}$ symmetric matrix, such that both the ith row and the ith column are equal to $\mathbf{g}(t_i)$, $i = 1 : N_{sc}$; $\mathbf{K}$ is an $N + 1 \times N$ matrix, such that the ith column is equal to $\mathbf{k}(x_i)$, x_i, $i = 1 : N$. The c_k's are loss functions over the constraints defined as $c_k(\mathbf{G}\,\Psi\,\mathbf{K}) = (\max(0, (l -$

---

* http://www-01.ibm.com/software/integration/optimization/cplex-optimizer

$\mathbf{1}_i^\top \mathbf{G} \, \Psi \, \mathbf{K} \mathbf{1}_j)))^2$ for same-class pairs of index i and j, or $= r \cdot (\max(0, (\mathbf{1}_i^\top \mathbf{G} \, \Psi \, \mathbf{K} \mathbf{1}_j - u)))^2$ otherwise, where $\mathbf{1}_i$ is an $N_{sc} \times 1$ vector with all zeros except at index i, and $\mathbf{1}_j$ is an $N \times 1$ vector with all zeros except at index j. This leads to the fact that $c_k(\mathbf{G} \, \Psi \, \mathbf{K})) = (\max(0, (l - \mathbf{g}(t_i)^\top \, \Psi \, \mathbf{k}(x_j)))^2$ for same-class pairs of index i and j, or $= r \cdot (\max(0, (\mathbf{g}(t_i)^\top \, \Psi \, \mathbf{k}(x_j) - u)))^2$ otherwise, where $u > l$, $r = nd/ns$, such that nd and ns are the number of pairs (i, j) of different classes and number of similar pairs, respectively. Finally, we used a Frobenius norm regularizer for $r(\Psi)$.

The objective function in Equation 5.8 controls the involvement of the constraints c_k by the term multiplied by λ_1, which controls its importance; we call it $C_{l,u}(\Psi)$.

In order to increase separability against seen classes, we adopted the inverse of the idea of the one-class kernel-SVM, whose main idea is to build a confidence function that takes only positive examples of the class. Our setting is the opposite scenario; seen examples are negative examples of the unseen class. In order to introduce our proposed adjustment method, we start by presenting the one-class SVM objective function. The Lagrangian dual of the one-class SVM [8] can be written as

$$\beta_+^* = \underset{\beta}{\text{argmin}}\big[\beta^\top \mathbf{K}' \beta - \beta^T \mathbf{a}\big]$$

$$\text{s.t.} : \beta^T \mathbf{1} = 1, 0 \le \beta_i \le C; \quad i = 1 \dots N$$

(5.9)

where $\mathbf{K}'$ is an $N \times N$ matrix, $\mathbf{K}'(i,j) = k(x_i, x_j)$, $\forall x_i, x_j \in \mathcal{S}_x$ (i.e., in the training data), $\mathbf{a}$ is an $N \times 1$ vector, $\mathbf{a}_i = k(x_i, x_i)$, and C is a hyper-parameter. It is straightforward to see that if β is aimed to be a negative decision function instead, the objective function would become

$$\beta_-^* = \underset{\beta}{\text{argmin}}\big[\beta^\top \mathbf{K}' \beta + \beta^T \mathbf{a}\big]$$

$$\text{s.t.} : \beta^T \mathbf{1} = -1, -C \le \beta_i \le 0; \quad i = 1 \dots N$$

(5.10)

While $\beta_-^* = -\beta_+^*$, the objective function in Equation 5.10 of the one-negative class SVM inspired us with the idea to adjust the kernel-classifier parameters to increase separability of the unseen kernel-classifier against the points of the seen classes, which leads to the following objective function:

$$\Phi(t_*) = \hat{\beta}(t_*) = \underset{\beta}{\text{argmin}}\big[\beta^\top \mathbf{K}' \beta - \zeta \hat{\beta}_{DT}(t_*)^\top \mathbf{K}' \beta + \beta^T \mathbf{a}\big]$$

$$\text{s.t.} : \beta^T \mathbf{1} = -1, \hat{\beta}_{DT}^\top \mathbf{K}' \beta > l, -C \le \beta_i \le 0; \quad \forall i$$

$$C, \zeta, l : \text{hyper-parameters,}$$

(5.11)

where $\hat{\beta}_{DT}$ is the first N elements in $\tilde{\beta}_{DT}(t^*) \in \mathbb{R}^{N+1}$ and $\mathbf{1}$ is an $N \times 1$ vector of ones. The objective function, in Equation 5.7, pushes the classifier of the unseen class to be highly correlated with the domain transfer prediction of the kernel classifier, while setting the points of the seen classes as negative examples. It is not hard to see that Equation 5.11 is a quadratic program in β, which could be solved using any quadratic solver. It is worth mentioning that the linear classifier prediction in Equation 5.7 (the best linear formulation in our results) predicts classifiers by solving an optimization problem of size $N + d_v + 1$ variables, $d_v + 1$ linear-classifier parameters, and N slack variables. In contrast, the kernelized objective function (Equation 5.11) solves a quadratic program of only N variables and predicts a kernel-classifier instead with fewer parameters. Using very high-dimensional features will not affect the optimization complexity.

5.4.3 Part-Based Model with Deep Convolutional Neural Network

In this sub-section, we show that unstructured text could be connected to images at the part level in a weekly supervised way. Connecting unstructured text into bird parts requires language and a visual representation that facilitates mutual transfer at the part level from text to images and vice versa. We also aim at a formulation that does not require text-to-part labeling at training time, nor does it require oracle part annotations at test time (e.g., [9]). Figure 5.3 shows an overview of our learning framework. Text articles are represented by a simple term frequency-inverse document frequency (TF-IDF) [10]. The text representation is then fed into a dimensionality reduction step followed by multi-part transformation to predict a visual classifier at the visual part level. The predicted classifier is applied on the part-based feature representations that are learned through a deep convolutional neural network (CNN). In the following sub-sections, we describe the text and visual part encoders and then the proposed approach.

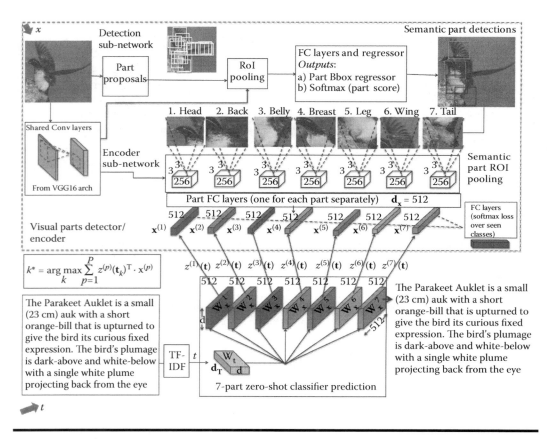

Figure 5.3   Part-based CNN approach (best seen in color): On the bottom is the core of the part-based CNN approach where the input is a pure text description and produces a classifier through a dimensionality reduction transformation W_t followed by part projections W_x^p, $p = 1 : P$, where P is the number of parts. The produced P classifiers are then applied on the part learning representation produced through detected parts from the top visual CNN. "RoI" refers to region-of-interest pooling [11]. "FC" refers to fully connected layers. "VGG conv layers" refers to the first five convolutional layers in VGGNet-16 [12].

Text Encoder: Similar to [13,14], text articles are first tokenized into words and the stop words are removed. Then, a simple TF-IDF feature vector is extracted [10]. We denote the TF-IDF representation of a text article t by $\mathbf{t} \in \mathbb{R}^{d_T}$, where d_T is the number of terms in the TF-IDF text representation.

Visual Parts CNN Detector/Encoder (VPDE): Detecting semantic parts facilitates modeling a representation that can be related to unstructured text terms at the part level. It was shown in Reference 15 that bird parts can be detected at a precision of 93.40% vs 74.0% with earlier methods [16]. We adopt a fast-RCNN framework [11] with VGG16 architecture [12] to detect seven small bird parts using the small-part proposal method proposed in Reference 15. The seven parts in order are (1) head, (2) back, (3) belly, (4) breast, (5) leg, (6) wing, and (7) tail; see Figure 5.3. We denote the input image to the visual part encoder as x. First, the image x is processed through VGG16 convolutional layers. The proposed regions by Zhang et al. [15] on x are then ROI pooled with a 3×3 grid. Then, they are then passed through an eight-way classifier (seven parts + background) and a bounding box regressor. Each part p is assigned to the region with the highest confidence of part p if that confidence is greater than a threshold (i.e., 1/7). If the highest confidence of part p is less than the threshold, part p is considered missing. The detected part regions are then passed to the visual encoder sub-network, in which ROI(3×3) pools these regions and eventually encodes each part into a 512-dimensional learning representation. When a part is missing, a region of all zeros is passed to the encoder sub-network. We denote these part-learning representations of a bird image x as $\mathbf{x}^{(1)}, \mathbf{x}^{(2)}, \dots, \mathbf{x}^{(P)}$; see the flow from x to the part representation in Figure 5.3 (top part starting from the blue arrow at the top left). We will detail later how the visual part detector/encoder (VPDE) network is trained. We denote the dimensionality of the part features as d_P, where $\mathbf{x}^{(p)} \in \mathbb{R}^{d_P} \forall p$ and $d_P = 512$ in our work.

During training, the information comes from images and text descriptions of K seen classes. We denote the learning representations of the detected parts of N training examples as $\{\mathbf{X}^{(p)} \in \mathbb{R}^{d_P \times N}\}, p = 1 : P$, where P is the number of parts. We denote the text representation of K seen classes as $\mathbf{T} \in \mathbb{R}^{d_T \times K}$. We define $Y \in \{0, 1\}^{N \times K}$ as the label matrix of each example in one-hot representation (i.e., each row in Y is a vector of zeros except at the corresponding class label index). At test time, the text features are given for $\hat{K}$ classes, where we need to assign the right label among them to each test image. Formally, the label assignment of an image x is defined as

$$k^* = \arg\max_k \sum_{p=1}^{P} z^{(p)}(\mathbf{t}_k)^{\top} \cdot \mathbf{x}^{(p)}, \ k = 1 : \hat{K} \tag{5.12}$$

where $\{\mathbf{x}^{(1)}, \mathbf{x}^{(2)}, \dots, \mathbf{x}^{(P)}\}$ is the part learned representation of image x, $\mathbf{t}_k$ is the text representation of class k, and $z^{(p)}(\mathbf{t})$ is a function that takes a text representation $\mathbf{t}$ and predicts a visual classifier weight for part p. In our work, we aim at jointly learning and regularizing $z^{(p)}(\cdot), \forall p \in 1 : P$ to encourage text terms to correlate with a sparse set of parts.

5.4.3.1 *Part Zero-Shot Classifier Prediction (PZSC)*

Part visual classifier prediction functions are defined as

$$z^{(p)}(\mathbf{t}) = \mathbf{t}^{\top} \mathbf{W}_{\mathbf{t}}^{\top} \mathbf{W}_{\mathbf{x}}^{p}, \quad \forall p \in 1 : P \tag{5.13}$$

where $\mathbf{W_t} \in \mathbb{R}^{d \times d_T}$ is a dimensionality reduction matrix, which projects the text representation $\mathbf{t} \in \mathbb{R}^{d_T}$ into a latent space. $\mathbf{W_x^p} \in \mathbb{R}^{d \times d_p}$ for each part p then regresses the projected text representation into a classifier for part p; see Figure 5.3 (bottom part starting from the blue arrow at the bottom left). Hence, $z^{(p)}(\mathbf{t})\forall p$ are mainly controlled by $\mathbf{W_x^p}$ and $\mathbf{W_t}$ since $\mathbf{t}$ is the input. We will elaborate next on how $\mathbf{W_t}$ and $\mathbf{W_x^p}\forall p$ are trained jointly. In this case, the predicted classifier $\Phi(t_*) = \boldsymbol{\rho}(t_*)$ is defined based on these predicted part-based classifiers as follows:

$$\Phi(t_*) = \boldsymbol{\rho}(t_*) = [z^{(1)}(\mathbf{t}_k), \dots, z^{(p)}(\mathbf{t}_*), \dots, z^{(P)}(\mathbf{t}_*)] \tag{5.14}$$

5.4.3.2 Model Optimization and Training

An interesting research direction regularizes zero-shot learning by introducing different structures to the learning parameters (e.g., [17,18]). In Reference 18, minimizing the variance of the projections from image to attribute space and vice versa was the key to improving attribute-based zero-shot prediction. Qiao et al. [17] used $l_{2,1}$ sparsity regularization, proposed in Reference 19, to encourage sparsity on the text terms, and they showed its capability to suppress noisy text terms and improve zero-shot classification from text. These regularization techniques inspired us to train our framework in Figure 5.3 with the following cost function:

$$\min_{\mathbf{W_x^1}, \dots, \mathbf{W_x^P}, \mathbf{W_t}} \left\| \left(\sum_{p=1}^{P} \mathbf{X}^{(p)\top} \mathbf{W_x^{p\top}} \right) \mathbf{W_t T} - \mathbf{Y} \right\|_F^2 + \lambda_1 \sum_{p=1}^{P} \left\| \mathbf{W_x^{p\top}} \mathbf{W_t T} \right\|_F^2 + \lambda_2 \sum_{p=1}^{P} \left\| \mathbf{W_x^{p\top}} \mathbf{W_t} \right\|_{2,1}$$

$$\tag{5.15}$$

where $||\cdot||_F$ is the Frobenius norm. The first term in Equation 5.15 encourages that for every image x_j, $\sum_{p=1}^{P} z^{(p)}(\mathbf{t}_k)^\top \cdot \mathbf{x}_j^{(p)} = \sum_{p=1}^{P} (\mathbf{t}_k^\top \mathbf{W_t^\top} \mathbf{W_x^p})^\top \cdot \mathbf{x}_j^{(p)}$ to be equal to 1 if k is the ground-truth class or 0 if other classes. This enables $z^{(p)}(\mathbf{t})$ to predict part classifiers for an arbitrary text $\mathbf{t}$ [i.e., high $(\rightarrow 1)$ for the right class, low $(\rightarrow 0)$ for others]. The second term bounds the variance of the functions $\{z^{(p)}(\mathbf{t}) = \mathbf{t}^\top \mathbf{W_t^\top} \mathbf{W_x^p} \ \forall p\}$. More importantly, the third term imposes structure on $\mathbf{W_t}$ and $\{\mathbf{W_x^p}\forall p\}$, to encourage connecting every text term with a sparse set of parts (i.e., every text term attends to as few parts as possible). The third term $\sum_{p=1}^{P} ||\mathbf{W_x^{p\top}} \mathbf{W_t}||_{2,1}$ is defined as $\sum_{p=1}^{P} \sum_{i=1}^{d_T} ||\mathbf{W_x^{p\top}} \mathbf{w_t^i}||_2$, $\mathbf{w_t^i}$ is the ith column in the $\mathbf{W_t}$ matrix that corresponds to the ith text term, and $\mathbf{W_x^{p\top}} \mathbf{w_t^i} \in \mathbb{R}^{d_X}$ are the weights that connect the pth part to ith text term. Hence, the third term encourages group sparsity over the parameter groups that connect every text term i to every part p (i.e., $\mathbf{W_x^{p\top}} \mathbf{w_t^i}$), which encourages terms to be connected to parts sparsely.

Optimization: The parameters of the part-based model include part detection sub-network parameters and part representation sub-network parameters for the VPDE network, and $\{\mathbf{W_x^p}, p = 1 : P\}$, $\mathbf{W_t}$ for the part zero-shot classifier predictor (PZSC) network. The VPDE network is trained by alternate optimization over the detector and the representation sub-networks with the training images. The detector sub-network is optimized through softmax loss over eight outputs (seven parts and background) and bounding box regression to predict the final box for each detected part. The representation sub-network is optimized over by softmax loss over the seen/training classes. The convolutional layers are shared between the detection and representation sub-networks (VGG16 conv layers in our work); see Figure 5.3 (top part). After training the VPDE network, we solve the objective function in Equation 5.15 to train the part zero-shot classifier predictor.

The cost function in Equation 5.15 is convex if optimized for either $\mathbf{W_t}$ or $\{\mathbf{W_x^p}, p = 1 : P\}$ individually but not convex on both. Hence, we solve Equation 5.15 by an alternate optimization, where we fix $\mathbf{W_t}$ and solve for $\{\mathbf{W_x^p}, p = 1 : P\}$; then we fix $\{\mathbf{W_x^p}, p = 1 : P\}$ and solve for $\mathbf{W_t}$.

Solving for $\mathbf{W_t}$: Following the efficient $l_{2,1}$ group sparsity optimization method in Reference 19, the solution to this sub-problem could be efficiently achieved by sequentially solving to the following problem until convergence:

$$\min_{\mathbf{W_t}, \{\mathbf{D}_l^p, \forall p\}} \left\| \left(\sum_{p=1}^P \mathbf{X}^{(p)^\mathsf{T}} \mathbf{W_x^{p\mathsf{T}}} \right) \mathbf{W_t T} - \mathbf{Y} \right\|_F^2 + \lambda_1 \sum_{p=1}^P \left\| \mathbf{W_x^{p\mathsf{T}}} \mathbf{W_t T} \right\|_F^2$$

$$+ \lambda_2 \sum_{p=1}^P \mathrm{Tr}(\mathbf{W_x^{p\mathsf{T}}} \mathbf{W_t} \mathbf{D}_l^p \mathbf{W_t^\mathsf{T}} \mathbf{W_x^p}) \tag{5.16}$$

where $\mathbf{D}_l^p$ is a diagonal matrix with the ith diagonal element is $1/(2||\mathbf{W_x^p}(\mathbf{w_z^i})^{(l-1)}||_2)^2$ at the lth iteration, where $(\mathbf{w_z^i})^{(l-1)}$ is the ith column of the $\mathbf{W_t}$ solution at iteration $l-1$. We realized that it is hard to find a closed-form solution to Equation 5.16. Hence, we solve Equation 5.16 by quasi-Newton with limited memory BFGS updating (i.e., gradient-based optimization).

Solving for $\mathbf{W_x^p}$: In this step, we solve the following sub-problem:

$$\min_{\{\mathbf{D}_l^p, \mathbf{W_x^p}, \forall p\}} \left\| \left(\sum_{p=1}^P \mathbf{X}^{(p)^\mathsf{T}} \mathbf{W_x^{p\mathsf{T}}} \right) \mathbf{W_t T} - \mathbf{Y} \right\|_F^2 + \lambda_1 \sum_{p=1}^P \left\| \mathbf{W_x^{p\mathsf{T}}} \mathbf{W_t T} \right\|_F^2$$

$$+ \lambda_2 \sum_{p=1}^P \mathrm{Tr}(\mathbf{W_x^{p\mathsf{T}}} \mathbf{W_t} \mathbf{D}_l^p \mathbf{W_t^\mathsf{T}} \mathbf{W_x^p}) \tag{5.17}$$

where $\mathbf{D}_l^p$ is a diagonal matrix with the ith diagonal element is $1/(2||(\mathbf{W_x^p})^{(l-1)} \mathbf{w_z^i}||_2)^2$ at the lth iteration, where $(\mathbf{W_x^p})^{(l-1)}$ is the solution of $\mathbf{W_x^p}$ for part p at iteration $l-1$. Similar to Equation 5.16, we solve Equation 5.17 by quasi-Newton with BFGS updating.

5.5 Experiments

Methods: In addition to the linear, kernel, and part-based versions, we also report the performance of four state-of-the-art methods: SJE [20], MCZSL [9], ZSLNS [17], and ESZSL [18]. Additionally, we used a state-of-the-art model [21] for image-sentence similarity by breaking down each text document into sentences and considering it as a positive sentence for all images in the corresponding class. Then we measure the similarities between an image and class by averaging its similarity to all sentences in that class. Images were encoded using VGGNet [12] and sentences were encoded by an RNN with GRU activations [22]. The purpose of this experiment is to study how RNN representation of the sentences performs in our setting with noisy text descriptions.

Datasets: We compare the discussed methods along with other competing methods from the literature on two datasets: CUB2011 [23] and NABirds [24]. Both are bird datasets for fine-grained classification. Important parts of the bird in each image are annotated with locations by experts. The CUB2011 dataset contains 200 categories of bird species with a total of 11,788 images. Compared with CUB2011, NABirds is a larger dataset of birds with 1011 classes and 48,562 images. It constructs a hierarchy of bird classes, including 555 leaf nodes and 456 parent nodes, starting from the root class "bird." Only leaf nodes are associated with images, and the images for the parent class can be collected by merging all the images of its children nodes. In practice, we found some pairs of classes merely differ in gender. For example, the parent node "American kestrel" is divided into "American kestrel (female, immature)" and "American kestrel (adult male)." Since we cannot find the Wikipedia articles for this subtle division of classes, we merged such pairs of classes to their parent. After such processing, we finally have 404 classes; each one is associated with a set of images, as well as the class description from Wikipedia. We collected the raw textual sources from English-language Wikipedia-v01.02.2016. We manually verified all the articles and augmented classes with limited descriptions from the all-about-birds website [25]. We plan to release these data and the NABird benchmarks that we set up.

SCS and SCE splits: As we discussed in Section 5.1, we have designed two kinds of splitting schemes, in terms of how close the seen classes are to the unseen classes: super-category-shared (SCS) splitting and super-category-exclusive (SCE) splitting. In the dataset, some classes are often the further division of one category. For example, both "black-footed albatross" and "Laysan albatross" belong to the category "albatross" in CUB2011, and both "Cooper's hawk" and "Harris's hawk" are under the category "Hawks" in NABirds. For SCS, unseen classes are deliberately picked on the condition that there exist seen classes with the same super-category. In this scheme, the relevance between seen classes and unseen classes is very high. On the contrary, in SCE, all classes under the same category as unseen classes would either belong to the seen or the unseen classes.

These strategies for zero-shot splits were used on the CUBirds dataset in the literature but in different works and were not compared to each other. For the SCS split on CUB2011, we use the same splitting as in [9,17], where 150 classes were used for training and 50 classes for testing. For the SCE split on CUB2011, we use the same splitting as in [30], where the first 80% of classes are considered as seen classes and used for training. To design these two splitting schemes in NABirds, we first check the class hierarchy. There exist 22 children nodes under the root category (bird) in the hierarchy. We found that the number of descendants under the 22nd children (perching birds) are much greater than the average descendants of the remaining 21 classes (205 vs 10). To eliminate this imbalance, we further divide this category into its children. With the combination of 29 children of this category and the other 21 children of the root, we ended up with 50 super-categories (21+29). For the SCS split, we randomly pick 20% of descendant classes under each super-category as unseen classes. For the SCE split, we randomly pick 20% of the super-categories and consider all of their descendant classes as unseen are considered the seen classes. For both splits, there are in total 323 training (seen) classes and 81 testing (unseen) classes, respectively. For ease of presentation, we sometimes refer to the SCS split as the easy split and to the SCE split as the hard split.

Textual representation for the linear, kernel, and part-based CNN approaches: We extract the text representation according to the scheme described in Section 3.1. The dimensionalities of the TF-IDF feature for CUB2011 and NABirds are 11,083 and 13,585, respectively. In the kernel approach, we used Gaussian rbf-kernel as a similarity measure between text description spaces [i.e., $g(t, t') = \exp(-\lambda||\mathbf{t} - \mathbf{t}||)$] (see Section 5.3.2), where $\mathbf{t}$ and $\mathbf{t}'$ are the TFIDF features for text descriptions t and t', respectively.

Image representation for the part-based CNN approach: The part regions are first detected and then passed to the VPDE network. A 512-dimensional feature vector is extracted for each semantic part. For the CUB2011 dataset, we only use seven semantic parts to train the VPDE network, as illustrated in Figure 5.3. For the NABird dataset, we used only six visual parts, with the "leg" part removed, since there are no annotations for the "leg" part in the NABirds dataset.

Image representation for the linear and kernel approaches: For the linear and kernel approaches, we used the feature activations for the FC7 features for the VGG16 architecture [26], the same backbone architecture as for the VPDE. In the kernel approach, we used Gaussian rbf-kernel as a similarity measure between image spaces [i.e., $k(x, x') = \exp(-\lambda||\mathbf{x} - \mathbf{x}'||)]$ (see Section 5.3.2), where $\mathbf{x}$ and $\mathbf{x}'$ are the deep features for images x and x', respectively.

5.5.1 Performance Evaluation

Zero-shot top-1 accuracy: For standard zero-shot image classification, we calculate the mean top-1 accuracy obtained on unseen classes. We performed comprehensive experiments on both SCS (easy) and SCS (hard) splits on both CUB2011 and NABirds. Note that some of these methods were applied on attribute prediction (e.g., ZSLNS [17], SynC [27], ESZSL [18]) or image-sentence similarity (e.g., order embedding [21]). We used the publicly available code of these methods and other text-based methods like ZSLNS [17]. Note that the conventional split setting for zero-shot learning is the SCS (easy) split. We think evaluating the performance for both the SCS (easy) and the SCE (hard) splits is complementary and hence we report the performance for both of them. In Table 5.2, we show the comparisons among linear, kernel, and part-based approaches, along with all the other baselines on the CUB2011 easy and hard benchmarks. The results show that the part-based method outperforms all the baselines by a noticeable margin on both the easy and the hard benchmarks. Note that the image-sentence similarity baseline (i.e., order embedding [21]) is among the worst-performing methods. We hypothesized that the reason is the level of noise, which is addressed by the other methods by regularizing the text information at the term level, while the representation unit in Reference 21 is the whole sentence. Similarly, Table 5.3 shows the

Table 5.2 Top-1 Accuracy (%) on CUB2011 Dataset in Two Different Split Settings

Methods	*SCS (Easy)*	*SCE (Hard)*
ESZSL [18]	28.5	7.4
SJE [20]	29.9	–
ZSLNS [17]	29.1	7.3
SynC$_{fast}$ [27]	28.0	8.6
SynC$_{OVO}$ [27]	12.5	5.9
Order embedding [21]	17.3	5.9
Linear	27.0	5.0
Kernel	33.5	7.7
Part-based CNN (detected parts)	37.2	9.7

Note: Note that some of these methods are attribute-based methods but applicable in our setting by replacing attribute vectors with text features.

Table 5.3   Top-1 Accuracy (%) on NABird Dataset Splits

Methods	SCS (Easy)	SCE (Hard)
ESZSL [18]	24.3	6.3
ZSLNS [17]	24.5	6.8
SynC$_{fast}$ [27]	18.4	3.8
Kernel [28]	11.4	6.0
Part-based CNN (detected parts)	30.3	8.1

results on NABirds easy and hard benchmarks, where the performance of the part-based approach is also superior over the competing methods. It is worth mentioning that the kernel approach is not scalable since its training parameters depend on the number of image-class pairs. We trained it for 6 days on a 64 GB RAM machine and report the results of the latest snapshot in Table 5.3. Notice also that the kernel approach preforms better than the linear approach, yet is still significantly outperformed by the part-based approach as shown in Tables 5.3 and 5.2.

Generalized zero-shot learning performance: The conventional zero-shot learning that we discussed earlier classifies test examples into unseen classes without considering the seen classes in the test phase. Because the seen classes are often the most common, it is hardly realistic to assume that we will never encounter them during the test phase [29]. To get rid of such an assumption, Chao et al. [29] recently proposed a more general metric for generalized zero-shot learning (GZSL). We here briefly review how it generally measures the capability of recognizing not only unseen data, but also seen data. Let $\mathcal{S}$ and $\mathcal{U}$ denote the label spaces of seen classes and unseen classes, respectively, and $\mathcal{T} = \mathcal{S} \cup \mathcal{U}$ the joint label space. $A_{\mathcal{U} \to \mathcal{T}}$ and $A_{\mathcal{S} \to \mathcal{T}}$ are the accuracies of classifying seen data and unseen data into joint label space. The labels are computed using the Equation 5.18:

$$y = \arg\max_{c \in \mathcal{T}} f(\mathbf{x}) - \lambda I[c \in \mathcal{S}] \qquad (5.18)$$

where $I[.] \in \{0, 1\}$ indicates whether c is a seen class and λ is the penalty factor. $\mathbf{x}$ is set to seen data or unseen data to calculate $A_{\mathcal{U} \to \mathcal{T}}$ and $A_{\mathcal{S} \to \mathcal{T}}$, respectively. As λ increases or decreases, data are encouraged to be classified into unseen classes or seen classes, respectively. In the cases where λ is extremely large or small, all data are assigned with an unseen class label or seen class label, respectively. Therefore, we can generate a series of pairs of classification accuracies ($\langle A_{\mathcal{U} \to \mathcal{T}}, A_{\mathcal{S} \to \mathcal{T}} \rangle$) by tuning values of λ. Considering these pairs as points with $A_{\mathcal{U} \to \mathcal{T}}$ as the x-axis and $A_{\mathcal{S} \to \mathcal{T}}$ as the y-axis, we can draw the seen-unseen accuracy curve (SUC). The area under SUC (AUSUC), as a widely used measure of curves, can well assess the performance of a classifier in the balance of the conflicting $A_{\mathcal{U} \to \mathcal{T}}$ and $A_{\mathcal{S} \to \mathcal{T}}$ measurements.

The seen-unseen accuracy curves of linear, kernel, part-based CNN and other state-of-the-art approaches are shown in Figure 5.4. The performance of part-based CNN is superior to all other methods in terms of the AUSUC score. Although the linear approach apparently achieves a high performance on seen classes, its poor performance of classifying unseen classes indicates that it doesn't learn much knowledge that can be effectively transferred to unseen classes. On the contrary, ZSLNS has a relatively good accuracy $A_{\mathcal{U} \to \mathcal{T}}$, but its lower $A_{\mathcal{S} \to \mathcal{T}}$ compared with other methods indicates that the success of unseen classes' classification may come from the overweighted regularizers. Part-based CNN remarkably outperforms other methods in terms of the classification

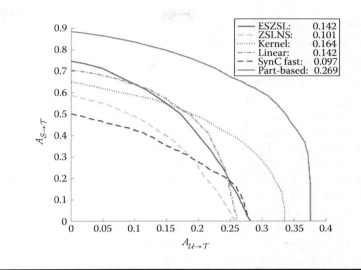

Figure 5.4 CUB2011 seen-unseen accuracy curve (SCE split).

of unseen classes, and it also achieves a relative high accuracy in the recognition of seen classes. The curves in Figure 5.4 demonstrate the part-based method's capability of balancing the classification of unseen classes and seen classes (0.304 AUSUC for Ours-DET compared to 0.239 for the best-performing baseline). We also demonstrated the performance of these methods on the NABirds dataset in Figure 5.5 (0.126 AUSUC for the part-based method compared to 0.093 for the best-performing baseline).

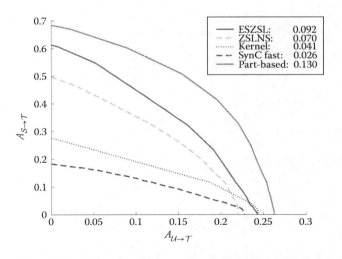

Figure 5.5 NABirds seen-unseen accuracy curve (SCS split).

5.5.2 Comparing Part-Based CNN to State-of-the Art Part-Based Method (MCZSL)

We here compare the part-based CNN approach with MCZSL, a competitive part-based approach. Both part-based CNN and MCZSL utilize part annotations provided by the CUB2011 dataset. However, in contrast to MCZSL, which directly uses part annotations to extract image features in the test phase, our part-based CNN is merely based on the detected semantic parts during both training and testing. Less accurate detection of semantic parts will surely degrade the accuracy for the final zero-shot classification. In order to make a fair comparison with MCZSL, we also report the performance of using the ground-truth annotations of semantic parts at test time. The results of our part-based CNN on the detected parts and ground-truth parts are denoted by "part-based-DET" and "part-based-ATN," respectively. In Table 5.4, we compared to the same benchmark reported in Reference 9, which is the SCS split on the CUB2011 dataset. The results show that the performance of "part-based-ATN" is 9% better than [9] (43.6% vs 34.7%), although we only used a simple TF-IDF text representation for the part-based-ATN compared to the multiple cues used in MCZSL like text, WordNet, and word2vec. Note also that the 34.7% achieved by Akata et al. [9] used 19 part annotations during training and testing (the whole image, head, body, full object, and 15 part locations annotated), while we only used 7 parts for part-based-ATN to achieve 43.6%. Table 5.4 also shows that part-based-DET still performs 2.5% better, even when using the detected parts at test time (37.2% Ours-DET vs 34.7% MCSZSL using ground-truth annotations). Note that in all the previous experiments, we used part-based-DET; that is, no ground-truth boxes were used at test time.

5.5.3 Part-Based CNN Model Analysis and Qualitative Examples

We also analyzed the connections between the terms and parts in the learned parameters, which are $\mathbf{W}_{\mathbf{x}}^{p\mathsf{T}}\mathbf{w}_{\mathbf{t}}^{i}$ for the connection between term i and part p in the CUB2011 dataset (SCS split); see Section 5.4.3. Figure 5.6 shows the l_2 norm of $\mathbf{W}_{\mathbf{x}}^{p\mathsf{T}}\mathbf{w}_{\mathbf{t}}^{i}$ for each part separately and only on the top

Table 5.4   Performance Comparison with Accuracy (%) on CUB2011 Dataset

Methods	Accuracy
MCZSL [9] (BoW)	26.0
MCZSL [9] (word2vec)	32.1
MCZSL [9] (Comb.)	34.7
part-based-DET	37.2
part-based-ATN	43.6

Note: In Reference 9, the approach is evaluated with different textual representations: BoW, word2vec, and their combination.

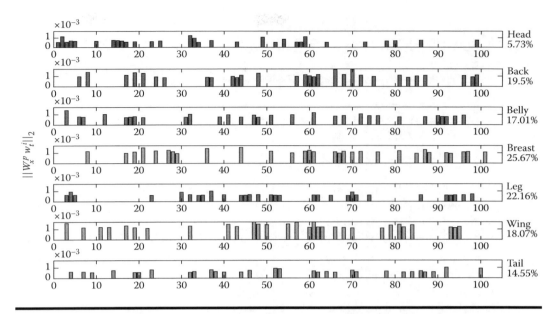

Figure 5.6   Connection to text terms (CUB2011 dataset, SCS split, with 37.2% Top1-Acc). On the right, Top1-Acc is shown per part.

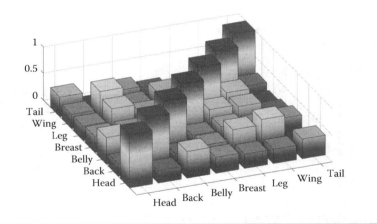

Figure 5.7   Top-30 terms overlap between every two parts (CUB2011 SCS).

30 terms for each part sorted by $\|\mathbf{W}_{\mathbf{x}}^{p\mathsf{T}}\mathbf{w}_{\mathbf{t}}^{i}\|_2$. Figure 5.7 shows the percentage of overlap between these terms for every pair of parts, which shows that every part focuses on its relevant concepts, yet there is still a shared portion that includes shared concepts like color and texture. In Figure 5.6, we show the summation of these connections for every part and compare between Ours-DET and Ours-ATN to analyze the effect of detecting the parts versus using part annotations. We observe that more concepts/terms are discovered and connected to "head" for Ours-ATN, while more concepts are learned for "breast" for Ours-DET. This is also consistent with the top-1 accuracy if each part is individually used for recognition; see the top-1 accuracy for each part separately in

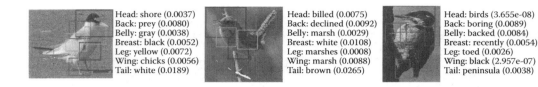

Head: shore (0.0037) Back: prey (0.0080) Belly: gray (0.0038) Breast: black (0.0052) Leg: yellow (0.0072) Wing: chicks (0.0056) Tail: white (0.0189)	Head: billed (0.0075) Back: declined (0.0092) Belly: marsh (0.0029) Breast: white (0.0108) Leg: marshes (0.0008) Wing: marsh (0.0088) Tail: brown (0.0265)	Head: birds (3.655e-08) Back: boring (0.0089) Belly: backed (0.0084) Breast: recently (0.0054) Leg: toed (0.0026) Wing: black (2.957e-07) Tail: peninsula (0.0038)

Figure 5.8 Part-to-term connectivity. Left to right: Least tern, marsh wren, and three-toed woodpecker from CUB2011 SCS split.

Figure 5.6 (right). This observation shows that if we have a perfect detector, "head" will be one of the most important parts to be connected to terms, which is intuitive. We also observed the same conclusion on both the SCS and SCE splits on NABirds and SCE on CUB2011. We further demonstrate this part-to-term connectivity by some qualitative examples in Figure 5.8. For each bird, the top related term for each part is printed based on ranking the terms by $\mathbf{x}^{(p)}\mathbf{W}_{\mathbf{x}}^{p^{\mathrm{T}}}\mathbf{w}_{\mathbf{z}}^{j}\mathbf{t}_{k}^{i}$, where $\mathbf{t}_{k}^{i}$ is the ith dimension of the text representation of the predicted class k (i.e., only the text terms that exist in the text description of class k are considered). The figure shows the capability of the part-based CNN method to ground concepts to its location in the image. In the right example, "toes" is strongly connected to leg—the connection strength is shown between parentheses. In the middle example, the "billed" concept is connected to head, "white" is connected to the breast, and "brown" is connected to the tail. In the left example, "yellow" is connected to leg.

5.6 Conclusion

We explored the problem of predicting visual classifiers from textual description of classes with no training images. We investigated and experimented with different approaches for the problem within the fine-grained categorization context (linear, kernel, and part-based approaches). The linear approach transforms the Wikipedia text feature vector into a linear visual classifier by mainly a domain transfer approach. The kernel approach is conceptually similar to the linear approach but predicts a generalized kernel-classifier instead, which introduces non-linearity that we found useful to relate text and visual space. We finally presented the part-based CNN approach, which uses deep CNN methods combined with bird databases to facilitate visual classifier prediction at the part level. We extensively studied the differences between these methods along with other state-of-the art approaches and our main findings could be summarized in the following two points.

1. Kernel visual classifier prediction outperforms the state-of-the art methods, including the linear approach presented in this chapter. This is due to the non-linearity introduced by the RBF-kernel in both the text and the visual spaces.
2. The part-based CNN approach improves upon kernel classifier prediction since it attends to the bird parts that are not captured by other competing methods. It also introduces a part-based noise suppression mechanism that encourages parts to be sparsely connected to text terms and vice versa. This suppresses the noise introduced by the large number of non-visual terms in the the Wikipedia bird articles.

References

1. A. Farhadi, I. Endres, D. Hoiem, and D.A. Forsyth. Describing objects by their attributes. In *CVPR*, 2009.
2. C.H. Lampert, H. Nickisch, and S. Harmeling. Learning to detect unseen object classes by between-class attribute transfer. In *CVPR*, 2009.
3. B. Schölkopf, R. Herbrich, and A.J. Smola. A generalized representer theorem. In *COLT*, 2001.
4. L. Duan, D. Xu, I.W.-H. Tsang, and J. Luo. Visual event recognition in videos by learning from web data. In *IEEE Transactions on Pattern Analysis and Machine Intelligence*, 2012.
5. B. Kulis, K. Saenko, and T. Darrell. What you saw is not what you get: Domain adaptation using asymmetric kernel transforms. In *CVPR*, 2011.
6. K. Saenko, B. Kulis, M. Fritz, and T. Darrell. Adapting visual category models to new domains. In *ECCV*, 2010.
7. J. Yang, R. Yan, and A.G. Hauptmann. Cross-domain video concept detection using adaptive SVMs. In *Proceedings of the 15th International Conference on Multimedia*, 2007.
8. P.F. Evangelista, M.J. Embrechts, and B.K. Szymanski. Some properties of the Gaussian kernel for one class learning. In *ICANN*, 2007.
9. Z. Akata, M. Malinowski, M. Fritz, and B. Schiele. Multi-cue zero-shot learning with strong supervision. In *Proceedings of the IEEE Conference on Computer Vision and Pattern Recognition*, 2016.
10. G. Salton and C. Buckley. Term-weighting approaches in automatic text retrieval. *Information processing & management*, **24**(5):513–523, 1988.
11. R. Girshick. Fast R-CNN. In *Proceedings of the IEEE International Conference on Computer Vision*, pp. 1440–1448, 2015.
12. K. Simonyan and A. Zisserman. Very deep convolutional networks for large-scale image recognition. In *ICLR*, 2015.
13. M. Elhoseiny, B. Saleh, and A. Elgammal. Write a classifier: Zero shot learning using purely textual descriptions. In *ICCV*, 2013.
14. J.L. Ba, K. Swersky, S. Fidler et al. Predicting deep zero-shot convolutional neural networks using textual descriptions. In *Proceedings of the IEEE International Conference on Computer Vision*, pp. 4247–4255, 2015.
15. H. Zhang, T. Xu, M. Elhoseiny, X. Huang, S. Zhang, A. Elgammal, and D. Metaxas. Spda-cnn: Unifying semantic part detection and abstraction for fine-grained recognition. In *Proceedings of the IEEE Conference on Computer Vision and Pattern Recognition*, 2016.
16. D. Lin, X. Shen, C. Lu, and J. Jia. Deep LAC: Deep localization, alignment and classification for fine-grained recognition. In *Proceedings of the IEEE Conference on Computer Vision and Pattern Recognition*, pp. 1666–1674, 2015.
17. R. Qiao, L. Liu, C. Shen, and A. van den Hengel. Less is more: Zero-shot learning from online textual documents with noise suppression. In *CVPR*, 2016.
18. B. Romera-Paredes and P.H.S. Torr. An embarrassingly simple approach to zero-shot learning. In *ICML*, 2015.
19. F. Nie, H. Huang, X. Cai, and C.H. Ding. Efficient and robust feature selection via joint 2, 1-norms minimization. In *Advances in Neural Information Processing Systems*, pp. 1813–1821, 2010.
20. Z. Akata, S. Reed, D. Walter, H. Lee, and B. Schiele. Evaluation of output embeddings for fine-grained image classification. In *CVPR*, 2015.
21. I. Vendrov, R. Kiros, S. Fidler, and R. Urtasun. Order-embeddings of images and language. In *ICLR*, 2016.
22. K. Cho, B. Van Merriënboer, C. Gulcehre, D. Bahdanau, F. Bougares, H. Schwenk, and Y. Bengio. Learning phrase representations using RNN encoder-decoder for statistical machine translation. In *EMNLP*, 2014.
23. C. Wah, S. Branson, P. Welinder, P. Perona, and S. Belongie. The Caltech-UCSD Birds-200-2011 dataset. Technical Report CNS-TR-2011-001, California Institute of Technology, 2011.
24. G. Van Horn, S. Branson, R. Farrell, S. Haber, J. Barry, P. Ipeirotis, P. Perona, and S. Belongie. Building a bird recognition app and large scale dataset with citizen scientists: The fine print in

fine-grained dataset collection. In *Computer Vision and Pattern Recognition (CVPR)*, Boston, MA, 2015.

25. The Cornell Lab Bird Academy. All About Birds, 2016. info.allaboutbirds.org, accessed June 19, 2016.
26. K. Simonyan and A. Zisserman. Very deep convolutional networks for large-scale image recognition. In *ICLR*, 2015.
27. S. Changpinyo, W.-L. Chao, B. Gong, and F. Sha. Synthesized classifiers for zero-shot learning. *arXiv* preprint arXiv:1603.00550, 2016.
28. M. Elhoseiny, A. Elgammal, and B. Saleh. Write a classifier: Predicting visual classifiers from unstructured text. In *TPAMI*, 2017.
29. W.-L. Chao, S. Changpinyo, B. Gong, and F. Sha. An empirical study and analysis of generalized zero-shot learning for object recognition in the wild, 2016.
30. Z. Akata, F. Perronnin, Z. Harchaoui, and C. Schmid. Label-embedding for attribute-based classification. In *Proceedings of the IEEE Conference on Computer Vision and Pattern Recognition*, pp. 819–826, 2013.

Chapter 6

Deep Learning for Font Recognition and Retrieval

Zhangyang Wang, Jianchao Yang, Hailin Jin, Zhaowen Wang, Eli Shechtman, Aseem Agarwala, Jonathan Brandt, and Thomas S. Huang

Contents

6.1 Introduction

Typography is a fundamental graphic design component and also a ubiquitous art form that affects our understanding and perception of what we read. Thousands of different font faces have been created with enormous variations in the characters. Graphic designers have the desire to identify the fonts they encounter in daily life for later use. While they might take a photo of the text of a particularly interesting font and seek out an expert to identify the font, the manual identification process is extremely tedious and error prone. Several websites allow users to search and recognize fonts by font similarity, including Identifont, MyFonts, WhatTheFont, and Fontspring. All of them rely on tedious humans interactions and high-quality manual preprocessing of images, and the accuracies are still unsatisfactory. On the other hand, the majority of font selection interfaces in existing software applications are simple linear lists, while exhaustively exploring the entire space of fonts using an alphabetical listing is unrealistic for most users.

This chapter mainly investigates the recent advances of exploiting the deep learning techniques to improve the experiences of browsing, identifying, selecting, and manipulating fonts. Two important and inter-linked tasks will be discussed in detail:

■ *Font recognition* from an image or photo effectively and automatically could greatly facilitate font organization and selection during the design process. It is usually formulated as a large-scale visual classification problem. Such a visual font recognition (VFR) problem is inherently difficult because of the huge number of possible fonts (online repositories provide hundreds of thousands); the dynamic and open-ended properties of font classes; and the very subtle and character-dependent differences among fonts (letter endings, stroke weights, slopes, size, texture, serif details, etc.).

■ *Font retrieval* arises when a target font is encountered and a user/designer wants to quickly browse and select visually similar fonts from a large selection. Compared to the recognition task, the retrieval task allows for more flexibility, especially when an exact match to the font seen may not be available, in which case similar fonts should be returned.

The recently shipped **DeepFont** system, described in References 1–3, has implemented the deep-learning-based font recognition and retrieval features, as part of the Adobe Photoshop software.* Note that the substantial processes of localizing, cropping, cleaning, centering and preprocessing the fonts from photographs is beyond the scope of this chapter.

In order for completeness, we introduce the **AdobeVFR Dataset**, in which a large set of *labeled real-world* images and a large corpus of unlabeled real-world data are collected for both training and testing, which is the first of its kind and is publicly released.† It can be leveraged together with a large training corpus of labeled synthetic data augmented in a specific way [1]. We also briefly discuss two relevant tasks, font generation and font emotion analysis, in the last part of this chapter.

6.2 Dataset

Besides the inherent difficulty of VFR as a larger-scale fine-grain classification problem, collecting real-world data for a large collection of font classes for training data-driven machine learning models is also extremely difficult. Most attainable real-world text images do not have font label information, while the error-prone font labeling task requires font expertise that is out of reach

---

* "Match fonts from an image," in Adobe Photoshop: https://helpx.adobe.com/photoshop/how-to/match-font-image.html
† http://www.atlaswang.com/deepfont.html

of most people. The few previous approaches [4–9] are mostly from the document analysis stand-point. These approaches only focus on a small number of font classes, and they are highly sensitive to noise, blur, perspective distortions, and complex backgrounds. In Reference 10, the authors proposed a large-scale, learning-based solution without dependence on character segmentation or OCR. The core algorithm is built on local feature embedding, local feature metric learning, and max-margin template selection. However, their results suggest that the robustness to real-world variations is unsatisfactory, and a higher recognition accuracy is still demanded.

6.2.1 Domain Mismatch between Synthetic and Real-World Data

To apply machine learning to the VFR problem, we require realistic text images with ground-truth font labels. However, such data are scarce and expensive to obtain. Moreover, the training data requirement is vast, since there are hundreds of thousands of fonts in use for Roman characters alone. One way to overcome the training data challenge is to synthesize the training set by rendering text fragments for all the necessary fonts. However, to attain effective recognition models with this strategy, we must face the domain mismatch between synthetic and real-world text images [10]. For example, it is common for designers to edit the spacing, aspect ratio or alignment of text arbitrarily, to make the text fit other design components. The result is that characters in real-world images are spaced, stretched, and distorted in numerous ways. For example, Figure 6.3a and b depict typical examples of *character spacing* and *aspect ratio* differences between (standard rendered) synthetic and real-world images. Other perturbations, such as background clutter, perspective distortion, noise, and blur, are also ubiquitous.

6.2.2 The AdobeVFR Dataset

Collecting and labeling real-world examples is notoriously hard and thus a labeled real-world dataset has been absent for a long time. A small dataset *VFRWild325* was collected in Reference 10, consisting of 325 real-world text images and 93 classes. However, the small size puts its effectiveness in jeopardy.

Chen et al. in Reference 10 selected 2,420 font classes to work on. We remove some script classes, ending up with a total of 2,383 font classes. We collected 201,780 text images from various typography forums, where people post these images seeking help from experts to identify the fonts. Most of them come with hand-annotated font labels that may be inaccurate. Unfortunately, only a very small portion of them fall into our list of 2,383 fonts. All images are first converted into grayscale. Those images with our target class labels are then selected and inspected by independent experts if their labels are correct. Images with verified labels are then manually cropped with tight bounding boxes and normalized proportionally in size, to be with the identical height of 105 pixels. Finally, we obtain 4,384 real-world test images with reliable labels, covering 617 classes (out of 2,383), as the VFR_real_test set. Compared to the synthetic data, these images typically have much larger appearance variations caused by scaling, background clutter, lighting, noise, perspective distortions, and compression artifacts. Removing the 4,384 labeled images from the full set, we are left with 197,396 unlabeled real-world images, which we denote as VFR_real_u.

To create a sufficiently large set of synthetic training data, we follow the same method as in Reference 10 to render long English words sampled from a large corpus and to generate tightly cropped, grayscale, and size-normalized text images. For each class, we assign 1,000 images for training, and 100 for validation, which are denoted as VFR_syn_train and VFR_syn_val, respectively. The entire **AdobeVFR dataset**, consisting of VFR_real_test, VFR_real_u, VFR_syn_train,

Table 6.1   Comparison of All VFR Datasets

Dataset Name	Source	Label?	Purpose	Size	Class
VFRWild325 [10]	Real	Y	Test	325	93
VFR_real_test	Real	Y	Test	4,384	617
VFR_real_u	Real	N	Train	197,396	/
VFR_syn_train	Syn	Y	Train	2,383,000	2,383
VFR_syn_val	Syn	Y	Test	238,300	2,383

and VFR_syn_val, are made publicly available.* The AdobeVFR dataset is the first large-scale benchmark set consisting of both synthetic and real-world text images, for the task of font recognition. To our best knowledge, VFR_real_test is the largest available set of real-world text images with reliable font label information (12.5 times larger than VFRWild325). The AdobeVFR dataset is super fine-grained, with highly subtle categorical variations, lending itself to be a new challenging dataset for object recognition. Moreover, the substantial mismatch between synthetic and real-world data makes the AdobeVFR dataset an ideal subject for general domain adaptation and transfer learning research. It is also related to the wider field of understanding styles [11] and aesthetics [12] with deep learning. The comparison among the above mentioned datasets could be found in Table 6.1.

6.3 Deep Font Recognition

Based on the AdobeVFR dataset, we develop the DeepFont system for the font recognition task of Roman alphabets [1–3]. Without any dependence on character segmentation or content text, the DeepFont system obtains an impressive performance on our collected large real-word dataset, covering an extensive variety of font categories. To combat the domain mismatch between available training and testing data, we introduce a convolutional neural network (CNN) decomposition approach, using a domain adaptation technique based on a stacked convolutional auto-encoder (SCAE) that exploits a large corpus of unlabeled real-world text images combined with synthetic data preprocessed in a specific way. Moreover, we study a novel learning-based model compression approach, in order to reduce the DeepFont model size without sacrificing its performance.

Figure 6.1 depicts the workflow of training and testing the DeepFont font recognition system. Figure 6.2 shows successful VFR examples using DeepFont. In (a) and (b), given the real-world query images, top-5 font recognition results are listed, within which the ground-truth font classes are marked out.† More real-world examples are displayed in (c). Although accompanied with high levels of background clutter, size, and ratio variations, as well as perspective distortions, they are all correctly recognized by the DeepFont system.

---

* http://www.atlaswang.com/deepfont.html
† Note that the texts are input manually for rendering purposes only. The font recognition process does not need any content information.

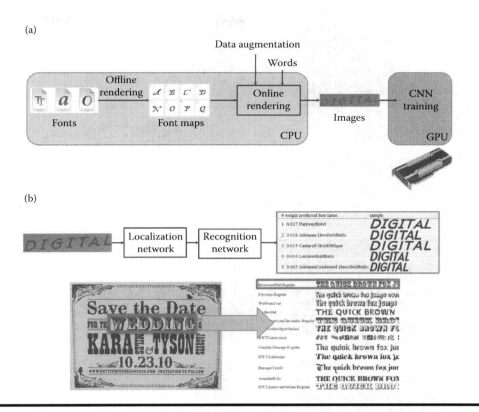

Figure 6.1   The system overview of DeepFont font recognition: (a) training; (b) testing.

6.3.1 Synthetic Data Augmentation

Before feeding synthetic data into model training, it is popular to artificially augment training data using label-preserving transformations to reduce overfitting. In Reference 13, the authors applied image translations and horizontal reflections to the training images, as well as altering the intensities of their RGB channels. The authors in Reference 10 added moderate distortions and corruptions to the synthetic text images:

- *Noise*: A small Gaussian noise with zero mean and standard deviation 3 is added to input.
- *Blur*: A random Gaussian blur with standard deviation from 2.5 to 3.5 is added to input.
- *Perspective Rotation*: A randomly parameterized affine transformation is added to input.
- *Shading*: The input background is filled with a gradient in illumination.

The above augmentations cover standard perturbations for general images and are adopted by us. However, as a very particular type of image, text images have various real-world appearances caused by specific handlings. Based on the observations in Figure 6.3, we identify two additional font-specific augmentation steps to our training data:

- *Variable Character Spacing*: When rendering each synthetic image, we set the character spacing (by pixel) to be a Gaussian random variable of mean 10 and standard deviation 40, bounded by [0, 50].

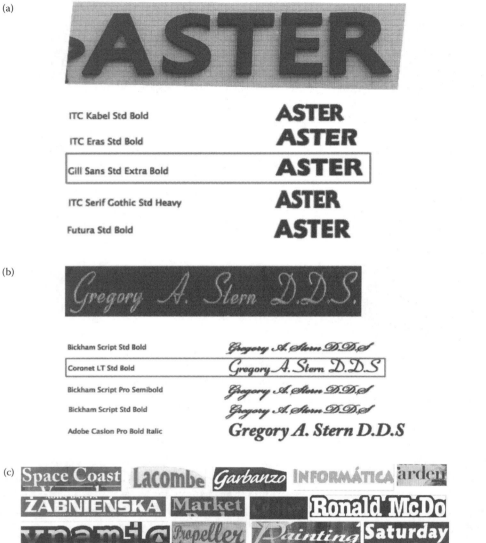

Figure 6.2 (a–b) Successful VFR examples with the DeepFont system. The top row are query images from VFR_real_test dataset. Below each query, the results (left column: font classes; right column: images rendered with the corresponding font classes) are listed in a high-to-low order in terms of likelihoods. The correct results are marked by the red boxes; (c) more correctly recognized real-world images with DeepFont.

■ *Variable Aspect Ratio*: Before cropping each image into an input patch, the image, with height fixed, is squeezed in width by a random ratio, drawn from a uniform distribution between $\frac{5}{6}$ and $\frac{7}{6}$.

Note that these steps are not useful for the method in Reference 10 because it exploits very localized features. However, as we show in our experiments, these steps lead to significant

(a)   (b)

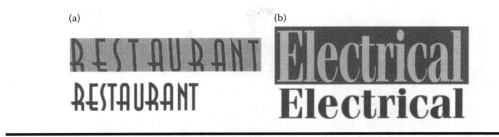

Figure 6.3 **(a) Different character spacings between a pair of synthetic and real-world images; (b) different aspect ratios between a pair of synthetic and real-world images.**

performance improvements in our DeepFont system. Overall, our data augmentation includes steps 1–6.

To leave a visual impression, we take the real-world image Figure 6.3a and synthesize a series of images in Figure 6.4, all with the same text but with different data augmentation methods. In particular, (a) is synthesized with no data augmentation; (b) is (a) with standard augmentation 1–4 added; (c) is synthesized with spacing and aspect ratio customized to be identical to those of Figure 6.3a; (d) adds standard augmentation 1–4 to (c). We input images (a–d) through the trained DeepFont model. For each image, we compare its layer-wise activations with those of the real image Figure 6.3a feeding through the same model, by calculating the normalized mean squared errors (MSEs). Figure 6.4e shows that those augmentations, especially the spacing and aspect ratio changes, reduce the gap between the feature hierarchies of real-world and synthetic data to a large extent. A few synthetic patches after full data augmentation 1–6 are displayed in Figure 6.5. It is observable that they possess a much more visually similar appearance to real-world data.

6.3.2 *Domain Adaptation by CNN Decomposition and SCAE*

Despite the fact that data augmentations are helpful in reducing the domain mismatch, enumerating all possible real-world degradations is impossible and may further introduce degradation bias in training. In this section, we propose a learning framework to leverage both synthetic and real-world data, using multi-layer CNN decomposition and SCAE-based domain adaptation. Our approach extends the domain adaptation method in Reference 14 to extract low-level features that represent both the synthetic and real-world data. We employ a CNN architecture, which is further decomposed into two sub-networks: a "shared" low-level sub-network that is learned from the composite set of synthetic and real-world data, and a high-level sub-network that learns a deep classifier from the low-level features.

The basic CNN architecture is similar to the popular ImageNet structure [13], as in Figure 6.6. The numbers along with the network pipeline specify the dimensions of outputs of corresponding layers. The input is a 105×105 patch sampled from a "normalized" image. Since a square window may not capture sufficient discriminative local structures and is unlikely to catch high-level combinational features when two or more graphemes or letters are joined as a single glyph (e.g., ligatures), we introduce a **squeezing** operation,* that scales the width of the height-normalized

---

* Note that squeezing is independent of the variable aspect ratio operation, as they are performed for different purposes.

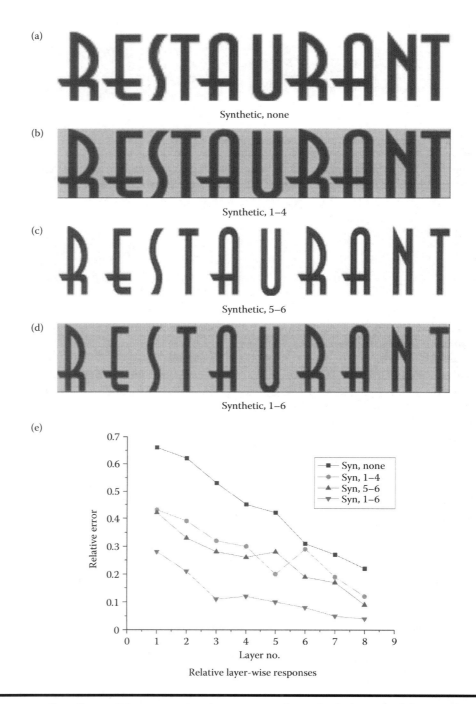

Figure 6.4   The effects of data augmentation steps: (a–d) synthetic images of the same text but with different data augmentation methods; (e) compares relative differences of (a–d) with the real-world image Figure 6.3a, in the measure of layer-wise network activations through the same DeepFont model.

Figure 6.5 Examples of synthetic training 105 × 105 patches after preprocessing steps 1–6.

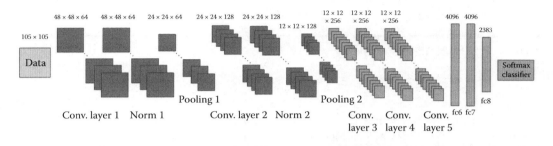

Figure 6.6 The CNN architecture in the DeepFont system, and its decomposition marked by different colors ($N = 8$, $K = 2$).

image to be of a constant ratio relative to the height (2.5 in all our experiments). Note that the squeezing operation is equivalent to producing "long" rectangular input patches.

When the CNN model is trained fully on a synthetic dataset, it witnesses a significant performance drop when testing on real-world data, compared to when it is applied to another synthetic validation set. This also happens with other models such as in Reference 10, which uses training and testing sets of similar properties to ours. It alludes to discrepancies between the distributions of synthetic and real-world examples. We propose to decompose the N CNN layers into two sub-networks to be learned sequentially:

■ *Unsupervised cross-domain sub-network* $\mathbf{C_u}$, which consists of the first K layers of CNN. It accounts for extracting low-level visual features shared by both synthetic and real-world data domains. $\mathbf{C_u}$ will be trained in an unsupervised way, using unlabeled data from both domains. It constitutes the crucial step that further minimizes the low-level feature gap, beyond the previous data augmentation efforts.

■ *Supervised domain-specific sub-network* $\mathbf{C_s}$, which consists of the remaining $N - K$ layers. It accounts for learning higher-level discriminative features for classification, based on the shared features from $\mathbf{C_u}$. $\mathbf{C_s}$ will be trained in a supervised way, using labeled data from the synthetic domain only.

We show an example of the proposed CNN decomposition in Figure 6.6. The $\mathbf{C_u}$ and $\mathbf{C_s}$ parts are marked by red and green colors, respectively, with $N = 8$ and $K = 2$. Note that the low-level shared features are implied to be independent of class labels. Therefore, in order to address the open-ended problem of font classes, one may keep reusing the $\mathbf{C_u}$ sub-network, and only retrain the $\mathbf{C_s}$ part.

Learning $\mathbf{C_u}$ *from SCAE.* Representative unsupervised feature learning methods, such as the auto-encoder and the denoising auto-encoder, perform a greedy layer-wise pretraining of weights using unlabeled data alone, followed by supervised fine-tuning [15]. However, they rely mostly

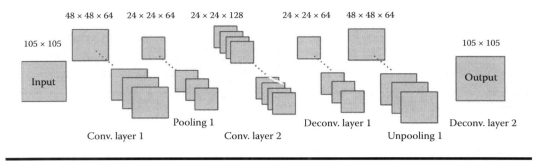

Figure 6.7　The SCAE architecture.

on fully connected models and ignore the 2D image structure. In Reference 16, a convolutional auto-encoder (CAE) was proposed to learn non-trivial features using a hierarchical unsupervised feature extractor that scales well to high-dimensional inputs. The CAE architecture is intuitively similar to the conventional auto-encoders in Reference 17, except that their weights are shared among all locations in the input, preserving spatial locality. CAEs can be stacked to form a deep hierarchy called the stacked convolutional auto-encoder (SCAE), where each layer receives its input from a latent representation of the layer below. Figure 6.7 plots the SCAE architecture for our $K = 2$ case.

Training Details. We first train the SCAE on both synthetic and real-world data in an unsupervised way, with a learning rate of 0.01 (we do not anneal it through training). MSE is used as the loss function. After SCAE is learned, its Conv. Layers 1 and 2 are imported to the CNN in Figure 6.6, as the C_u sub-network, and fixed. The C_s sub-network, based on the output by C_u, is then trained in a supervised manner. We start with the learning rate at 0.01, and follow a common heuristic to manually divide the learning rate by 10 when the validation error rate stops decreasing with the current rate. The "dropout" technique is applied to fc6 and fc7 layers during training. Both C_u and C_s are trained with a default batch size of 128, momentum of 0.9, and weight decay of 0.0005. The network training is implemented using the CUDA ConvNet package [13] and runs on a workstation with 12 Intel Xeon 2.67 GHz CPUs and 1 GTX680 GPU. It takes around 1 day to complete the entire training pipeline.

Testing Details. We adopt multi-scale multi-view testing to improve the result robustness. For each test image, it is first normalized to 105 pixels in height, but squeezed in width by three different random ratios, all drawn from a uniform distribution between 1.5 and 3.5, matching the effects of squeezing and variable aspect ratio operations during training. Under each squeezed scale, five 105×105 patches are sampled at different random locations. That constitutes in total fifteen test patches, each of which comes with different aspect ratios and views, from one test image. As every single patch could produce a softmax vector through the trained CNN, we average all fifteen softmax vectors to determine the final classification result of the test image.

6.3.2.1 Connections to Other Works

We are not the first to look into an essentially "hierarchical" deep architecture for domain adaption. In Reference 18, the proposed transfer learning approach relies on the unsupervised learning of representations. Bengio et al. hypothesized in Reference 19 that more levels of representation can give rise to more abstract, more general features of the raw input, and that the lower layers of the predictor constitute a hierarchy of features that can be **shared** across variants of the input distribution. The authors of Reference 14 used data from the union of all domains to learn their shared features, which is different from many previous domain adaptation methods that focus on learning features in an unsupervised way from the target domain only. However, their entire network hierarchy is learned in an unsupervised fashion, except for a simple linear classier trained on top of the network, that is, $K = N - 1$. In Reference 20, the CNN learned a set of filters from raw images as the first layer, and those low-level filters are fixed when training higher layers of the same CNN, that is, $K = 1$. In other words, they either adopt a simple feature extractor ($K = 1$) or apply a shallow classifier ($K = N - 1$). Our CNN decomposition is different from prior work in that

- Our feature extractor $\mathbf{C_u}$ and classier $\mathbf{C_s}$ are both deep sub-networks with more than one layer (both K and $N - K$ are larger than 1), which means that both are able to perform more sophisticated learning. More evaluations can be found in Section 5.2.
- We learn "shared-feature" convolutional filters rather than fully connected networks such as in Reference 14, the former of which is more suitable for visual feature extractions.

The domain mismatch between synthetic and real-world data on the lower-level statistics can occur in more scenarios, such as real-world face recognition from rendered images or sketches, recognizing characters in real scenes with synthetic training, and human pose estimation with synthetic images generated from 3D human body models. Lately, the authors of [21] adopted both simulated and unsupervised real data to train models for gaze estimation and hand pose estimation, where labeled real-world data are scarce but synthetic data can be easily rendered.

6.3.3 Learning-Based Model Compression

The architecture in Figure 6.6 contains a huge number of parameters. It is widely known that the deep models are heavily over-parameterized [22], and thus those parameters can be compressed to reduce storage by exploring their structure. For a typical CNN, about 90% of the storage is taken up by the dense connected layers, which shall be our focus for mode compression.

One way to shrink the number of parameters is using matrix factorization [23]. Given the parameter $W \in R^{m \times n}$, we factorize it using singular-value decomposition (SVD):

$$W = USV^T \qquad (6.1)$$

where $U \in R^{m \times m}$ and $V \in R^{n \times n}$ are two dense orthogonal matrices and $S \in R^{m \times n}$ is a diagonal matrix. To restore an approximate W, we can utilize $\widetilde{U}$, $\widetilde{V}$, and $\widetilde{S}$, which denote the sub-matrices corresponding to the top k singular vectors in U and V along with the top k eigenvalue in S:

$$\widetilde{W} = \widetilde{U}\widetilde{S}\widetilde{V}^T \qquad (6.2)$$

The compression ratio given m, n, and k is $k(m + n + 1)/mn$, which is very promising when $m, n \gg k$. However, the approximation of SVD is controlled by the decay along the eigenvalues in S. Even the eigenvalues of CNN weight matrices usually decay fast; the truncation inevitably leads to information loss and potential performance degradations compared to the uncompressed model (Figure 6.8).

Instead of first training a model and then lossy-compressing its parameters, we propose to directly learn a **losslessly compressible** model (the term "lossless" means there is no further loss

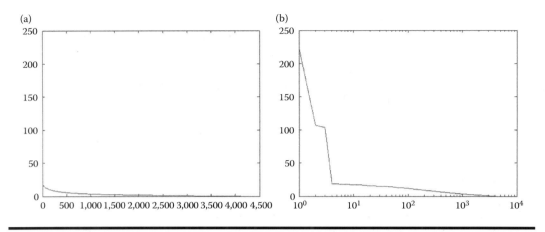

Figure 6.8 **The plots of eigenvalues for the fc6 layer weight matrix in Figure 6.6. This densely connected layer takes up 85% of the total model size. (a) Standard scale; (b) logarithm scale.**

after a model is trained). Assuming the parameter matrix W of a certain network layer, our goal is to make sure that its rank is **exactly no more than a small constant** k. In terms of implementation, in each iteration, an extra hard thresholding operation [24] is executed on W after it is updated by a conventional back-propagation step:

$$W_k = U \mathcal{T}_k(S) V^T \qquad (6.3)$$

where $\mathcal{T}_k$ will keep the largest k eigenvalues in S while setting others to zero. W_k is the best rank-k approximation of W, similar to Equation 6.2. However, different from Equation 6.2, the proposed method incorporates a low-rank approximation into the model training and jointly optimizes them as a whole, guaranteeing a rank-k weight matrix that is ready to be compressed losslessly by applying (6.1). Note that other alternatives, such as vector quantization methods [25], have been applied to compress deep models with appealing performances. We will investigate utilizing them together to further compress our model in the future.

6.3.4 *Experiments on Font Recognition*

6.3.4.1 *Analysis of Domain Mismatch*

We first analyze the domain mismatch between synthetic and real-world data and examine how our synthetic data augmentation can help. First we define five dataset variations generated from VFR_syn_train and VFR_real_u. These are denoted by the letters N, S, F, R, and FR, which are explained in Table 6.2.

We train five separate SCAEs, all with the same architecture as in Figure 6.7, using the above five training data variants. The training and testing errors are all measured by relative MSEs (normalized by the total energy) and compared in Table 6.2. The testing errors are evaluated on both the unaugmented synthetic dataset N and the real-world dataset R. Ideally, the better the SCAE captures the features from a domain, the smaller the reconstruction error will be on that domain.

As revealed by the training errors, real-world data contain rich visual variations and are more difficult to fit. The sharp performance drop from N to R of SCAE N indicates that the

Table 6.2   Comparison of Training and Testing Errors (%) of Five SCAEs ($K = 2$)

Methods	Training Data	Train	Test N	Test R
SCAE N	**N**: VFR_syn_train, no data augmentation	0.02	3.54	31.28
SCAE S	**S**: VFR_syn_train, standard augmentation 1–4	0.21	2.24	19.34
SCAE F	**F**: VFR_syn_train, full augmentation 1–6	1.20	1.67	15.26
SCAE R	**R**: VFR_real_u, real unlabeled dataset	9.64	5.73	10.87
SCAE FR	**FR**: Combination of data from **F** and **R**	6.52	2.02	14.01

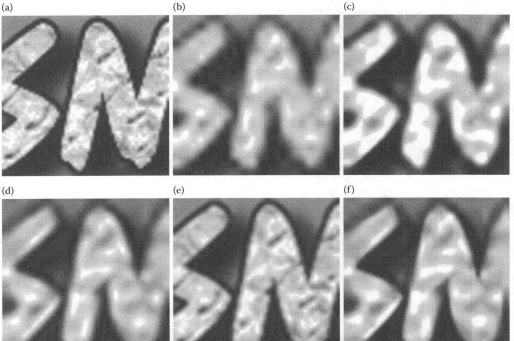

Figure 6.9   A real-world patch and its reconstruction results from the five SCAE models. (a) Original; (b) SCAE N; (c) SCAE S; (d) SCAE F; (e) SCAE R; (f) SCAE FR.

convolutional features for synthetic and real data are quite different. This gap is reduced in SCAE S, and further in SCAE F, which validates the effectiveness of adding font-specific data augmentation steps. SCAE R fits the real-world data best, at the expense of a larger error on N. SCAE FR achieves an overall best reconstruction performance of both synthetic and real-world images.

Figure 6.9 shows an example patch from a real-world font image of highly textured characters, and its reconstruction outputs from all five models. The gradual visual variations across the results confirm the existence of a mismatch between synthetic and real-world data and verify the benefit of data augmentation as well as learning shared features.

6.3.4.2 Analysis of Network Structure

Fixing Network Depth N. Given a fixed network complexity (N layers), one may ask about how to best decompose the hierarchy to maximize the overall classification performance on real-world data. Intuitively, we should have sufficient layers of lower-level feature extractors as well as enough subsequent layers for good classification of labeled data. Thus, the depth K of C_u should be neither too small nor too large.

Table 6.3 shows that while the *classification* training error increases with K, the testing error does not vary monotonically. The best performance is obtained with $K = 2$ (3 slightly worse), where smaller or larger values of K give a substantially worse performance. When $K = 5$, all layers are learned using SCAE, leading to the worst results. Rather than learning all hidden layers by unsupervised training, as suggested in Reference 14 and other DL-based transfer learning work, our CNN decomposition reaches its optimal performance when higher-layer convolutional filters are still trained by supervised data. A visual inspection of reconstruction results of a real-world example in Figure 6.10, using SCAE FR with different K values, shows that a larger K causes less information loss during feature extraction and leads to a better reconstruction. But in the meantime, the classification result may become worse since noise and irrelevant high-frequency details (e.g., textures) might hamper recognition performance. The optimal $K = 2$ corresponds to a proper "content-aware" smoothening, filtering out "noisy" details while keeping recognizable structural properties of the font style.

Fixing C_s or C_u Depth. We investigate the influences of K (the depth of C_u) when the depth of C_s (e.g., $N - K$) remains fixed. Table 6.4 reveals that a deeper C_u contributes little to the results.

Table 6.3 Top-5 Testing Errors (%) for Different CNN Decompositions (Varying K, $N = 8$)

K	0	1	2	3	4	5
Train	8.46	9.88	11.23	12.54	15.21	17.88
VFR_real_test	20.72	20.31	18.21	18.96	22.52	25.97

(a) (b) (c) (d)

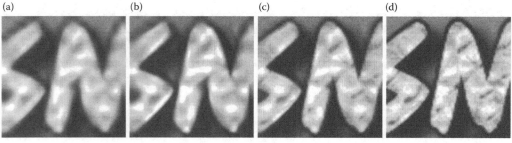

Figure 6.10 The reconstruction results of a real-world patch using SCAE FR, with different K values. (a) $K = 1$; (b) $K = 2$; (c) $K = 4$; (d) $K = 5$.

Table 6.4 Top-5 Testing Errors (%) for Different CNN Decompositions (Varying K, $N = K + 6$)

K	1	2	3	4
Train	11.46	11.23	10.84	10.86
VFR_real_test	21.58	18.21	18.15	18.24

Similar trends are observed when we fix K and adjust N (and thus the depth of C_s). Therefore, we choose $N = 8$, $K = 2$ to be the default setting.

6.3.4.3 Recognition Performances on VFR Datasets

We implemented and evaluated the local feature embedding-based algorithm (LFE) in Reference 10 as a baseline, and we include the four different DeepFont models as specified in Table 6.5. The first two models are trained in a fully supervised manner on **F**, without any decomposition applied. For each of the latter two models, its corresponding SCAE (SCAE FR for DeepFont CAE_FR and SCAE R for DeepFont CAE_R) is first trained and then it exports the first two convolutional layers to **C$_u$**. All trained models are evaluated in term of top-1 and top-5 classification errors, on the VFR_syn_val dataset for validation purposes. Benefiting from a large learning capacity, it is clear that DeepFont models fit synthetic data significantly better than LFE. Notably, the top-5 errors of all DeepFont models (except for DeepFont CAE_R) reach zero on the validation set, which is quite impressive for such a fine-grained classification task.

We then compare DeepFont models with LFE on the original VFRWild325 dataset in Reference 10. As seen from Table 6.5, while DeepFont S fits the synthetic training data best, its performance is the poorest on real-world data, showing a severe overfitting. With two font-specific data augmentations added in training, the DeepFont F model adapts better to real-world data, outperforming LFE by roughly 8% in top-5 error. An additional gain of 2% is obtained when unlabeled real-world data are utilized in DeepFont CAE_FR. Next, the DeepFont models are evaluated on the new VFR_real_test dataset, which is more extensive in size and class coverage. A large margin of around 5% in top-1 error is gained by the DeepFont CAE_FR model over the second

Table 6.5 Comparison of Training and Testing Errors on Synthetic and Real-World Datasets (%)

Methods	Training Data		Training Error	VFR_syn_val		VFRWild325		VFR_real_test	
	C$_u$	**C$_s$**		Top-1	Top-5	Top-1	Top-5	Top-1	Top-5
LFE	/	/	/	26.50	6.55	44.13	30.25	57.44	32.69
DeepFont S	/	F	0.84	1.03	0	64.60	57.23	57.51	50.76
DeepFont F	/	F	8.46	7.40	0	43.10	22.47	33.30	20.72
DeepFont CAE_FR	FR	F	11.23	6.58	0	38.15	20.62	28.58	18.21
DeepFont CAE_R	R	F	13.67	8.21	1.26	44.62	29.23	39.46	27.33

Figure 6.11   Failure VFR examples using DeepFont.

best (DeepFont F), with its top-5 error as low as 18.21%. We will use DeepFont CAE_FR as the default DeepFont model.

Although SCAE R has the best reconstruction result on the real-world data on which it is trained, it has large training and testing errors on synthetic data. Since our supervised training relies fully on synthetic data, an effective feature extraction for synthetic data is also indispensable. The error rates of DeepFont CAE_R are also worse than those of DeepFont CAE_FR and even DeepFont F on the real-world data because of the large mismatch between the low-level and high-level layers in the CNN.

Another interesting observation is that all methods get similar top-5 errors on VFRWild325 and VFR_real_test, showing their statistical similarity. However, the top-1 errors of DeepFont models on VFRWild325 are significantly higher than those on VFR_real_test, with a difference of up to 10%. In contrast, the top-1 error of LFE rises more than 13% on VFR_real_test than on VFRWild325. For the small VFRWild325, the recognition result is easily affected by "bad" examples (e.g., low-resolution* or highly compressed images) and class bias (less than 4% of all classes are covered). On the other hand, the larger VFR_real_test dataset dilutes the possible effect of outliers and examines many more classes.

For more results with respect to tuning the network architecture, as well as the efforts to compress the DeepFont model, please refer to [1].

Figure 6.11 lists some failure cases of DeepFont. For example, the top left image contains extra "fluff" decorations along text boundaries that are nonexistent in the original fonts, which make the algorithm incorrectly map it to some "artistic" fonts. Others are affected by 3-D effects and strong obstacles in the foreground and background. Being considerably difficult to adapt, those examples fail mostly because there are neither specific augmentation steps handling their effects, nor enough examples in VFR_real_u to extract corresponding robust features.

6.3.4.4 DeepFont Model Compression

Since the fc6 layer takes up 85% of the total model size, we first focus on its compression. We start from a well-trained DeepFont model (DeepFont CAE_FR) and continue tuning it with

---

* A more recent study on how to improve font recognition under low resolution can be found in Reference 26.

Table 6.6 Performance Comparisons of Lossy and Lossless Compression Approaches

	fc6 Size	*Total Size*	*Ratio*	*Method*	*Error*
Default	150,994,944	177,546,176	NA	NA	18.21
$k = 5$	204,805	26,756,037	6.64	Lossy	20.67
				Lossless	19.23
$k = 10$	409,610	26,960,842	6.59	Lossy	19.25
				Lossless	18.87
$k = 50$	2,048,050	28,599,282	6.21	Lossy	19.04
				Lossless	18.67
$k = 100$	4,096,100	30,647,332	5.79	Lossy	18.68
				Lossless	18.21

the hard thresholding (6.3) applied to the fc6 parameter matrix W in each iteration, until the training/validation errors reach the plateau again.

Table 6.6 compares the DeepFont models compressed using conventional matrix factorization (denoted as the "lossy" method), and the proposed learning-based method (denoted as the "lossless" method), under different compression ratios (fc6 and total size counted by parameter numbers). The last column of Table 6.6 lists the top-5 testing errors (%) on VFR_real_test. We observe a consistent margin of the "lossless" method over its "lossy" counterpart, which becomes more significant when the compression ratio goes low (more than 1% when $k = 5$). Notably, when $k = 100$, the proposed "lossless" compression suffers no visible performance loss, while still maintaining a good compression ratio of 5.79.

In practice, it takes around 700 megabytes to store all the parameters in our uncompressed DeepFont model, which is quite huge to be embedded or downloaded into most customer software. More aggressively, we reduce the output sizes of both fc6 and fc7 to 2048, and further apply the proposed compression method ($k = 10$) to the fc6 parameter matrix. The obtained "mini" model, with only 9,477,066 parameters and a high compression ratio of 18.73, becomes less than 40 megabytes in storage. Being portable even on mobiles, it manages to keep a top-5 error rate around 22%.

6.3.5 Software Integration

The DeepFont system features advanced machine-learning algorithms that send pictures of typefaces from Photoshop software on a user's computer. Later, it was significantly extended to cover a huge database of over 20,000 fonts in the cloud. Within seconds, results are sent back to the user, akin to the way the music discovery app Shazam works. The user interaction is intuitive: you highlight the text area that you want recognized, and it will give you a list of the top fonts that match what you highlighted. The PC version Adobe Photoshop implementation, a mobile phone iOS app implementation, and a tablet iOS app implementation are depicted in Figure 6.12.

(a)

(b)

(c)

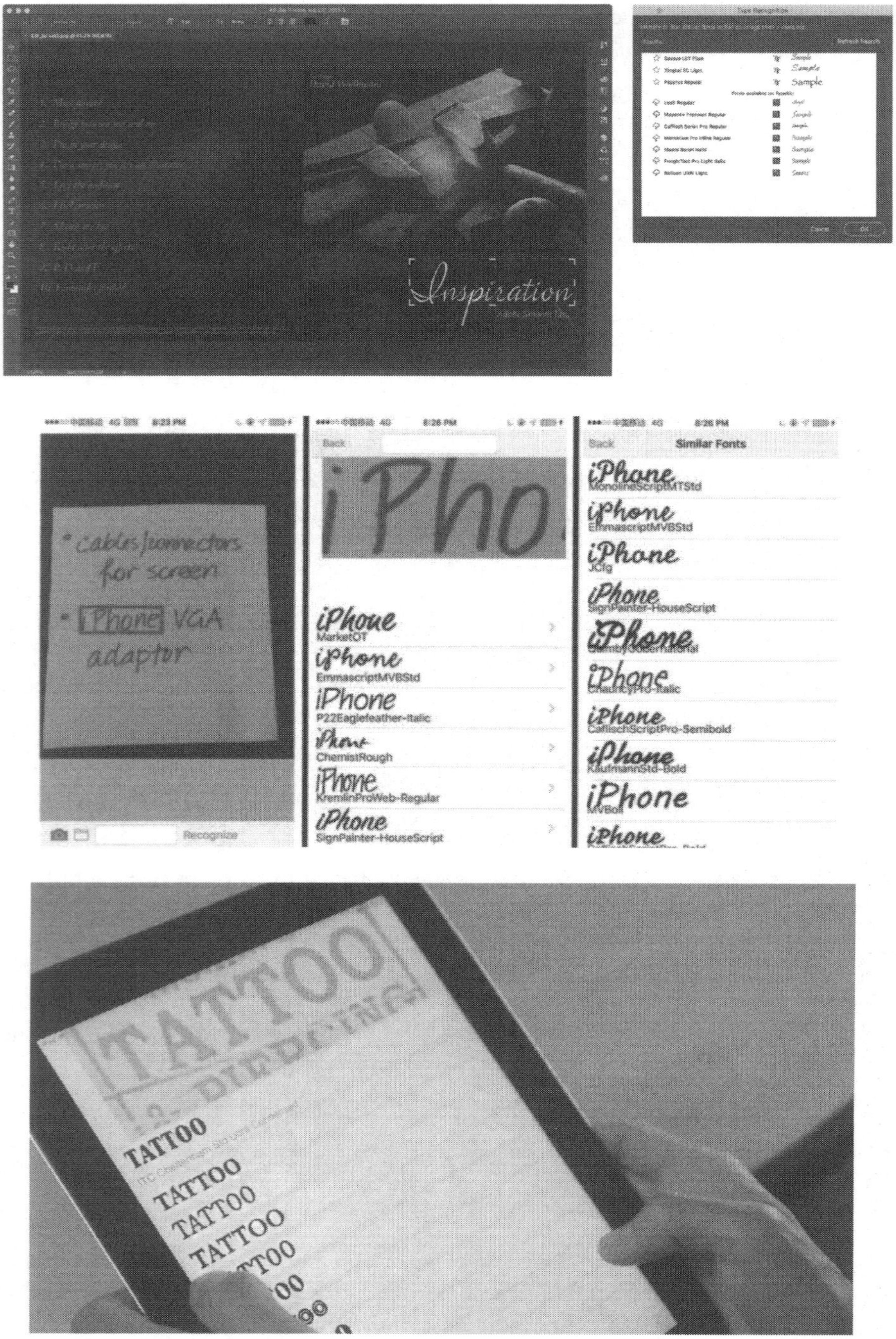

Figure 6.12 The DeepFont implementations on (a) Adobe Photoshop software (PC version); (b) an iOS app on the mobile phone; (c) an iOS app on the tablet.

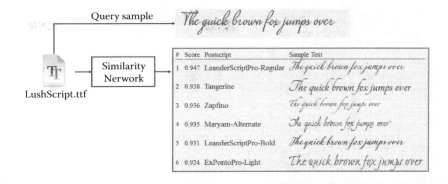

Figure 6.13 **The system overview of DeepFont-based font retrieval.**

6.4 DeepFont Retrieval

There are a variety of font selection tasks with different goals and requirements. Among them, the font similarity measure is very helpful for font selection, organization, browsing, and suggestion. One designer may wish to match a font to the style of a particular image. Another may wish to find a free font that looks similar to a commercial font such as Helvetica. A third may simply be exploring a large set of fonts such as Adobe TypeKit or Google Web Fonts. Exhaustively exploring the entire space of fonts using an alphabetical listing is unrealistic for most users. The authors of Reference 27 proposed to select fonts based on online crowdsourced attributes and to explore *font similarity*, in which a user is enabled to explore other visually similar fonts given a specific font. While the list of font attributes cannot really be exhaustive, their experimental results suggest that font evaluation is highly subjective for both novices and professionals.

Based on our DeepFont font recognition system described above, we are able to build up measures of font similarity. The system overview is depicted in Figure 6.13. We use the 4096 × 1 outputs of the fc7 layer as the high-level feature vectors describing font visual appearances. We then extract such features from all samples in the VFR_syn_val dataset, obtaining 100 feature vectors per class. Next for each class, the 100 feature vectors are averaged to a representative vector. Finally, we calculate the Euclidean distance between the representative vectors of two font classes as their similarity measure. Two visualized examples are demonstrated in Figure 6.14. For each example, the top is the query image of a known font class; the most similar fonts obtained by the font similarity measures are sorted below. Note that although the result fonts can belong to different font families from the query, they share identifiable visual similarities by human perception.

6.5 Related Research Topics

A recent blog post* discussed the task to generate (unseen) characters with a given font. The author tried to create a "font vector" in some latent space that "defines" a certain font in such a way that one can embed all fonts in a space where similar fonts have similar vectors. The author further interpolated between different fonts in the continuous embedding space. In this way, one can generate completely new fonts. For example, the authors modeled the distribution of font vectors as

---

* https://erikbern.com/2016/01/21/analyzing-50k-fonts-using-deep-neural-networks/

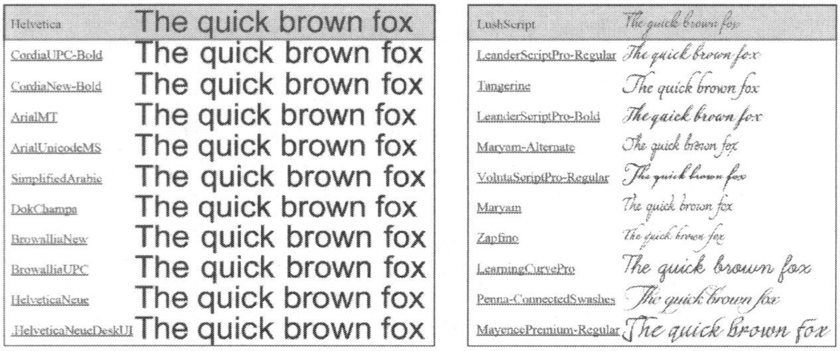

Figure 6.14 Examples of the font similarity. For each one, the top is the query image, and the renderings with the most similar fonts are returned.

a multivariate normal one, sampled random vectors from it, and looked at the fonts they generated. Readers are referred to the original post for many interesting visualizations and animations.

The author of [28] worked on a similar problem: learning the style of a font by analyzing a small subset of only four letters. The author utilized deep models to learn two tasks:

1. *A discrimination task*: Given the four letters and a new candidate letter, does the new letter belong to the same font?
2. *A generative task*: Given the four basis letters, can one generate all of the other letters with the same characteristics as those in the basis set?

Their quantitative and qualitative experiments present promising results.

Lately, the authors of [29] investigated the potential use of typefaces for emotional representation by which people can feel nonverbal signals. The authors constructed a dataset of various typefaces and conducted a large-scale crowd-sourced user study to investigate the relationship between typefaces and emotional signals based on commonly used psychological emotion models. From the user study, they determined that several visual characteristics of typefaces have weak/strong emotional influences on viewers and verified that certain emotions and feelings can be conveyed in text messages.

References

1. Z. Wang, J. Yang, H. Jin, E. Shechtman, A. Agarwala, J. Brandt, and T. S. Huang. DeepFont, Identify your font from an image. In *Proceedings of the 23rd ACM International Conference on Multimedia*, pages 451–459. ACM, 2015.
2. Z. Wang, J. Yang, H. Jin, E. Shechtman, A. Agarwala, J. Brandt, and T. S. Huang. Real-world font recognition using deep network and domain adaptation. *arXiv preprint arXiv:1504.00028*, 2015.
3. Z. Wang, J. Yang, H. Jin, J. Brandt, E. Shechtman, A. Agarwala, Z. Wang, Y. Song, J. Hsieh, S. Kong et al. Deepfont: A system for font recognition and similarity. In *Proceedings of the 23rd ACM International Conference on Multimedia*, pages 813–814. ACM, 2015.
4. C. Avilés-Cruz, R. Rangel-Kuoppa, M. Reyes-Ayala, A. Andrade-Gonzalez, and R. Escarela-Perez. High-order statistical texture analysis-font recognition applied. *Pattern Recognition Letters*, **26**(2):135–145, 2005.

5. M.-C. Jung, Y.-C. Shin, and S. N. Srihari. Multifont classification using typographical attributes. In *Document Analysis and Recognition, 1999. ICDAR'99. Proceedings of the Fifth International Conference on*, pages 353–356. IEEE, 1999.

6. H. Ma and D. Doermann. Gabor filter based multi-class classifier for scanned document images. In *2013 12th International Conference on Document Analysis and Recognition*, volume **2**, page 968. IEEE Computer Society, 2003.

7. R. Ramanathan, K. P. Soman, L. Thaneshwaran, V. Viknesh, T. Arunkumar, and P. Yuvaraj. A novel technique for English font recognition using support vector machines. In *Advances in Recent Technologies in Communication and Computing, 2009. ARTCom'09. International Conference on*, pages 766–769. IEEE, 2009.

8. H.-M. Sun. Multi-linguistic optical font recognition using stroke templates. In *ICPR 2006. 18th International Conference on Pattern Recognition*, volume **2**, pages 889–892. IEEE, 2006.

9. Y. Zhu, T. Tan, and Y. Wang. Font recognition based on global texture analysis. *IEEE Transactions on Pattern Analysis and Machine Intelligence*, **23**(10):1192–1200, 2001.

10. G. Chen, J. Yang, H. Jin, J. Brandt, E. Shechtman, A. Agarwala, and T. X. Han. Large-scale visual font recognition. In *Computer Vision and Pattern Recognition (CVPR), 2014 IEEE Conference on*, pages 3598–3605. IEEE, 2014.

11. J. Johnson, A. Alahi, and L. Fei-Fei. Perceptual losses for real-time style transfer and super-resolution. In *European Conference on Computer Vision*, pages 694–711. Springer, 2016.

12. Z. Wang, S. Chang, F. Dolcos, D. Beck, D. Liu, and T. S. Huang. Brain-inspired deep networks for image aesthetics assessment. *arXiv preprint arXiv:1601.04155*, 2016.

13. A. Krizhevsky, I. Sutskever, and G. E. Hinton. ImageNet classification with deep convolutional neural networks. In *Advances in Neural Information Processing Systems*, pages 1097–1105, 2012.

14. X. Glorot, A. Bordes, and Y. Bengio. Domain daptation for large-scale sentiment classification: A deep learning approach. In *Proceedings of ICML*, pages 513–520, 2011.

15. Y. Bengio, P. Lamblin, D. Popovici, and H. Larochelle. Greedy layer-wise training of deep networks. *Proceedings of NIPS*, **19**:153, 2007.

16. J. Masci, U. Meier, D. Cireşan, and J. Schmidhuber. Stacked convolutional auto-encoders for hierarchical feature extraction. In *Proceedings of ICANN*, pages 52–59. Springer, 2011.

17. P. Vincent, H. Larochelle, Y. Bengio, and P.-A. Manzagol. Extracting and composing robust features with denoising autoencoders. In *Proceedings of ICML*, pages 1096–1103. ACM, 2008.

18. R. Raina, A. Battle, H. Lee, B. Packer, and A. Y. Ng. Self-taught learning: Transfer learning from unlabeled data. In *Proceedings of ICML*, pages 759–766. ACM, 2007.

19. Y. Bengio. Learning deep architectures for AI. *Foundations and Trends in Machine Learning*, **2**(1):1–127, 2009.

20. T. Wang, D. J. Wu, A. Coates, and A. Y. Ng. End-to-end text recognition with convolutional neural networks. In *Proceedings of ICPR*, pages 3304–3308. IEEE, 2012.

21. A. Shrivastava, T. Pfister, O. Tuzel, J. Susskind, W. Wang, and R. Webb. Learning from simulated and unsupervised images through adversarial training. *arXiv preprint arXiv:1612.07828*, 2016.

22. M. Denil, B. Shakibi, L. Dinh, and N. de Freitas. Predicting parameters in deep learning. In *Advances in Neural Information Processing Systems*, pages 2148–2156, 2013.

23. E. L. Denton, W. Zaremba, J. Bruna, Y. LeCun, and R. Fergus. Exploiting linear structure within convolutional networks for efficient evaluation. In *Advances in Neural Information Processing Systems*, pages 1269–1277, 2014.

24. Z. Lin, M. Chen, and Y. Ma. The augmented Lagrange multiplier method for exact recovery of corrupted low-rank matrices. *arXiv preprint, arXiv:1009.5055*, 2010.

25. Y. Gong, L. Liu, M. Yang, and L. Bourdev. Compressing deep convolutional networks using vector quantization. *arXiv preprint arXiv:1412.6115*, 2014.

26. Z. Wang, S. Chang, Y. Yang, D. Liu, and T. S. Huang. Studying very low resolution recognition using deep networks. In *Proceedings of the IEEE Conference on Computer Vision and Pattern Recognition*, pages 4792–4800, 2016.

27. P. O'Donovan, J. Lıbeks, A. Agarwala, and A. Hertzmann. Exploratory font selection using crowd-sourced attributes. *ACM Transactions on Graphics (TOG)*, **33**(4):92, 2014.

28. S. Baluja. Learning typographic style. *arXiv preprint arXiv:1603.04000*, 2016.

29. S. Choi, T. Yamasaki, and K. Aizawa. Typeface emotion analysis for communication on mobile messengers. In *Proceedings of the 1st International Workshop on Multimedia Alternate Realities*, pages 37–40. ACM, 2016.

Chapter 7

Chapter 7

A Distributed Secure Machine-Learning Cloud Architecture for Semantic Analysis

Arun Das, Wei-Ming Lin, and Paul Rad

Contents

7.1 Introduction

Machine learning (ML) has come a long way, as such has become a part of our everyday lives. Personal assistants like "Google Now" and "Apple Siri" to novel cybersecurity applications [1] use machine learning at their core. Deep learning, a form of machine learning, has enabled convolutional neural networks (CNNs) [2,3] to carry out classification of handwritten digits [4], complex face detection [5], self-driving cars [6], speech recognition [7], and much more. Coding by hand a problem such as speech recognition is nearly impossible because of the sheer amount of variance in the data. The way the human brain interprets these kinds of problems is complex, but they can be modeled to an extent using artificial neural networks (ANNs) with a substantial amount of accuracy, which sometimes even beat humans [8]. The whole concept of ANN started evolving after the 1950s. Artificial neurons gradually evolved from a simple perceptron to sigmoid neurons and then to many other forms. Earlier neurons were able to provide binary output to the many inputs that were provided. Newer algorithms and activation functions allow artificial neural networks to make complex predictions by learning on their own [2,3].

Machine learning, for example, by using deep neural networks (DNNs) or CNNs, is endowed by the availability of big data. The term *big data* refers to large, diverse, complex datasets generated from various instruments or software ranging from sensors, camera feeds, Internet transactions, email, video or audio streams, etc. [9]. The scientific, biomedical, and engineering research communities are in an imperative shift with access to these datasets. For example, big data analytics with machine learning in health care allows better research and development by predictive modeling using various statistical tools, algorithms, and analysis. It helps analyze disease patterns, develop targeted vaccines, and allow for better genomic analysis [10]. However, processing, analyzing, and working with big data is computationally intensive.

Over the years, researchers have come up with impressive and ambitious concepts that target the high computation requirement. Training a deep-learning model requires a significant amount of computing power, which was restricted to focused academic research groups and industries in the past. Studies show that the accuracy of a DNN improves significantly by increasing the number of training examples and changing the model parameters accordingly [11,12]. Nevertheless, this increases the computational requirement even more. With the availability of GPUs specialized for deep-learning purposes, as described in Reference 13, the time required to train a DNN model has decreased tremendously.

High-performance computing (HPC) is one of the main catalysts of deep learning. However, the cost-to-performance ratio does not always balance while scaling compute nodes vertically. Also, parallel implementations of many machine-learning and deep-learning algorithms are still in their infancy [14,15] and are slowly catching up. Networking and synchronization in a multi-cluster environment is challenging. It is economical, in most cases, to leverage cloud services for computationally intensive tasks, which would not be feasible otherwise. To add to that, in most HPC use cases, users have to configure the software environment with the right kernel, drivers, machine-learning and deep-learning packages from scratch, which is usually a tedious process.

The growing interest among academic and commercial HPC users to utilize cloud computing [16,17] as an economical tool has generated many HPC optimized clouds such as Magellan [18] and Amazon EC2 Cluster Compute [19], offering compute nodes with GPU support. However, most of these solutions are bounded by virtualization software like Xen, KVM, etc. These virtualization layers introduce performance overheads to HPC applications [20,21]. On the other hand, bare-metal cloud servers are single-tenant systems that can be provisioned within minutes. This allows users to pay by the minute and also gives end users the full processing power of the physical server without using a virtual layer. The tenants do not share the server with anyone else; users know the exact hardware specifications of their own machines [22–24].

To tackle the challenges of deep learning and aid academic and industrial research, we propose the Scalable Cloud AI Framework, an open-source cloud architecture tailored for deep-learning applications. The proposed architecture is implemented on bare-metal OpenStack cloud nodes connected through high-speed interconnects. They are deep-learning ready systems with NVIDIA M40, K80, and P100 GPUs. The GPUs strengthen machine learning on big data. The AI framework also hosts state-of-the-art high-speed object storage (OpenStack Swift) nodes to store huge datasets for quick retrieval. Popular machine-learning and deep-learning frameworks are prebuilt as cloud images on an operating system of choice. They are collectively called an "appliance." These appliances can be spun up in minutes and provide users with an ML-ready system with the required packages preinstalled. Several layers work in tandem to provide end users with a comprehensive, easy-to-use, complete, and readily deployable machine-learning platform. Also, the cloud AI framework can be deployed on a well-maintained datacenter to transform it to a cloud tailor-fit for deep learning. A high-speed web interface is developed to train, validate, and visualize ML models right from the website.

7.2 Scalable Cloud AI Framework

The Scalable Cloud AI Framework is built specifically for big-data scale platform and framework independent machine learning in the cloud. It facilitates cluster computing and distributed deep learning by the use of various frameworks such as Apache Hadoop [25] and Apache Spark [26], Distributed TensorFlow [27] by Google, CaffeOnSpark [28] and TensorFlowOnSpark [29] by Yahoo, MXNet [30] by Apache and Amazon, etc., and single-node solutions using popular frameworks such as TensorFlow [27], Caffe [31], Theano [32], Keras [33], TFLearn [34], etc.

The architecture employs a data-centric approach and uses fast object storage nodes to handle the high volume of data required for machine learning. Furthermore, in the case of requirements such as bigger local storage, network attachable storage devices are used to support the local filesystem, strengthening the data-centric approach. This allows numerous compute nodes to access and write data from a centralized location, which can be crucial for parallel programs.

An API interface drives the cloud AI framework and allows for easily deployable AI applications on a web interface called the Machine Learning Dashboard. Various AI applications can be configured to run as independent applications that can be selected from the API list. This also allows easy integration of the cloud AI framework with edge and Internet-of-things (IOT) devices. For example, an AI application can be run in an edge device using the respective API to support edge computing, rather than doing all computations in the edge device itself.

In summary, the architecture described has three distinct use cases. First, it can be used as a cloud service tailored for deep-learning applications to train resource-intense deep-learning models fast and easily. Second, it can be used as a data warehouse to host petabytes of datasets and trained models. Third, the API interface can be used to deploy trained models as AI applications on the web interface or in edge and IOT devices.

The architecture, which is illustrated in Figure 7.1, consists of several layers which work in tandem to create a holistic machine learning framework. Some of the main components includes:

1. A *Machine Learning Dashboard* for managing projects and visualizations.

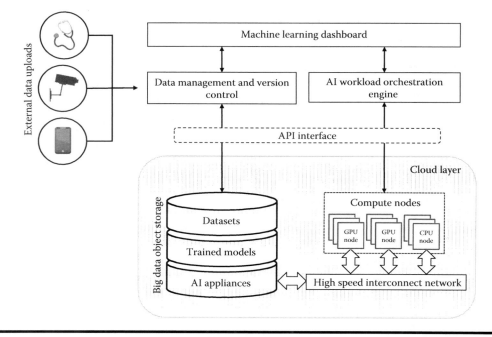

Figure 7.1   Scalable Cloud AI Framework.

2. Bare-metal *GPU and CPU Compute Nodes* to carry out resource-intensive machine-learning training and inference.
3. An *AI Workload Orchestration Engine* to efficiently provision and manage the compute nodes for different projects.
4. A *Big Data Storage* node for storing datasets, trained AI models, and metadata for high-speed data retrieval.
5. A *Data Management and Version Control* layer for data manipulation, preprocessing, and automatic versioning of datasets and trained AI models.

7.2.1 Machine Learning Dashboard

The ML Dashboard provides the entire stack of operations of the proposed cloud framework in a user-friendly website. Enrolled users can launch cloud instances with GPU support to train neural networks of their choice, preprocess and manage datasets, version-control trained models, visualize different projects' training curves, and test the models by giving new inputs right from the web interface using the proper APIs. The ML Dashboard is thus the primary user interface (UI) of the cloud AI framework.

Every operation carried out in the ML Dashboard is communicated with the rest of the cloud using APIs. This allows for a flexible and scalable ecosystem that can add or remove components as required. For example, if a user wants to add an IOT/edge compute service, it can be done by developing it locally and integrating the API service with the cloud AI platform without having to statically bind the services as such.

Users can train neural network models from the web interface by either coding them live in interactive terminal sessions or by pushing scripts. By choosing the number of nodes to train on and the deep-learning framework, users can spin multiple bare-metal compute nodes to carry out distributed deep learning. Once the training is done, the training logs can be used to visualize the training curves. Each training is versioned and logged automatically to ensure proper research and comparisons.

The trained models can be wrapped around an API to be pushed to production. Thus, the trained models can be used for inference. For example, in future sections, we show how trained models' AI applications can be pushed to production and used to make inferences by selecting the proper API from the API list. This enables automated software deployment for deep-learning research activities and many other workloads. At the time of writing this chapter, a few components of the ML Dashboard were in active development, which are mentioned in the Conclusion and Future Work section.

7.2.2 Bare-Metal GPU and CPU Compute Nodes

The core idea of a bare-metal cloud server is to give end users the full processing power of the physical server without using a virtual layer. They are single-tenant servers and are provisioned in minutes, allowing the user to know the exact hardware they are working on. Consequently, they provide more control over the hardware and system configurations than virtual machines (VMs). The bare-metal cloud servers are interconnected through a high-speed network to facilitate clustering of the compute nodes rather easily. As mentioned earlier, Apache Hadoop, Spark, and in-house distributed libraries in deep-learning frameworks like TensorFlow, TensorFlowOnSpark, CaffeOnSpark, and MXNet are used to create the distributed deep-learning cluster.

Within this proposed architecture, the bare-metal cloud servers provide four flavors: a CPU node and three GPU nodes. All compute nodes are equipped with Dual Intel(R) Xeon(R) CPU E5-2670 v3, 2.30 GHz processors. Also they host 128 GB of RAM in all flavors. The GPU nodes differ from the CPU nodes only on the additional NVIDIA GPUs. Together, the four flavors of bare-metal cloud servers provide users with distinct choices of hardware for different machine-learning or deep-learning problems, some of which are explained in Section 7.5. A thorough benchmark of the architecture is discussed in Section 7.4.2 for the three GPU flavors. The hardware specifications of these servers are described in Table 7.1.

7.2.3 AI Workload Orchestration Engine

Clustering compute nodes efficiently requires a smart orchestration engine. The idea of the orchestration service is to choose the right compute nodes for the task at hand, allocate them for the user, and manage them properly. Also, using powerful orchestration engines like OpenStack Heat [35], we can bring up cloud instances according to our need. Additional support from automation scripts

Table 7.1 Bare-Metal Server Specifications

Specifications	CPU Node	K80 Node	M40 Node	P100 Node
GPU available	None	NVIDIA K80	NVIDIA M40	NVIDIA P100
Processor	Dual Intel(R) Xeon(R) CPU E5-2670 v3 @ 2.30GHz			
RAM	8 × 16 GB = 128 GB, 2133 MHz			

and popular deployment software applications like Jenkins [36] and Ansible [37] are developed to help set up the deep-learning cluster automatically.

For advanced users, a web interface is also added to the OpenStack side of the cloud AI framework. It performs three major roles:

1. Providing a user interface for using and managing the OpenStack-based cloud services, including an additional object storage file system viewer
2. Providing a programming interface with secure shell login to user environments and an interactive console
3. Enabling complete control and integration over the available instances and also visualization of resources, files, and object storage nodes

Once users have an idea about the number of compute nodes required and the flavor of compute nodes, they can spin the required resources from the web interface manually. Also, users are given the option to choose an appliance of choice while launching the instances. An appliance is a ready-to-deploy image of a system with the required OS, drivers, and relevant deep-learning framework. Once users choose the appliance, they will be redirected to a website with a console interface and interactive terminal access to the launched instances.

7.2.4 Object Storage Using OpenStack Swift

OpenStack Swift is a distributed object storage system that is designed to scale from a single machine to thousands of servers. It allows for massively scalable and highly redundant storage on commodity hardware and provides the underlying storage system and computational resources. In the proposed cloud AI framework, unlike traditional deep-learning systems, the object storage node is heavily utilized to store datasets and train deep-learning models. As OpenStack has native support with the Hadoop distributed file system (HDFS), the use of Hadoop and Spark lend themselves to machine learning on scale.

The cloud AI framework is configured to allow bidirectional data flow between Hadoop and Spark with the object storage node. This translates to less or no data replication by the Hadoop cluster to store data locally since critical data are always hosted in the object storage node, which has a data replication factor of three, and are readily available. Deep-learning frameworks, while in the training phase, can utilize the object storage nodes in two different ways:

1. To download the entire dataset to local storage before training
2. To fetch data from an object storage node in real time during training

The perks of using object storage can be justified by closely studying these options. To extract the whole performance of the cloud frameworks' hardware, datasets should be hosted locally in a format best suited for the deep-learning software. The overhead of downloading huge datasets of hundreds of GBs from object storage to a local file system before training is a substantial factor to consider. Alternatively, to train very large models on very huge datasets, since the cloud AI framework is configured with OpenStack Swift, any deep-learning framework can essentially utilize the object storage equivalent to a normal filesystem, thereby using data stored in it during training instead of downloading large files locally. This can be done by mounting the object storage as a network-attached-storage solution, which makes it incredibly versatile and offers flawless networking using the high-speed network interconnects.

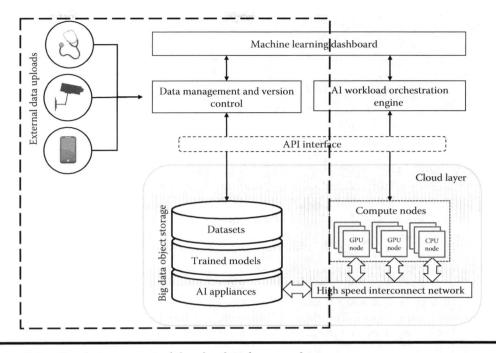

Figure 7.2 Cloud storage part of the cloud AI framework.

The highlighted portion in Figure 7.2 illustrates the cloud storage part of OCML architecture. The object store node is benchmarked using the Intel COS benchmark [38] and results are tabulated in the experiment section. In traditional workloads, the majority of data input/output (I/O) operations are read operations such as reading entries from datasets during training. Write operations happen frequently; however, the amount of data being written is much less than read operations in most cases. The benchmark also covers upload conditions such as archiving logs of training, uploading trained models to the object storage, etc.

7.2.5 Data Management and Version Control

Deep-learning platforms require data from external streams such as IOT camera feeds, sensors or data sent from users to be preprocessed to a proper format required by the deep-learning platforms. Proper versioning and logging of data are also huge requirements as the data used to train a specific model, in its original form, are required to reproduce results later.

The data management and version control layer versions each dataset and updates the same with newer data while associating proper versions with the trained AI model metadata. This ensures that the trained AI models can be reused and retrained on the same data with different parameters. The trained models are also versioned in the same way. This process aids in teaching pretrained neural networks to learn a new task on a new dataset. This process is called transfer learning.

We show here an easily configurable algorithm for dataset preprocessing in Algorithm 7.1. The algorithm will search for available CPU instances and if found will look for a user given the preprocessing script. If a script is provided, it will be run in an attached CPU node. Otherwise, a script will be chosen by checking the data type and output type required. If no combinations are found, users will have to provide the preprocessing script manually. Scripts for converting from

---

Algorithm 7.1 Dataset preprocessing pipeline.

Input: new task t_i
      name of the container in object storage: *container-name*
      input datatype: *in-type* and output datatype: *out-type*
      optional preprocessing script defined by user: *user-script*
      preprocessing scripts available in system: *preprocess-script-list*
      existing cpu instances: *cpu-total*
Output: task t_i assignment
Ensure: *free-cpu-instance* = *Find-Free(cpu-total)* $\neq 0$
 1: **for** each task t_i **do**:
 2:    *chosen-instance* = Choose(*free-cpu-instance*)
 3:    **if** *chosen-instance* is NULL **then**
 4:        Raise exception and exit
 5:    **end if**
 6:    **if** Exist(*user-script*) **then**
 7:        Run *user-script(container-name, in-type, out-type)* in *chosen-instance*
 8:    **else if** True(Check-Script(*in-type, out-type, preprocess-script-list*)) **then**
 9:        Run *system-available-script(in-type, out-type)* in *chosen-instance*
10:    **else**
11:        Raise exception and request manual entry
12:    **end if**
13: **end for**

---

image datasets to many different formats are available. Inputs are expected in different folders such as training, validation, and testing, or a proper split should be specified; otherwise, they default to a split of 70, 15, and 15 for train, test, and validation splits, respectively.

7.3 Deep Learning: An Overview

Deep learning is a representation-learning method which uses multiple levels of representations. Non-linear modules convert each representation more abstractly than the other modules, allowing them to learn complex functions [39]. If data used for learning are labeled properly, we can use supervised learning methods to train a deep-learning model because certain outputs may be associated with the input labels. This method is used in a variety of problems, most popularly in image recognition. For example, in an image classification problem, we input labeled images and train a network on an algorithm to create a vector of real number outputs, one for each category of input images.

7.3.1 Convolutional Neural Networks

CNNs are widely used for image recognition, pattern recognition, speech recognition, natural language problems, etc. CNNs consist of one or more convolution layers, pooling layers and subsampling layers together to form a network. Convolution is an important operation, widely used in signal processing applications. It expresses the amount of overlap of one function, for example function A, over the other, function B and can be calculated as the integral of point-wise

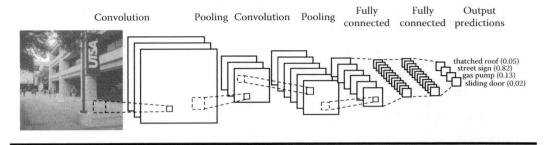

Figure 7.3   A typical convolutional neural network architecture. Image credits: UTSA Instagram @utsa.

multiplication of the functions. For images, convolution operation is done between a source image and a smaller filter, often called a convolution kernel. The small kernel is slid across the source image and convolution operation is carried out on each position of the kernel. The result of the convolution operation is a multidimensional image, often called an activation map. The basic convolution operation can be described as simple two-dimensional (2D) convolutions in discrete form:

$$f[x,y] * g[x,y] = \sum_{n_1=-\infty}^{\infty} \sum_{n_2=-\infty}^{\infty} f[n_1,n_2] \cdot g[x-n_1,y-n_2] \tag{7.1}$$

where f and g are the functions that are convolved together.

The convolution layers work as the feature extractor, extracting local features of each layer and making complex features as they progress to more hidden layers. This means that the high-level features are obtained from the low-level features when they pass through many convolution layers on their way to the output layer. Thus, CNNs favor applications where inputs have local correlation [39]. The networks typically have one or more fully connected layers toward the output side. Figure 7.3 illustrates a typical CNN architecture with multiple convolution and pooling layers followed by fully connected layers.

Consider an example of a forward pass on an $N \times N$ image with a $K \times K$ kernel. A convolution happens between the $K \times K$ kernel and the image. The kernel is, in steps, slid across the image, thus performing convolution across the entire image. A non-linearity is applied to this convolution. If the kernel is w, then the output of the convolution layer will be

$$y_{ij}^{l} = \sigma \left(\sum_{p=0}^{k} \sum_{q=0}^{k} w_{pq} \cdot y_{(i+p)(i+q)}^{(l-1)} \right) \tag{7.2}$$

where σ is the non-linearity applied. The size of this convolution layer will be $(N-K+1) \times (N-K+1)$ and each of these convolutions, in the software level, involves numerous matrix multiplications that account for 80%–90% of the execution time. Hence, convolutions are very important operations that make training a CNN possible. They make up the majority of floating point operations per second (FLOPS) in neural networks designed for images and videos that enable image classification, object recognition, speech analysis, natural language modeling, etc.

Assume $G = \{g_1, g_2, \ldots, g_k\}$ denotes the activation function of the penultimate layer, and $W = \{w_{s,t} | 1 \leq s \leq n, 1 \leq t \leq m\}$ are the weights of neurons connecting that layer to the Softmax layer, where n and m are the number of nodes in the penultimate and last layer, respectively. Assume there are $K = m$ number of output classes such that true labels $y \in k_1 : class_1, \ldots, k_m : class_m$. The probability of observation set x^i belonging to class $k_j \in \{1, \ldots, K\}$ is

$$p\left(y = k_j\right) = \frac{e^{g_k(x;w_k)}}{\sum_j^K e^{g_k(x;w_k)}} \tag{7.3}$$

with the constraint of $\sum_{i=1}^K p\left(y = k_i\right) = 1$. The objective is to maximize the log-likelihood of the classifier:

$$L = -\sum_{i=1}^l \ln\left(p\left(y = k_j\right)\right) = \sum_{i=1}^l \ln\left(\sum_j^K e^{g_k(x;w_k)}\right) - g_{y^i}\left(x; w_{y^i}\right) \tag{7.4}$$

To update the weights $w_{s,t} \in W$ between nodes in the penultimate layer and node t in the Softmax layer, the cost function is calculated as

$$\frac{\partial L}{\partial w_{s,t}} = \sum_{i=1}^l \frac{\partial G\left(x^i; W\right)}{\partial w_{s,t}} \left(p\left(k\right)\right) - \partial_{y^i=k} \sum_{i=1}^l \frac{\partial G\left(x^i; W\right)}{\partial w_{s,t}} \tag{7.5}$$

Therefore, the updating law is defined as

$$w_{s,t}[r+1] = w_{s,t}[r] - \eta \frac{\partial L}{\partial w_{s,t}} \tag{7.6}$$

where η is the learning rate and r is the index number.

7.3.2 Recurrent Neural Networks

A recurrent neural network (RNN) is used mainly to model sequential data such as sound [40–42] or text [43,44]. It is a standard feed-forward neural network with many hidden layers and non-linearity modeled especially for that purpose. The primary difference between a feed-forward neural network (e.g., a CNN) and an RNN is that, in RNNs, each of the hidden layers are connected back to themselves additionally. Weights in each of these connections can be different in different directions (say, the forward weight is W_1 and backward weight is W_2 such that $W_1 \neq W_2$). Thus, the output of each case is dependent on the previous one.

The RNN is fed with inputs during each time step and updates the hidden state, making a prediction. This concept can be thought of as the network having an internal memory of its own. The memory holds the information about previous computations and can thus act as a buffer to future computations that are dependent on it. Theoretically, this property of RNNs storing information about previous computations can be arbitrarily long and is exploited to create models for text generation or sequence generation. Figure 7.4 shows an RNN structure described well in Reference 39. Parameters U, V, and W define the state of the RNN. The objective of training an RNN is to find optimal values for these parameters. Accurate predictions can be made by properly designing the RNN with multiple hidden layers and non-linearity and training them over many time steps.

In a simple RNN network with an input x_t and an output o_t, the hidden state at any time step t is calculated by using both the current input x_t and the previous hidden state s_{t-1}. The first hidden

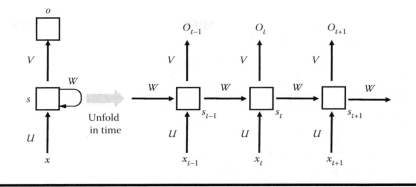

Figure 7.4   Unfolding an RNN cell in time.

state s_{t-1} is typically initialized to zeros. Thus,

$$s_t = f\left(Ux_t + W_{s_{t-1}}\right) \tag{7.7}$$

where the function f is usually a *tanh* or *ReLU* non-linearity. *tanh* is a widely used activation function for RNN networks with the mathematical property

$$f(x) = tanh(x) = \frac{2}{1 + e^{-2x}} - 1 \tag{7.8}$$

The parameters U, V, and W are the same across all time steps, such that the RNN cell learns the same or similar tasks with multiple input vectors. The next output in a sequence would be a probability vector across the input. Thus, if we train an RNN on a stock market dataset to predict stock values, the next data point predicted will be according to the parameter V_{s_t} such that $o_t = softmax\left(V_{s_t}\right)$.

Back-propagation in RNN can be achieved by the similar gradient descend algorithms used in CNNs. However, gradient descend becomes ineffective for large RNNs as the gradient starts to decay exponentially as it is back-propagated [45,46] and the network fails to store information for longer periods of time. One way to overcome this is to include a memory that stores information over long time periods so that long-term memory requirements can be effectively dealt with. This approach is known as long-short term memory (LSTM) [47]. Since they are good at learning long-term dependencies, LSTMs have been widely and successfully applied across many sequence modeling tasks.

An LSTM layer contains an additional forget gate along with the input and output gates. Each layer acts as a memory cell that learns when to open and close the three gates to learn a specific task. They do this by storing the temporal state of the network in the recurrent self-connections and using the input and output gates to flow information that is required. The input gate controls the flow of input activations into the memory cell, whereas the output gate controls the flow of cell activations from the memory cell to the rest of the neural network. The forget gate learns to reset (forget) the memory cell when the information stored in them is no longer useful for proper learning. Thus a mapping is created between the input sequence $x = (x_1, \ldots, x_T)$ and the output sequence $y = (y_1, \ldots, y_T)$ by calculating the network unit activations using the following equations iteratively from $t = 1$ to T:

$$i_t = \sigma\left(W_{ix}x_t + W_{im}m_{t-1} + W_{ic}c_{t-1} + b_i\right) \tag{7.9}$$

$$f_t = \sigma \left(W_{fx} x_t + W_{mf} m_{t-1} + W_{cf} c_{t-1} + b_f \right) \tag{7.10}$$

$$f_t = f_t \odot c_{t-1} + i_t \odot g \left(W_{cx} x_t + W_{cm} m_{t-1} + b_c \right) \tag{7.11}$$

$$o_t = \sigma \left(W_{ox} x_t + W_{om} m_{t-1} + W_{oc} c_{t-1} + b_o \right) \tag{7.12}$$

$$m_t = o_t \odot h \left(c_t \right) \tag{7.13}$$

$$y_t = W_{ym} m_t + b_y \tag{7.14}$$

where the W terms denote weight matrices between corresponding gates and connections, the b terms denote bias vectors, and σ is the logistic sigmoid function. The terms i, f, o, and c are respectively the input gate, forget gate, output gate, and cell activation vectors. They are the same size as the cell output activation vector m. The terms g and h are the cell input and cell output activation functions, generally *tanh*. The symbol $\odot$ is the element-wise product of the vectors [48].

7.4 Benchmarking the Cloud AI Framework

The proposed cloud AI framework is a collection of closely knit services working together to provide a user-friendly, compute-intensive cloud environment. It provides easy access to petabytes of object storage enabling users to store huge datasets, carry out streaming operations, and enable deep-learning training on data stored in an object storage node without downloading the entire dataset locally. GPU-enabled compute nodes bolster the deep-learning hardware, which, in tandem with the software stack, allows researchers to perform deep-learning training in less time while collaborating easily using appliances and the cloud marketplace.

First, to evaluate the importance of the object storage node and its performance, we use Intel COSBench to benchmark our object storage node. COSBench is widely used to benchmark cloud storage systems and provides easy configurations to test object storage performance of varying object and container sizes.

Then, we use Baidu's DeepBench [49] to benchmark our GPU-based M40, K80, and P100 instances on low-level deep-learning operations like deep matrix multiplication, convolution, and recurrent layer operations for parameters such as different input and kernel sizes. Baidu's Deep-Bench, rather than training a neural network end to end, provides time and TeraFLOPS for a particular operation and parameters. This ensures a fair ground of comparison of all GPU instances and gives users an estimate of the performance of each flavor of cloud instance provided.

7.4.1 Benchmarking the Big-Data Object Storage

The majority of I/O operations on object storage are read operations, for example, reading datasets to train a neural network. In order to benchmark the object storage properly, separate read and write benchmarks have been carried out for many different workloads, starting from tiny file sizes to large sizes. Objects of sizes 4KB, 128KB, and 512KB will simulate small datasets with tiny images or text files. Objects of sizes 1 MB, 4 MB, and 8 MB are chosen to replicate large image files, sound, and large text corpus used to train neural networks and also for streaming applications while data are continuously transferred from an array of sensors, etc. Objects of sizes 128 MB, 256 MB, and 512 MB will benchmark the object storage for transferring large files, like trained models, back and forth.

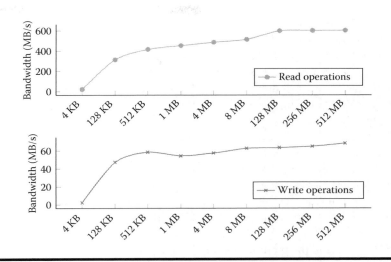

Figure 7.5   Intel COSBench benchmark results.

The Scalable Cloud AI Framework is more concerned with big data and hence big datasets. While dealing with huge datasets, it is a good practice to partition the whole dataset into segments while uploading them to object storage. This ensures better data resiliency and reduces the strain on object storage while dealing with huge datasets. In the benchmark, object sizes of 128 MB, 256 MB, and 512 MB are chosen as the segmentation size to account for huge datasets. For example, the ImageNet 2012 dataset is roughly 250 GB, which could be written as 1,950 segments of 128 MB size, 976 segments of 256 MB size, etc. Thus, the benchmark covers many possible scenarios while using datasets stored in an object storage node. Figure 7.5 illustrates the bandwidth achieved for different object sizes for both read and write operations from and to the object storage node.

From the results, it can be seen that an average of 446 MB/s read speed is achieved for the entire stack of input object sizes chosen for the benchmark. This will essentially result in seamless data transfer from the object storage to the bare-metal instances while training. A high read speed is also desired if one chooses to download the entire dataset to the bare-metal instance for offline training. Also, an average of 52.4 MB/s write speed ensures that the trained models, backed-up logs, and archives can be written to an object storage node with ease. Thus, an object storage node backed by OpenStack Swift is a wonderful option for storing and retrieving huge datasets and training logs to and from its petabyte storage.

7.4.2 Benchmarking the Cloud Hardware Using DeepBench

Deep learning is a computationally intensive process. Training a deep neural network on a large dataset might require days or even weeks of resource-intensive computing hours. In a fast-paced research institute, using CPUs alone for training might not be feasible. CPUs are optimized to carry out tasks serially. Over the years, CPUs evolved from SimpleScalar processors to simultaneous multi-threading (SMT) processors, exploiting thread-level parallelism as well as instruction-level parallelism [50]. SMT processors offer very low latency by using a high-speed cache and sophisticated control logic. CPUs are getting better with every iteration. However, in this decade when Amdahl's law struggles to be relevant, for a deep-learning problem, CPUs have little role to play when compared to GPUs.

DeepBench [49] is an application developed by Baidu to benchmark operations that are critical to deep learning on different hardware platforms involving GPUs. In a diverse architecture like the proposed cloud AI framework that supports standalone as well as distributed deep-learning environments, the fundamental computations required for a neural network can vary by a large margin. For example, in a distributed deep-learning problem, there can be either data parallelism or model parallelism. These kinds of options may be compute bound, bandwidth bound, or in some cases occupancy bound.

DeepBench benchmarks the performance of many basic operations carried out in any deep-learning problem for different sets of hardware and mitigates the issue of comparing different architectures. Thus, rather than focusing on the time required to train a model, DeepBench benchmarks the underlying operations of a variety of deep-learning problems like computer vision, face recognition, optical character recognition, speech recognition, machine translation, language modeling, etc. [49], on single compute nodes. By adding proper benchmarks, one can have a comprehensive understanding of the architecture.

Both the GPU nodes in the proposed cloud AI framework are benchmarked using DeepBench. The basic operations carried out in the benchmarking process are the following:

1. General matrix-matrix multiplication (GEMM) operation
2. Convolutions of different filter and input sizes
3. Recurrent layer operations of various hidden unit and input sizes

Each of these operations gives users specific information about various applications that they might run on the cloud AI framework's hardware. The following section describes each of these operations briefly.

7.4.2.1 General Matrix-Matrix Operation

Matrix multiplication is an essential mathematical computation in any deep-learning problem. It forms the backbone of fully connected layers, recurrent layers of vanilla RNNs. Also, GEMM benchmarks make use of underlying deep-learning and neural network libraries like cuDNN, MKL, etc., along with other BLAS libraries to carry out multiplication of matrices of different sizes. For example, a matrix of size $M \times N$ is multiplied by another matrix of size $N \times K$, resulting in a matrix of size $M \times K$. The FLOPS of these operations can be calculated using the equation, FLOPS $= (2 \times M \times N \times K)/t$, where M, N, and K are the respective sizes of the matrices and t is the wall time required for the multiplication. These matrices can then be transposed independently to introduce additional sizes of matrices and hence a variety of results.

Table 7.2 lists the different kernels used for the benchmark. Each kernel corresponds to a unique matrix size. A^T refers to whether kernel A is transposed or not, and similarly for B^T. TF is the teraflops achieved for the GEMM operation. For example, consider the first entry in Table 7.2, where $M = 1760$, $N = 7133$, $K = 1760$, A^T is N (not true), and B^T is T (true). Here, two matrices A and B of size (1760×7133) and (7133×1760) are multiplied together, with the condition that matrix B is transposed to size (1760×7133). Table 7.3 shows the wall time required to compute matrix multiplications for various kernel sizes and the respective teraflops.

The results provide interesting insight into choosing the right hardware for deep-learning problems such as speech recognition. The kernel sizes are increased and transposed to give a mix of input conditions. The kernel sizes indicate typical matrix sizes that are associated with deep-learning problems in the Baidu research group, specifically the DeepSpeech speech recognition engine. It

Table 7.2   Benchmark Kernel Specifications for GEMM Benchmark*

Sl. No.	Kernel	A^T	B^T
1	$M = 1760, N = 7133, K = 1760$	N	T
2	$M = 1760, N = 7000, K = 1760$	T	N
3	$M = 1760, N = 128, K = 1760$	N	N
4	$M = 2048, N = 7133, K = 2048$	N	T
5	$M = 2048, N = 7000, K = 2048$	N	N
6	$M = 2048, N = 7000, K = 2048$	T	N
7	$M = 2048, N = 128, K = 2048$	T	N
8	$M = 2560, N = 7133, K = 2560$	N	T
9	$M = 2560, N = 7000, K = 2560$	N	N
10	$M = 2560, N = 128, K = 2560$	N	N
11	$M = 2560, N = 128, K = 2560$	T	N
12	$M = 4096, N = 7133, K = 4096$	N	T
13	$M = 4096, N = 128, K = 4096$	N	N
14	$M = 4096, N = 7000, K = 4096$	N	N
15	$M = 4096, N = 7000, K = 4096$	T	N

* A^T is a transpose of matrix A specified by T for true and N for not true, and similarly for B^T.

can be seen from the data that NVIDIA M40 performs better than K80, with a peak of 5.27 teraflops. However, the P100 GPU node outperforms both M40 and K80 with a peak TFLOPS of 8.96. This means that it should perform well for convolutional neural networks since the major part of operations involving CNNs are matrix multiplications given a deep network with usage of many fully connected layers.

It should be noted that the K80 node has twice the amount of GPU memory as the M40 node. This means that we will be able to perform much bigger matrix multiplications albeit a bit slower. This is a crucial point that makes more sense in the coming sections involving neural network training on a cloud AI framework. The amount of GPU memory is important since it decides how big of a neural network it can train without overflowing the memory and the amount of training examples it can hold in one batch (batch size) for each iteration of the training process. If the GPU cannot hold large networks, then one has to explore model parallelism. Also, having a lower batch size will generally take longer to train the neural network.

7.4.2.2 Convolution Operations

As mentioned in Section 7.3.1, most of the mathematical operations carried out during convolutions are dense matrix multiplications. The framework is benchmarked on a variety of

Table 7.3   GEMM Benchmark

	K80		M40		P100	
Sl. No.	Time	TF	Time	TF	Time	TF
1	17.73	2.49	11.44	3.86	5.22	8.47
2	18.37	2.36	13.28	3.26	5.74	7.55
3	0.53	1.51	0.28	2.84	0.15	5.36
4	22.71	2.63	11.36	5.27	6.73	8.90
5	20.55	2.86	46.62	5.04	6.82	8.61
6	25.55	2.30	14.76	3.98	6.93	8.48
7	0.81	1.33	0.32	3.31	0.21	5.09
8	35.03	2.67	18.02	5.19	10.45	8.95
9	34.55	2.66	17.99	5.10	10.60	8.65
10	0.84	1.99	0.35	4.52	0.27	6.28
11	0.81	1.33	0.49	3.46	0.30	5.54
12	88.30	2.71	45.84	5.22	26.72	8.96
13	1.87	2.29	0.84	5.11	0.61	7.06
14	89.10	2.64	46.62	5.04	27.01	8.69
15	104.24	2.25	66.95	3.51	27.37	8.58

convolution conditions involving many different input sizes, kernel sizes, stride, padding, and so on. Stride is the distance by which the kernel is moved when performing convolution across the image. Padding is the additional area added to an image to make up for different image and window sizes.

Instead of concentrating on the accuracy of each model architecture used for benchmarking, DeepBench focuses on the performance of data that are presented in the *NCHW* format, where N corresponds to the batch size, C corresponds to the number of channels, H is the height of the image, and W is the width. In addition, different techniques like matrix-multiplication, FFT, and Winograd-based techniques are used to compute convolutions that can give researchers vivid insight into the right hardware to choose.

Results from the benchmark are tabulated in Table 7.4 for various input sizes, kernel (filter) sizes, and different numbers of filters for varying padding and stride. Table 7.5 provides the benchmark results for the different kernel sizes for the K80, M40, and P100 GPU nodes. The respective benchmark results are illustrated in Figure 7.6 for quick reference. This gives insight into which hardware to choose given the network architecture and corresponding performance required.

The kernels listed in Table 7.4 cover a variety of convolution operations usually found in computer-vision problems. The kernels are chosen to show the impact of the number of filters, different filter sizes, etc., on similarly shaped images. The kernels are also square in shape, since

Table 7.4 Benchmark Kernel Specifications for Convolution Benchmark*

Sl. No.	Input Size	Filter Size	No. of Filters	P(h, w)	S(h, w)
1	$W=7, H=7, C=832, N=16$	$R=5, S=5$	128	2,2	1,1
2	$W=7, H=7, C=512, N=16$	$R=3, S=3$	512	1,1	1,1
3	$W=7, H=7, C=512, N=8$	$R=3, S=3$	512	1,1	1,1
4	$W=7, H=7, C=832, N=16$	$R=1, S=1$	256	0,0	1,1
5	$W=14, H=14, C=512, N=16$	$R=3, S=3$	512	1,1	1,1
6	$W=14, H=14, C=512, N=8$	$R=3, S=3$	512	1,1	1,1
7	$W=14, H=14, C=512, N=16$	$R=1, S=1$	192	0,0	1,1
8	$W=14, H=14, C=512, N=16$	$R=5, S=5$	48	2,2	1,1
9	$W=28, H=28, C=256, N=16$	$R=3, S=3$	512	1,1	1,1
10	$W=28, H=28, C=256, N=8$	$R=3, S=3$	512	1,1	1,1
11	$W=28, H=28, C=192, N=16$	$R=5, S=5$	32	2,2	1,1
12	$W=28, H=28, C=192, N=16$	$R=1, S=1$	64	0,0	1,1
13	$W=56, H=56, C=128, N=16$	$R=3, S=3$	256	1,1	1,1
14	$W=56, H=56, C=128, N=8$	$R=3, S=3$	256	1,1	1,1
15	$W=112, H=112, C=64, N=16$	$R=3, S=3$	128	1,1	1,1
16	$W=112, H=112, C=64, N=8$	$R=3, S=3$	128	1,1	1,1
17	$W=224, H=224, C=3, N=16$	$R=7, S=7$	64	3,3	2,2
18	$W=224, H=224, C=3, N=16$	$R=3, S=3$	64	1,1	1,1
19	$W=224, H=224, C=3, N=8$	$R=3, S=3$	64	1,1	1,1

* $P(h, w)$ are the different heights and widths for padding. $S(h, w)$ are the different heights and widths for strides.

most computer-vision problems such as object detection, classification, etc., work on square images and square kernels.

7.4.2.3 RNN Layer Operations

Benchmarking an RNN operation is extremely challenging because of the sheer number of optimizations that can be applied to the process. From Equation 7.8, we know that the state of the current hidden layer depends on the previous state and current input. The equation also suggests that the recurrent layers are made up of matrix multiplications, some form of convolutions, and basic unary or binary operations.

Both GEMM and convolution operations play a part in RNN, but both operations are relatively small. However, because of the recurrence, these operations play a crucial role in deciding

Table 7.5 Convolution Benchmark for GPU Nodes*

Sl. No.	K80				M40				P100			
	Total Time	FwdTF	BwdTF	BwdPmTF	Total Time	FwdTF	BwdTF	BwdPmTF	Total Time	FwdTF	BwdTF	BwdPmTF
1	14.49	0.94	0.76	0.91	4.34	3.61	2.14	3.39	2.75	5.81	3.94	4.30
2	12.30	0.89	1.01	0.83	4.67	3.25	3.43	1.51	3.00	5.25	5.31	2.32
3	5.09	0.92	1.06	1.38	2.13	2.72	2.95	2.25	1.49	4.09	4.18	3.11
4	1.12	1.44	0.71	0.81	0.47	2.07	2.35	1.99	0.42	1.51	3.75	3.12
5	29.92	1.53	1.48	1.45	7.33	7.11	7.52	4.51	4.60	13.22	13.34	6.23
6	15.24	1.48	1.48	1.41	4.06	6.98	7.42	3.69	2.73	12.39	12.58	4.80
7	1.82	1.56	0.80	0.94	0.63	3.44	3.39	2.28	0.41	4.34	4.97	4.31
8	12.18	0.76	1.10	1.07	7.11	1.43	1.21	3.09	3.18	4.73	2.44	4.93
9	51.95	1.78	1.68	1.68	13.53	7.54	8.18	4.94	8.39	13.41	14.05	7.27
10	26.00	1.77	1.28	1.51	6.99	7.48	8.28	4.59	4.56	13.11	13.78	6.29
11	3.21	4.06	3.65	3.21	2.41	3.66	5.98	5.39	1.66	4.84	7.86	10.44
12	1.18	0.87	0.80	0.70	0.44	2.63	2.30	1.61	0.30	4.28	3.95	2.10
13	38.49	1.57	1.55	1.12	26.17	2.93	2.85	5.20	13.24	6.42	6.20	7.68
14	64.24	1.20	1.70	0.85	11.26	2.27	8.40	4.98	6.16	4.87	13.65	7.29
15	50.91	1.81	2.00	1.50	13.11	8.51	9.10	4.64	8.78	12.34	13.75	7.01
16	29.67	1.77	1.68	1.67	6.67	8.46	9.10	4.49	4.53	12.21	13.66	6.63
17	9.16	0.89	N/A*	0.77	2.68	4.18	N/A*	2.12	1.46	6.74	N/A*	4.19
18	11.72	0.54	N/A*	0.42	4.64	1.98	N/A*	0.86	2.33	4.50	N/A*	1.62
19	5.86	0.54	N/A*	0.42	2.39	1.94	N/A*	0.83	1.26	4.32	N/A*	1.48

* All times are in ms. FwdTF is the forward teraflops, BwdTF is the backward teraflops, and BwdPmTF is the backward teraflops for parameters.

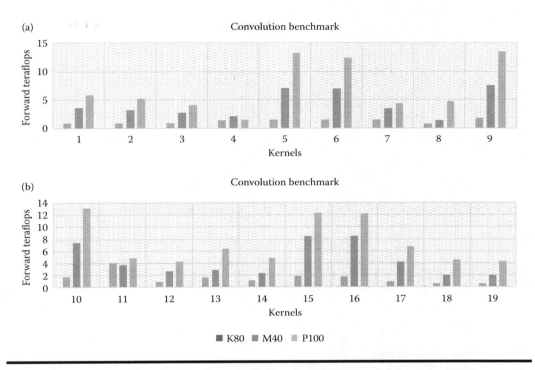

Figure 7.6 CNN benchmark for all GPU nodes: (a) CNN benchmark for all GPU nodes for kernels 1 to 9; (b) CNN benchmark for all GPU nodes for kernels 10 to 19.

the overall performance of the RNN layer. Another factor that is prominent is the input data in real time converted to newer, faster formats recognizable by the RNN layer during training. Thus, the benchmark focuses on only one recurrent layer unlike the convolution benchmark.

From Equation 7.8, we can also see that factor Ux_t is calculated for every time t. Since this calculation can be done all at once, we do not have to take into account the time required to carry out this multiplication, leaving us with the time required for the actual recurrent calculation. Both vanilla RNNs and LSTM are benchmarked on the cloud AI framework using DeepBench. Vanilla RNN uses *ReLU* non-linearity, and the LSTM uses sigmoid for gates and *tanh* for activations. Table 7.6 summarizes the different kernels used for the benchmark and Figure 7.7 illustrates the results from the benchmark process.

7.5 Exploring ML Applications Using the Proposed Cloud AI Framework

Machine-learning applications are experiencing the same dynamic shift that ML research has in this decade. More and more AI applications have been deployed in many aspects of life that are both personal and otherwise to humans [51]. From improving speech recognition engines to enabling self-driving cars and its subsystems [52], ML is at the heart of many technologies that we take for granted [53,54]. We present a few examples on using the cloud AI framework to develop and deploy ML applications. The cloud AI framework makes it easy to train and validate deep

Table 7.6   RNN Benchmark Kernels

Sl. No.	Batch Size	Hidden Units	
		Vanilla RNN	*LSTM*
1	16	1760	512
2	32	1760	512
3	64	1760	512
4	128	1760	512
5	16	2048	1080
6	32	2048	1080
7	64	2048	1080
8	128	2048	1080
9	16	2560	1080
10	32	2560	1080
11	64	2560	1080
12	128	2560	1080

neural networks and also provides a storage-centric architecture with a web back-end called the ML Dashboard. The ML Dashboard interacts with the cloud AI framework using APIs and thus makes it highly scalable. It also allows integrating edge devices to the platform with ease. In a context-aware semantic application, the role of the right hardware is important for high-speed inference during deployment. The architecture enables research in various types of cross-platform research including fog computing, edge computing, and deep-learning control [55]. We show how the architecture can be used to build AI applications utilizing its many features.

7.5.1 Speaker Recognition and Identification Using DNNs

Speaker recognition (SR) is an important tool in today's connected world. Verifying a person's identity over the phone for security purposes, authentication systems, etc., relies on powerful and accurate speaker recognition systems [56,57]. Voice identification (VI) is a subset of SR that uses voice as a form of biometric in determining the identities of different people. Thus, in general, the two primary goals of a speaker recognition problem are verification and identification. Speaker verification is a way to verify whether a speaker is truly who he or she claims to be and identification systems try to identify an enrolled speaker from a pool of preregistered speakers. Both can be either text-dependent and text-independent applications [58].

The recent popularity of using ML and DL techniques for speech recognition [7] and speaker recognition [59] has boosted the accuracy of both, even beating human-level performance [8]. The project described here uses fully connected deep neural networks to recognize and verify speakers with much less computational cost [60]. Instead of using very deep neural networks to do the heavy lifting, the raw audio is preprocessed into the mel-frequency cepstral coefficients (MFCCs), which are extracted to specifically define the audio that is being used.

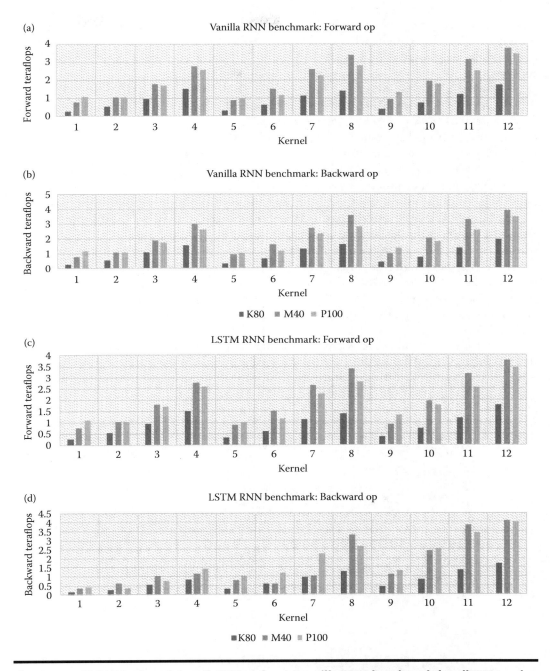

Figure 7.7   RNN Benchmark for all GPU nodes: (a) vanilla RNN benchmark for all GPU nodes, forward op; (b) vanilla RNN benchmark for all GPU nodes, backward op; (c) LSTM benchmark for all GPU nodes, forward op; (d) LSTM benchmark for all GPU nodes: backward op.

MFCCs are representations of the short-term power spectrum of a sound and are used frequently in speech recognition systems [61]. Even though audio signals are constantly changing, given a sufficiently short amount of time, the signal's characteristics can be assumed to be fairly constant. This type of analysis is known as short-time spectral analysis and is the type of analysis used when calculating MFCCs. Human voice typically ranges in frequency between 85 and 255 Hz. MFCCs have the ability to be less impressionable to variations in speech patterns and effectively extract the features of the human voice [62].

A simple DNN model is trained on the extracted MFCCs to distinguish between subtle changes in speech patterns between speakers. An example DNN model is shown in Figure 7.8. Initial experiments were carried out using data sets from LibriSpeech [63], an open-source corpus of almost 1000 hours of open-source speech data. To increase the accuracy of our model, as studied by Ahmad, Khan Suhail et al. [64], a 75% overlap is done between consecutive frames of audio.

The proposed cloud AI model is used to convert raw audio data to MFCC using a preprocessing script and help from the dataset preprocessing pipeline introduced in Section 7.2.4. As such, users need to provide the name of the object storage container in which the raw audio files are saved, the input datatype, and the output datatype. Since our system did not have a preprocessing script to convert from *wav* files to MFCCs, we provided one to the dataset preprocessing pipeline. Once these details are provided, the data management service will spin cloud instances to convert the raw audio to MFCCs, and the preprocessed data will be made available in the object storage after completion.

To initialize the training procedure, the training scripts are prepared and information about the dataset is added. As mentioned in the architecture section, training can be done in either a single node or distributed fashion. Since the network is small, we chose to train the network in a single node. Once the training starts, we can view the training statistics on the ML Dashboard.

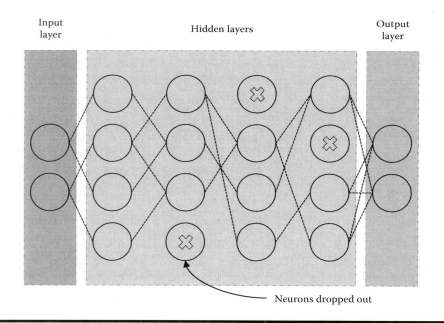

Figure 7.8 Typical DNN architecture with input, hidden, and output layers with dropout.

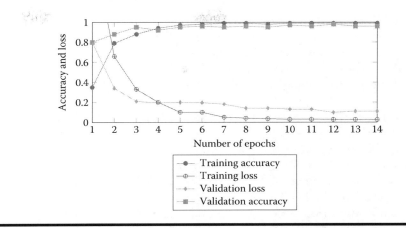

Figure 7.9   Training and validation curves of speaker recognition project.

This helps in deciding whether the neural network is learning properly. After training, the weights of the neural network are saved for future use. The trained models are versioned manually (to be automated in future builds of the architecture).

The trained model can then be pushed to an edge device to do speaker identification. Despite its high accuracy, using the model as a standalone authentication system is not recommended as recorded voices of the speaker will trigger the neural network. Hence, currently the speaker recognition AI model is used for multi-factor authentication systems. The training curves, including accuracy and loss values for both training and validation, over different epochs are given in Figure 7.9. An epoch is reached when the training algorithm iterates through the entire training dataset.

7.5.2 Facial Emotion Recognition Using CNNs

Understanding human emotions at a personal level is important in many aspects of life. Mapping human emotions from a variety of sources such as facial images, audio and video streams are essential for numerous security and affective computing projects. However, complex emotions or feelings such as pain or a change in emotions according to context cannot be registered using traditional closed-form learning algorithms. One aspect of our research is in applying deep learning to multiple domains of complex human emotions and finding patterns in them.

We discuss here a neural network capable of predicting basic human emotions such as anger, sadness, disgust, fear, etc. and the use of the proposed cloud AI model in streamlining the process of preparing the dataset and training and publishing the AI model. In our case, the dataset contains images of human faces, which are cropped, and the emotions in each face are properly labeled. As discussed in Section 7.3.1, CNNs act as feature extractors that learn to abstract the many data points available in the training dataset as the data flows through the hidden convolutional layers. This property helps the first few layers of the neural network to learn the edges and sharp contrast features of the human face. The further hidden layers learn to combine these edges to make shapes that are understandable by humans such as eyes, nose, or ears. It is often hard to generalize what a convolution layer learns, so proper visualization of each layer is required to fully understand the learning process of a CNN. At their heart, neural network models are still a black box that works wonders, and we are only starting to understand their learning process better.

The first step is in cleaning the dataset and preprocessing it to suit the application at hand. We make use of the data preprocessing pipeline to preprocess the datasets. Since we are not converting from one format to the other, we used existing scripts to reshape the dataset to the required size. Once the dataset is preprocessed, it is uploaded to the object storage with proper versioning. This allows us to track any changes in the dataset over time and also to tag the dataset with an AI model trained on it.

Training a neural network for emotion recognition requires careful crafting of the number of layers, kernel sizes, etc. We can gain insights about the raw performance of some of these kernels from the convolution benchmarks discussed in previous sections. To properly train a network, along with these metrics, we should gain the intuition to choose proper kernel sizes according to the application. Proper selection of kernels for the CNN layers comes from experience and experimentation. The powerful P100 nodes allow users to quickly run training scripts for a small portion of data and see the performance to gain fruitful insights without spending hours developing and debugging on laptops and CPU-based servers. We run multiple algorithms on the same dataset on multiple nodes to access the performance of each. Once an architecture is chosen, further changes are made to make it tailor-fit for the task at hand. The cloud AI framework allows users to do this process easily by proper versioning of trained models, visualization engines, and access to interactive shells and notebooks within the cloud servers.

The trained neural model can be deployed in the Machine Learning Dashboard (see Section 7.2) and the API can be used to drive numerous projects for affective computing. One example image of the ML Dashboard is illustrated in Figure 7.10. Here, an image can be dragged and dropped into one window to view it. Any computer vision API can then be selected from the dropdown menu to carry out inferences using the AI model that the API corresponds to. The example shows that an emotion recognition API can be used to extract the basic human emotions from an image of a person.

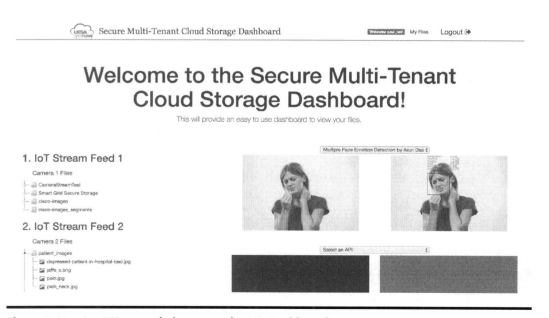

Figure 7.10   An API example image on the ML Dashboard.

7.5.3 *Music Genre Classification Using CNN-RNN Networks*

Deep-learning methods have been aggressively applied in the field of music tagging retrieval [65,66]. Genre categorization, mood classification, and chord detection are the most common applications designed from local spectral to temporal structure of music audio files. CNNs extract the local features that are in different levels of hierarchy within the music, while RNNs discover the global features to understand the temporal context. CNN-RNN architecture, or C-RNN for short, works as a powerful music tagging network with the benefits of both the CNN and RNN structures.

A C-RNN-based model designed to classify genres of an input music file [67] and the use of the proposed cloud AI framework to aid in the process of training and publishing the AI model is described in the following paragraphs. The MagnaTagATune dataset is used to train the network and it has 188 different tags (genre of music, gender of singer, instruments used, etc.) as raw music in *mp3* format. The *mp3* format is converted to a power-based *mel-spectrogram* signal in the data preprocessing stage by providing preprocessing scripts to the data management engine. As discussed in the speaker recognition example (Section 7.5.1), converting the raw audio file to proper formats can significantly boost the performance of the classifier and decrease the network complexity.

Here, we choose mel-spectograms as they over-perform compared to MFCCs in genre classification in our tests. Since the amount of training data is very large and because of the C-RNN architecture, the network takes a long time to converge. Hence, the network is trained on the labeled dataset in a distributed fashion by spinning up multiple bare-metal cloud instances.

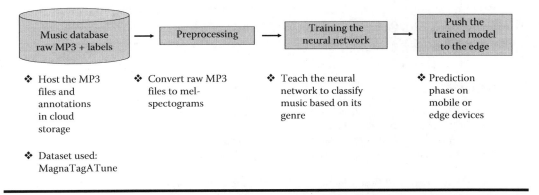

Figure 7.11   The implemented music genre classification pipeline.

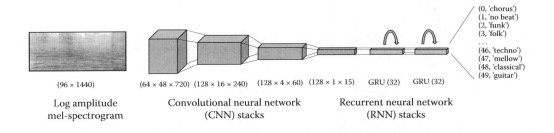

Figure 7.12   C-RNN architecture for music genre classification.

The AI workload orchestration engine is used to properly manage the cloud instances and terminate them after the training is done. Overall, the network is trained on the mel-spectogram data of corresponding music files and is allowed to learn the local and temporal structure of the audio files. The whole pipeline is illustrated in Figure 7.11. An illustration of the C-RNN model is also provided in Figure 7.12. The final AUC-ROC index for the proposed architecture is 0.893, which shows its superiority over traditional network structures on the same database.

7.6 Conclusion and Future Work

A scalable cloud architecture to train and deploy machine-learning models has been discussed. Use cases and other examples were given to show how the architecture integrates as a cloud AI framework. Several benchmarks have been carried out and illustrated to validate the framework in compute-intensive machine-learning tasks. The primary user interface, called the Machine Learning Dashboard, provides the ability to train, test, and deploy machine-learning models from the web interface itself. The data-centric architecture also hosts high-speed object storage nodes for quick data retrieval and also for archiving datasets and trained models with proper versioning. This aids researchers in keeping track of the dataset used to train specific models and allows data to be modified later on for other research. Overall, the cloud AI framework works as a holistic machine-learning cloud capable of meeting the needs of research-oriented and industry-oriented workloads with ready-to-deploy AI ecosystems.

Some of the components of the framework have been in active development while this chapter was being written. The AI workload orchestration engine 7.2.3 and data management engine 7.2.5 are constantly redefined to meet the new needs of AI and edge computing scenarios. Also, the ML Dashboard 7.2.1 goes through constant iterations to be as user friendly as possible, with the addition of newer APIs.

References

1. MIT Technology Review. https://www.technologyreview.com/s/602115/machine-learning-algorithm-combs-the-darknet-for-zero-day-exploits-and-finds-them/.
2. Michael A Nielsen. Neural networks and deep learning, 2015.
3. Richard Lippmann. An introduction to computing with neural nets. *IEEE ASSP Magazine*, **4**(2):4–22, 1987.
4. Yann LeCun, Bernhard Boser, John S Denker, Donnie Henderson, Richard E Howard, Wayne Hubbard, and Lawrence D Jackel. Backpropagation applied to handwritten zip code recognition. *Neural Computation*, **1**(4):541–551, 1989.
5. Haoxiang Li, Zhe Lin, Xiaohui Shen, Jonathan Brandt, and Gang Hua. A convolutional neural network cascade for face detection. In *Proceedings of the IEEE Conference on Computer Vision and Pattern Recognition*, pages 5325–5334, 2015.
6. Raia Hadsell, Pierre Sermanet, Jan Ben, Ayse Erkan, Marco Scoffier, Koray Kavukcuoglu, Urs Muller, and Yann LeCun. Learning long-range vision for autonomous off-road driving. *Journal of Field Robotics*, **26**(2):120–144, 2009.
7. Geoffrey Hinton, Li Deng, Dong Yu et al. Deep neural networks for acoustic modeling in speech recognition: The shared views of four research groups. *IEEE Signal Processing Magazine*, **29**(6):82–97, 2012.
8. Dario Amodei, Sundaram Ananthanarayanan, Rishita Anubhai et al. Deep speech 2: End-to-end speech recognition in English and Mandarin. In *International Conference on Machine Learning*, pages 173–182, 2016.

9. NSF-NIH Interagency Initiative et al. Core techniques and technologies for advancing big data science and engineering (bigdata), 2012.

10. Wullianallur Raghupathi and Viju Raghupathi. Big data analytics in healthcare: Promise and potential. *Health information science and systems*, **2**(1):3, 2014.

11. Adam Coates, Andrew Ng, and Honglak Lee. An analysis of single-layer networks in unsupervised feature learning. In *Proceedings of the Fourteenth International Conference on Artificial Intelligence and Statistics*, pages 215–223, 2011.

12. Jiquan Ngiam, Adam Coates, Ahbik Lahiri, Bobby Prochnow, Quoc V Le, and Andrew Y Ng. On optimization methods for deep learning. In *Proceedings of the 28th International Conference on Machine Learning (ICML-11)*, pages 265–272, 2011.

13. Rajat Raina, Anand Madhavan, and Andrew Y Ng. Large-scale deep unsupervised learning using graphics processors. In *Proceedings of the 26th Annual International Conference on Machine Learning*, pages 873–880. ACM, 2009.

14. Jeffrey Dean, Greg Corrado, Rajat Monga et al. Large scale distributed deep networks. In *Advances in Neural Information Processing Systems*, pages 1223–1231, 2012.

15. Li Deng, Dong Yu, and John Platt. Scalable stacking and learning for building deep architectures. In *Acoustics, Speech and Signal Processing (ICASSP), 2012 IEEE International Conference on*, pages 2133–2136. IEEE, 2012.

16. Edward Walker. Benchmarking Amazon EC2 for high-performance scientific computing. *USENIX Login*, **33**(5):18–23, 2008.

17. Aniruddha Marathe, Rachel Harris, David K Lowenthal, Bronis R De Supinski, Barry Rountree, Martin Schulz, and Xin Yuan. A comparative study of high-performance computing on the cloud. In *Proceedings of the 22nd International Symposium on High-Performance Parallel and Distributed Computing*, pages 239–250. ACM, 2013.

18. Lavanya Ramakrishnan, Piotr T Zbiegel, Scott Campbell, Rick Bradshaw, Richard Shane Canon, Susan Coghlan, Iwona Sakrejda, Narayan Desai, Tina Declerck, and Anping Liu. Magellan: Experiences from a science cloud. In *Proceedings of the 2nd International Workshop on Scientific Cloud Computing*, pages 49–58. ACM, 2011.

19. EC Amazon. Amazon web services. Available in: http://aws.amazon.com/es/ec2/ (November 2012), 2015.

20. Pradeep Padala, Xiaoyun Zhu, Zhikui Wang et al. Performance evaluation of virtualization technologies for server consolidation. *HP Labs Tec. Report*, 137, 2007.

21. Ludmila Cherkasova and Rob Gardner. Measuring CPU overhead for I/O processing in the Xen virtual machine monitor. In *Proceedings of the 2005 USENIX Annual Technical Conference*, volume **50**, pages 387–390, Anaheim, CA, 2005.

22. Paul Rad, A T Chronopoulos, Mahendra P Lama, Pranitha Madduri, and Cameron Loader. Benchmarking bare metal cloud servers for HPC applications. In *Cloud Computing in Emerging Markets (CCEM), 2015 IEEE International Conference on*, pages 153–159. IEEE, 2015.

23. Paul Rad, Rajendra V Boppana, Palden Lama, Gilad Berman, and Mo Jamshidi. Low-latency software defined network for high performance clouds. In *System of Systems Engineering Conference (SoSE), 2015 10th*, pages 486–491. IEEE, 2015.

24. Aun Haider, Richard Potter, and Akihiro Nakao. Challenges in resource allocation in network virtualization. In *20th ITC Specialist Seminar*, volume **18**, Hoi An, Veitnam, 2009.

25. Apache. Hadoop. Available: http://hadoop.apache.org, 2009.

26. Apache. Apache spark: Lightning-fast cluster computing. Available: http://spark.apache.org, 2016.

27. Martín Abadi, Ashish Agarwal, Paul Barham et al. Tensorflow: Large-scale machine learning on heterogeneous distributed systems. *arXiv preprint arXiv:1603.04467*, 2016.

28. Cyprien Noel, Jun Shi, and Andy Feng. Large scale distributed deep learning on Hadoop clusters. Available: http://yahoohadoop.tumblr.com/post/129872361846/large-scale-distributed-deep-learning-on-hadoop, 2016.

29. Lee Yang, Jun Shi, Bobbie Chern, and Andy Feng. Open sourcing tensorflowonspark: Distributed deep learning on big-data clusters. Available: http://yahoohadoop.tumblr.com/post/157196317141/open-sourcing-tensorflowonspark-distributed-deep, 2017.

30. Tianqi Chen, Mu Li, Yutian Li, Min Lin, Naiyan Wang, Minjie Wang, Tianjun Xiao, Bing Xu, Chiyuan Zhang, and Zheng Zhang. Mxnet: A flexible and efficient machine learning library for heterogeneous distributed systems. *arXiv preprint arXiv:1512.01274*, 2015.

31. Yangqing Jia, Evan Shelhamer, Jeff Donahue, Sergey Karayev, Jonathan Long, Ross Girshick, Sergio Guadarrama, and Trevor Darrell. Caffe: Convolutional architecture for fast feature embedding. In *Proceedings of the 22nd ACM International Conference on Multimedia*, pages 675–678. ACM, 2014.

32. Frédéric Bastien, Pascal Lamblin, Razvan Pascanu, James Bergstra, Ian Goodfellow, Arnaud Bergeron, Nicolas Bouchard, David Warde-Farley, and Yoshua Bengio. Theano: New features and speed improvements. *arXiv preprint arXiv:1211.5590*, 2012.

33. François Chollet. Keras. Available, https://github.com/fchollet/keras.

34. Yuan Tang. Tf. learn: Tensorflow's high-level module for distributed machine learning. *arXiv preprint arXiv:1612.04251*, 2016.

35. OpenStack. Heat: Openstack orchestration. Available: https://wiki.openstack.org/wiki/Heat, 2017.

36. Jenkins. Available: https://jenkins.io/, 2017.

37. Ansible. Ansible is simple IT automation. Available: https://www.ansible.com/, 2017.

38. Qing Zheng, Haopeng Chen, Yaguang Wang, Jiangang Duan, and Zhiteng Huang. COSBench: A benchmark tool for cloud object storage services. In *Cloud Computing (CLOUD), 2012 IEEE 5th International Conference on*, pages 998–999. IEEE, 2012.

39. Yann LeCun, Yoshua Bengio, and Geoffrey Hinton. Deep learning. *Nature*, 521(7553):436–444, 2015.

40. Sharath Adavanne, Giambattista Parascandolo, Pasi Pertilä, Toni Heittola, and Tuomas Virtanen. Sound event detection in multichannel audio using spatial and harmonic features. *arXiv preprint arXiv:1706.02293*, 2017.

41. Giambattista Parascandolo, Heikki Huttunen, and Tuomas Virtanen. Recurrent neural networks for polyphonic sound event detection in real life recordings. In *Acoustics, Speech and Signal Processing (ICASSP), 2016 IEEE International Conference on*, pages 6440–6444. IEEE, 2016.

42. Chang-Hyun Park, Dong-Wook Lee, and Kwee-Bo Sim. Emotion recognition of speech based on RNN. In *Machine Learning and Cybernetics, 2002. Proceedings. 2002 International Conference on*, volume 4, pages 2210–2213. IEEE, 2002.

43. Ilya Sutskever, James Martens, and Geoffrey E Hinton. Generating text with recurrent neural networks. In *Proceedings of the 28th International Conference on Machine Learning (ICML-11)*, pages 1017–1024, 2011.

44. Alex Graves. Generating sequences with recurrent neural networks. *arXiv preprint arXiv:1308.0850*, 2013.

45. Sepp Hochreiter. The vanishing gradient problem during learning recurrent neural nets and problem solutions. *International Journal of Uncertainty, Fuzziness and Knowledge-Based Systems*, 6(02):107–116, 1998.

46. Sepp Hochreiter, Yoshua Bengio, Paolo Frasconi et al. Gradient flow in recurrent nets: The difficulty of learning long-term dependencies, 2001.

47. Sepp Hochreiter and Jürgen Schmidhuber. Long short-term memory. *Neural computation*, 9(8):1735–1780, 1997.

48. Haşim Sak, Andrew Senior, and Françoise Beaufays. Long short-term memory based recurrent neural network architectures for large vocabulary speech recognition. *arXiv preprint arXiv:1402.1128*, 2014.

49. Sharan Narang. Deepbench. Available: https://svail.github.io/DeepBench/, 2017.

50. Dean M Tullsen, Susan J Eggers, and Henry M Levy. Simultaneous multithreading: Maximizing on-chip parallelism. In *ACM SIGARCH Computer Architecture News*, volume 23, pages 392–403. ACM, 1995.

51. Mehdi Roopaei, Paul Rad, and Kim-Kwang Raymond Choo. Cloud of things in smart agriculture: Intelligent irrigation monitoring by thermal imaging. *IEEE Cloud Computing*, 4(1):10–15, 2017.

52. Rohith Polishetty, Mehdi Roopaei, and Paul Rad. A next-generation secure cloud-based deep learning license plate recognition for smart cities. In *Machine Learning and Applications (ICMLA), 2016 15th IEEE International Conference on*, pages 286–293. IEEE, 2016.

53. Deep features class activation map for thermal face detection and tracking. In *Human System Interactions (HSI), 2017 10th International Conference on*, pages 41–47. IEEE, 2017.

54. Jonathan Lwowski, Prasanna Kolar, Patrick Benavidez, Paul Rad, John J Prevost, and Mo Jamshidi. Pedestrian detection system for smart communities using deep convolutional neural networks. In *System of Systems Engineering Conference (SoSE), 2017 12th*, pages 1–6. IEEE, 2017.

55. Mehdi Roopaei, Paul Rad, and Mo Jamshidi. Deep learning control for complex and large scale cloud systems. In *Intelligent Automation & Soft Computing*, pages 1–3, 2017.

56. Nilu Singh, RA Khan, and Raj Shree. Applications of speaker recognition. *Procedia Engineering*, **38**:3122–3126, 2012.

57. Joseph P Campbell. Speaker recognition: A tutorial. *Proceedings of the IEEE*, **85**(9):1437–1462, 1997.

58. Tomi Kinnunen and Haizhou Li. An overview of text-independent speaker recognition: From features to supervectors. *Speech communication*, **52**(1):12–40, 2010.

59. Yun Lei, Nicolas Scheffer, Luciana Ferrer, and Mitchell McLaren. A novel scheme for speaker recognition using a phonetically-aware deep neural network. In *Acoustics, Speech and Signal Processing (ICASSP), 2014 IEEE International Conference on*, pages 1695–1699. IEEE, 2014.

60. Andrew Boles and Paul Rad. Voice biometrics: Deep learning-based voiceprint authentication system. In *System of Systems Engineering Conference (SoSE), 2017 12th*, pages 1–6. IEEE, 2017.

61. Md Rashidul Hasan, Mustafa Jamil, Md Golam Rabbani, and Md Saifur Rahman. Speaker identification using mel frequency cepstral coefficients. *Variations*, **1**(4):2004.

62. Ronald J Baken and Robert F Orlikoff, *Clinical measurement of speech and voice*, Speech Science. Singular Thomson Learning, 2000.

63. Vassil Panayotov, Guoguo Chen, Daniel Povey, and Sanjeev Khudanpur. LibriSpeech: An ASR corpus based on public domain audio books. In *Acoustics, Speech and Signal Processing (ICASSP), 2015 IEEE International Conference on*, pages 5206–5210. IEEE, 2015.

64. Khan Suhail Ahmad, Anil S Thosar, Jagannath H Nirmal, and Vinay S Pande. A unique approach in text independent speaker recognition using MFCC feature sets and probabilistic neural network. In *Advances in Pattern Recognition (ICAPR), 2015 Eighth International Conference on*, pages 1–6. IEEE, 2015.

65. Philippe Hamel and Douglas Eck. Learning features from music audio with deep belief networks. In *ISMIR*, pages 339–344. Utrecht, The Netherlands, 2010.

66. Keunwoo Choi, George Fazekas, and Mark Sandler. Automatic tagging using deep convolutional neural networks. *arXiv preprint arXiv:1606.00298*, 2016.

67. Sharaj Panwar, Arun Das, Paul Rad, and Mehdi Roopaei. A deep learning approach for mapping music genres. In *12th System of Systems Engineering Conference (SoSE)*, pages 1–5. Waikoloa, HI, IEEE, 2017.

# Chapter 8

A Practical Look at Anomaly Detection Using Autoencoders with H2O and the R Programming Language

Manuel Amunategui

Contents

Christensen always encouraged me to focus on anomalies—where theory doesn't explain something, or where there is disagreement around a prediction. Why is that? What accounts for the difference in views? The most compelling contributions to knowledge often come from pursuing those anomalies, from driving to the root of such disagreements.

James Allworth on his mentor,
Professor Clayton Christensen (Allworth J., 2017)

8.1 Anomaly Detection and Neural Networks

Anomaly detection, according to Wikipedia, is the "identification of items, events or observations which do not conform to an expected pattern or other items in a dataset" (Anomaly detection, 2017). In this chapter, we will use the R programming language to explore different ways of applying autoencoding techniques to quickly find anomalies in data at both the row and cell level. We will also explore ways of improving classification accuracy by removing extremely abnormal data to help focus a model on the most relevant patterns.

Figure 8.1 from H2O's freely downloadable "Training Book" on Github, shows the typical three layers associated with autoencoders. The first layer is the original feature set contained in the data, the second is the reduction of those features, and the last one is the reconstruction of the features from the learned weights and derived formula back to its original dimension. The autoencoder isn't a stand-alone tool; instead, it is created by tuning a neural network in a specific way. Conventional deep learning tends to blow up a feature space to capture non-linearities and subtle interactions hidden in the data. Autoencoders take a different path and reduce the feature space to focus only on the essential aspects of the data.

According to Geoffrey Hinton, godfather of "deep learning" (Lee, 2016), feeding high-dimensional data into a smaller central layer and rebuilding it back into its original size is a much more efficient and powerful method at feature reduction than principal component analysis (PCA) (Hinton and Salakhutdinov, 2006).

Autoencoding is used in digital data compression such as music compression, where ancillary information is stripped away, leaving only the essential bits to reproduce music at an acceptable level of fidelity while reducing its digital footprint.

8.2 Dimensionality Reduction

To understand how an autoencoder works, one must understand dimensionality reduction: "Dimensionality reduction is the transformation of high-dimensional data into a meaningful

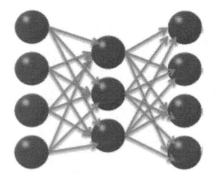

Figure 8.1   Typical autoencoder. (Adapted from h2oai/h2o-training-book.)

representation of reduced dimensionality. Ideally, the reduced representation should have a dimensionality that corresponds to the intrinsic dimensionality of the data. The intrinsic dimensionality of data is the minimum number of parameters needed to account for the observed properties of the data" (Laurens van der Maaten, 2009).

Being plagued with more data than we can handle is a timeless problem. We have access to huge stores of data and can only imagine all the great discoveries we could reach if only we could fit it on a computer. This is all about doing as much as we can by reducing the data to the smallest footprint possible while retaining the interesting properties of the data. Many techniques have been developed to attempt to address this problem. On the simple end of the dimensionality reduction spectrum, we have techniques like correlation filters and variable-importance selection that aim at removing features from the data that aren't deemed essential (Isabelle Guyon, 2003). On the more complex end exists techniques like singular value decomposition (SVD) and PCA that reduce the feature space by taking bits and pieces from many existing features and creating new reduced composite features (Ghodsi, 2006). The simpler techniques are easy to interpret, while the more complex ones can require a great deal of additional work (Abdi Hervé, 2010).

8.3 Autoencoders to Anomaly Detection

So, how do autoencoders and anomaly detection fit together? One of the most powerful and mysterious aspects of deep learning is that algorithms learn patterns in different ways than humans. This can make the output of complex deep models difficult, if not impossible, to interpret (Nielsen, 2017). Autoencoders traditionally have only one hidden layer (Hinton and Salakhutdinov, 2006). This makes it much easier to interpret what the autoencoder did and didn't do. As stated earlier, the autoencoder will take a feature space, reduce it, and blow it back up to its original size to the best of the autoencoder's abilities. By analyzing how well the model rebuilt the data to the original feature-space size, we determine what falls within a threshold of pattern acceptability and what doesn't. What cannot be rebuilt or what is missing from the reconstructed data is what we label an anomaly (Jinwon An, 2015). This chapter not only looks at practical uses of autoencoders, but also at approaches to automate the extraction of anomalies.

8.4 Autoencoders in R

Let's get practical and see how to implement autoencoders in the R programming language. R has been somewhat of a second-class citizen compared to other languages with regards to GPU support and availability of advanced neural and deep-belief networks (Python or R . . . a debate, 2013). H2O offers an interesting solution to this problem by enabling the R programming language to interface directly with its Java-based platform (Package 'h2o', 2017). This allows R users to benefit from additional modeling algorithms and the ability to work in distributed and clustered environments. It also endows R users with a powerful and easy-to-use autoencoder.

8.5 H2O's Autoencoder

The autoencoder we will use is a straightforward, unsupervised, and non-linear extension of the H2O deep-learning model. H2O is an open-source software for machine learning and big-data analysis. It offers various models such as generalized linear modeling, gradient boosting machine, and random forest modeling, but of pertinence for us here, it offers a deep-learning neural network.

H2O is written in and runs on Java so you will need to have Java and Java SDK installed on your machine. Because it runs as a self-contained service, it allows you to do all your data wrangling in R, send the transformed data to H2O to perform modeling and predictions, and finally harvest the results back into R for analysis and reporting. This architecture allows R to benefit from distributed computing (H2O can be chained with other H2O instances and can also run on Spark clusters) and from powerful neural network models.

The H2O autoencoder offers functions to easily access row- and feature-level reconstruction values. It also returns a mean square error (MSE) ranking to better understand what can be rebuilt and with what level of accuracy. The focus in this article is to quantitatively analyze those differences as an investigative tool in the search for and understanding of anomalies in data.

R-code snippets will be presented here, but the complete source can be found on GitHub at https://github.com/amunategui/practical-look-at-anomaly-detection.

8.6 Two Autoencoding Techniques Applied to Healthcare Data

To illustrate the autoencoder's capabilities, we will use a great healthcare dataset from the University of California, Irvine Machine Learning Repository (http://archive.ics.uci.edu/ml/). This publicly available dataset is very similar to the protected healthcare data that medical data scientists use on a daily basis:

Diabetes 130-U.S. hospitals for years 1999–2008 Dataset

The data hold electronic medical records (EMR) on diabetic patients along with a flag stating whether or not they were readmitted to the hospital.

Readmissions are a big deal for hospitals in the United States. Medicare and Medicaid will scrutinize reimbursement claims from participating hospitals and may decline payment if it is for a patient who was readmitted for the same problem under a time threshold.

Here is a look at the first row from the diabetes dataset:

```
head(diabetes,1)

##   encounter_id patient_nbr       race gender     age weight
##       2278392     8222157 Caucasian Female [0-10)    <NA>
##   admission_type_id discharge_disposition_id admission_source_id
##                 6                       25                   1
##   time_in_hospital payer_code     medical_specialty num_lab_procedures
##               1       <NA> Pediatrics-Endocrinology               41
##   num_procedures num_medications number_outpatient number_emergency
##               0               1                 0                0
##   number_inpatient number_diagnoses max_glu_serum A1Cresult metformin
##               0                1          None      None        No
##   repaglinide nateglinide chlorpropamide glimepiride acetohexamide
##          No          No             No          No            No
##   glipizide glyburide tolbutamide pioglitazone rosiglitazone acarbose
##        No        No          No           No            No       No
##   miglitol troglitazone tolazamide insulin glyburide.metformin
##        No           No         No      No                  No
##   glipizide.metformin glimepiride.pioglitazone metformin.rosiglitazone
##                  No                       No                      No
##   metformin.pioglitazone change diabetesMed readmitted
##                      No     No          No          0
```

We apply the customary data transformation and wrangling functions to make the diabetes data model-ready. This includes creating binary columns for all the categorical data, removing columns with extremely high variance, and taking care of missing data. After the data-cleaning process, we end up with a data set that is 51 features wide by 101,766 rows long.

8.7 Finding Out-of-the-Norm Patient Behavior in Healthcare Data

We start by using the unsupervised autoencoder to identify patients with out-of-the-norm values contained in their medical history. This is an unsupervised technique, meaning we are not focusing on or guiding our model toward a particular outcome. Instead, we are letting the algorithm roam over the data, find major patterns, and alert us of any cases going against those major patterns. The results found won't necessarily pertain to hospital readmissions or even diabetes; instead, they will highlight any anomaly found within the data regardless of the type. As with any unsupervised modeling, you're never sure what you'll end up with, and when you do get something, you will need to investigate further to understand what it means (Ghahramani, 2004).

Let's take a high-level look at some R code to understand how we call the H20 autoencoder and what type of information it returns (find the complete code on GitHub at https://github.com/amunategui/practical-look-at-anomaly-detection).

8.8 Per Row (or Patient) Reconstruction Error

The snippet below is a typical function call to an H2O modeling algorithm. We start by removing non-applicable fields such as the patient number and the encounter number. Then we upload the data to H2O by calling the **as.h2o** function:

```
# feed into h2o but remove non-modeling variables first

diabetes_ready_h2o <-as.h2o(dplyr::select(diabetes_ready_df, -encounter_id,
-patient_nbr,-readmitted) , destination_frame="diabetes.hex")


# model using the autoencoder-enabled deeplearning
anomaly_model <- h2o.deeplearning(x=feature_names,
                        training_frame = diabetes_ready_h2o,
                        hidden=c(20),
                        epoch=1,
                        activation="Tanh",
                        autoencoder=T,
                        reproducible=T,
                        ignore_const_cols=F)
```

We then call the **h2o.deeplearning** function. We pass the diabetes-h2o data to the deep learning model. In terms of parameters, the most important ones are enabling the **autoencoder** option and choosing one hidden layer with **20 neurons.** The other settings are kept simple. **Epoch** is set to 1, meaning the model will train over one iteration. The activation function is set to **Tanh**, meaning the model's output value will be between 1 and −1. Setting **reproducible** to true ensures that every run yields the same score (but will make the model run much slower). Setting **ignore_const_cols** to false will ensure that all columns are evaluated by the model.

What is interesting here is that the diabetes dataset fed into the model contains 51 features and we force it down to 20 features (referred to as 20 "neurons" in neural-network terms). Imagine a vice squeezing those 51 features until they are reduced down to 20. This unsupervised and non-linear dimensional reduction process makes the model drop weaker features so that the remaining ones are the most representative of the original data.

We then attempt to reconstruct the original data by calling the **h2o.anomaly** function:

```
reconstruction_error   = as.data.frame(h2o.anomaly(anomaly_model,
diabetes_ready_h2o, per_feature=FALSE))
```

This will use the trained neural-network model and its tuned weights to reconstruct the data. It first shrinks it down to the essential 20 features discovered earlier and rebuilds the features back to its original size of 51 features. It will return the MSE of the reconstruction, i.e., how far away the reconstructed rows are from the original ones. (An error of 0 is preferred and means the model rebuilt the data perfectly.) The rows of data that the autoencoder struggled to rebuild will have a higher error rate, and these will be the patients with out-of-the-norm values, i.e., our anomalies. This is an important point worth reiterating: our primary goal isn't perfect compression; instead, it is highlighting the outliers that failed to be compressed.

We'll see later how to get errors at the feature level by turning on parameter **per_feature**. Here we are looking at the reconstruction error for each row (i.e., the patient).

```
head(reconstruction_error)
```

```
##    Reconstruction.MSE
## 1          0.031500631
## 2          0.009943395
## 3          0.012556488
## 4          0.005279311
## 5          0.009574552
## 6          0.011859194
```

From the above list showing a sample of first six errors, the fourth row has the most accurate reconstruction while the first row has the worst. In the search for anomalies, one would start investigating the third row. Below is a plot of all the errors for the full data set. Looking at the chart, a logical next step toward investigating anomalous patients would be looking at patients with a reconstruction error above 0.08.

```
plot(sort(reconstruction_error$Reconstruction.MSE[sample(nrow(reconstruction_
error), 1000)]))
```

We attach the reconstruction error back to its corresponding row in the original dataset (Figure 8.2).

```
# attach error score to row

diabetes_ready_df$Reconstruction_Error <-
reconstruction_error$Reconstruction.MSE
```

Here is a look at the first patient row. The last column in the row is the reconstruction error.

```
# show one full row with attached reconstruction error

head(diabetes_ready_df, 1)
```

In this case, patient number 8222157 for encounter ID 2278392 has a reconstruction error of 0.03496385:

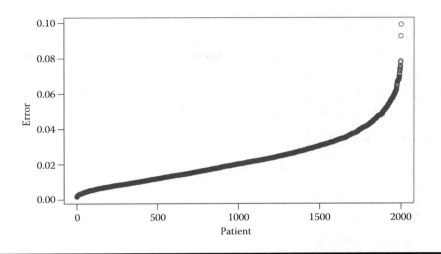

Figure 8.2   Reconstruction error.

```
##    encounter_id patient_nbr time_in_hospital num_lab_procedures
##       2278392      8222157                 1                 41
##    num_procedures num_medications number_outpatient number_emergency
##              0                1                 0                 0
##    number_inpatient number_diagnoses readmitted race_Caucasian
##              0                1                 0                 1
##    race_AfricanAmerican gender_Female gender_Male age_.40.50. age_.50.60.
##              0                1                 0                 0          0
##    age_.60.70. age_.70.80. age_.80.90. admission_type_id_6
##          0           0           0                 1
##    admission_type_id_1 admission_type_id_2 admission_type_id_3
##              0                 0                 0
##    discharge_disposition_id_1 discharge_disposition_id_3
##              0                      0
##    discharge_disposition_id_6 admission_source_id_1 admission_source_id_7
##              0                      1                  0
##    admission_source_id_17 payer_code_NA payer_code_MC payer_code_HM
##              0                  1             0             0
##    medical_specialty_NA medical_specialty_InternalMedicine
##              0                          0
##    medical_specialty_Family.GeneralPractice medical_specialty_Cardiology
##                      0                                  0
##    medical_specialty_Emergency.Trauma max_glu_serum_None A1Cresult_None
##                      0                          1             1
##    A1Cresult_.8 metformin_No metformin_Steady glimepiride_No glipizide_No
##          0           1             0                 1             1
##    glipizide_Steady glyburide_No glyburide_Steady pioglitazone_No
##              0           1             0                 1
##    pioglitazone_Steady rosiglitazone_No rosiglitazone_Steady insulin_No
##              0               1                 0                 1
##    insulin_Up insulin_Steady insulin_Down change_No change_Ch
##          0           0             0           1           0
##    diabetesMed_No diabetesMed_Yes Reconstruction_Error
##          1               0                 0.03496385
```

If we sort the data by reconstruction error, we can look at the first and last row, the highest and lowest error in the dataset:

```
# sort diabetes dataset by errors

diabetes_ready_df <- dplyr::arrange(diabetes_ready_df,
desc(Reconstruction_Error))
```

Patient number 104923179 for encounter ID of 218381862 has the highest reconstruction error:

```
Reconstruction Error: 0.1153027 # highest found


# show biggest error

head(diabetes_ready_df, 1)


##    encounter_id patient_nbr time_in_hospital num_lab_procedures
##     218381862    104923179                5                  5
##    num_procedures num_medications number_outpatient number_emergency
##                0              12                 0                0
##    number_inpatient number_diagnoses readmitted race_Caucasian
##                0                4          0              0
##    race_AfricanAmerican gender_Female gender_Male age_.40.50. age_.50.60.
##                    0             0           1           1           0
##    age_.60.70. age_.70.80. age_.80.90. admission_type_id_6
##              0           0           0                 0
##    admission_type_id_1 admission_type_id_2 admission_type_id_3
##                    0                   0                   1
##    discharge_disposition_id_1 discharge_disposition_id_3
##                          1                          0
##    discharge_disposition_id_6 admission_source_id_1 admission_source_id_7
##                          0                     0                     1
##    admission_source_id_17 payer_code_NA payer_code_MC payer_code_HM
##                        0             0             0             0
##    medical_specialty_NA medical_specialty_InternalMedicine
##                    0                                  0
##    medical_specialty_Family.GeneralPractice medical_specialty_Cardiology
##                                        0                              0
##    medical_specialty_Emergency.Trauma max_glu_serum_None A1Cresult_None
##                                    1                  1              1
##    A1Cresult_.8 metformin_No metformin_Steady glimepiride_No glipizide_No
##              0            1                0              0            1
##    glipizide_Steady glyburide_No glyburide_Steady pioglitazone_No
##                  0            1                0               1
##    pioglitazone_Steady rosiglitazone_No rosiglitazone_Steady insulin_No
##                    0                0                    1          1
##    insulin_Up insulin_Steady insulin_Down change_No change_Ch
##            0              0            0         0         1
##    diabetesMed_No diabetesMed_Yes Reconstruction_Error
##                0               1            0.1153027
```

Patient number 41411286 for encounter ID of 122802492 has the lowest reconstruction error:

```
Reconstruction Error: 0.001130284 # lowest found
```

```
# shot smallest error

tail(diabetes_ready_df, 1)
```

```
##    encounter_id patient_nbr time_in_hospital num_lab_procedures
##      122802492    41411286                3                 36
##    num_procedures num_medications number_outpatient number_emergency
##                1               8                 0                0
##    number_inpatient number_diagnoses readmitted race_Caucasian
##                  0                8          0              1
##    race_AfricanAmerican gender_Female gender_Male age_.40.50.
##                      0             0           1           0
##    age_.50.60. age_.60.70. age_.70.80. age_.80.90. admission_type_id_6
##              0           0           1           0                   0
##    admission_type_id_1 admission_type_id_2 admission_type_id_3
##                      1                   0                   0
##    discharge_disposition_id_1 discharge_disposition_id_3
##                             1                          0
##    discharge_disposition_id_6 admission_source_id_1
##                             0                     0
##    admission_source_id_7 admission_source_id_17 payer_code_NA
##                        1                      0             0
##    payer_code_MC payer_code_HM medical_specialty_NA
##                1             0                    1
##    medical_specialty_InternalMedicine
##                                     0
##    medical_specialty_Family.GeneralPractice
##                                           0
##    medical_specialty_Cardiology medical_specialty_Emergency.Trauma
##                               0                                  0
##    max_glu_serum_None A1Cresult_None A1Cresult_.8 metformin_No
##                     1              1            0            1
##    metformin_Steady glimepiride_No glipizide_No glipizide_Steady
##                   0              1            1                0
##    glyburide_No glyburide_Steady pioglitazone_No pioglitazone_Steady
##              1                0               1                   0
##    rosiglitazone_No rosiglitazone_Steady insulin_No insulin_Up
##                   1                    0          1          0
##    insulin_Steady insulin_Down change_No change_Ch diabetesMed_No
##                 0            0         1         0              1
##    diabetesMed_Yes Reconstruction_Error
##                  0          0.001130284
```

The differences between both patients are very interesting. The patient with the largest error went to the hospital 5 times, had 5 laboratory procedures, was on 12 medications, and received 4 diagnoses. The patient with the lowest error went to the hospital 3 times, had 36 laboratory procedures, was on 8 medications, and received 8 diagnoses. Keep in mind that this is a purely unsupervised algorithm where we aren't telling the model to look for something specific. Anomaly detection doesn't mean "at risk of readmission" or "at risk of diabetes"; instead, it simply means that the high-reconstruction scoring rows are very different from the norm. One anomaly that can be spotted is that the high-reconstruction scoring patient is in the youngest bucket. Relatively speaking, young sick patients are rarer than older ones.

Let's continue investigating anomalies by taking 10 patients with the most errors and comparing them with 10 patients with the least errors. We then average each feature group to pinpoint the features that diverge the most from each other. Below is the simple loop needed to achieve this experiment and its resulting plot.

```
# take 10 rows with highest reconstruction errors and compare with 10 rows
with the least errors

difference <- c()
for (feature in feature_names) {
  high_errors <- mean(head(diabetes_ready_df[,feature], 10))
  low_errors <- mean(tail(diabetes_ready_df[,feature],10))
  difference <- c(difference, high_errors - low_errors)
}


plot(sort(difference),type="l", col="Blue", pch=2, main='Directional
Differences between\n High Error & Low Error Features', ylab='Variable Average
Difference',xlab='Feature')

abline(h = 0, col='gray')
```

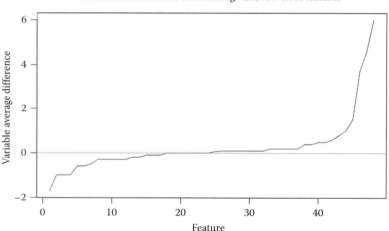

Directional differences between high and low error features

```
head(feature_divergeance_set,3)
```

```
##                 feature avg_difference
## 1 num_lab_procedures            6.6
## 2    time_in_hospital           3.6
## 3     num_medications           3.0
```

Per the above list, patient rows with a higher reconstruction error will have spent more time in the hospital along with many more lab tests than those with a low reconstruction error.

```
tail(feature_divergeance_set,3)
```

```
##                 feature avg_difference
## 46      payer_code_MC           -1.0
## 47          change_No            -1.0
## 48 number_diagnoses            -1.7
```

On the other end of the range, we see that patient rows with a higher reconstruction error have smaller quantities of diagnoses than those with lower error rates.

According to our simple analysis based on reconstruction scores, high-error rows may appear to contain more patients with chronic problems that require lab work, treatment, and time in the hospital to keep a disease under control, while those with a lower rate may be undergoing more exploratory diagnosing. Obviously, much more analysis, investigation, and data are needed to objectively come to such a conclusion.

It is important to remember that H2O's autoencoder has already captured most of the patterns, so using a pattern-based approach to pinpoint non-pattern abiding data may not be the most effective approach. The highest reconstruction error rows tend to behave more chaotically with less discernable patterns. This may be one of those cases where automation may not be a substitute for manual analysis; instead, domain knowledge and hard work may find insights that automation may miss.

8.9 Per-Feature Reconstruction Error

Another way of finding the difference between high and low reconstruction-error rates is through the **h2o.anomaly** function. We used it earlier with the **per_feature** parameter set to false, which returns an aggregated reconstruction-error value for the entire row. We can set that parameter to true and the function will output an error associated with each value instead of each row.

```
reconstruction_error  = as.data.frame(h2o.anomaly(anomaly_model,
diabetes_ready_h2o, per_feature=TRUE))

head(reconstruction_error,1)
```

This approach returns an error reading for every single value in the data set, so be ready to analyze a huge amount of data! Here are the errors for just the first row:

```
##    reconstr_time_in_hospital.SE reconstr_num_lab_procedures.SE
##             0.09302193                 0.0001673066
##    reconstr_num_procedures.SE reconstr_num_medications.SE
##             0.1027586                 0.03207709
##    reconstr_number_outpatient.SE reconstr_number_emergency.SE
##             8.236768e-05                 6.84568e-06
##    reconstr_number_inpatient.SE reconstr_number_diagnoses.SE
##             0.0006967247                 0.1489505
##    reconstr_race_Caucasian.SE reconstr_race_AfricanAmerican.SE
##             0.003761122                 0.000771504
##    reconstr_gender_Female.SE reconstr_gender_Male.SE
##             0.0001267885                 0.0001267933
##    reconstr_age_.40.50..SE reconstr_age_.50.60..SE reconstr_age_.60.70..SE
##             0.009513522           0.04405965                 0.0415845
##    reconstr_age_.70.80..SE reconstr_age_.80.90..SE
##             0.04783303           0.0861111
##    reconstr_admission_type_id_6.SE reconstr_admission_type_id_1.SE
##                 0.5345339                     4.25157e-05
##    reconstr_admission_type_id_2.SE reconstr_admission_type_id_3.SE
##                 0.05012827                     0.2541179
##    reconstr_discharge_disposition_id_1.SE
##                     0.07399473
##    reconstr_discharge_disposition_id_3.SE
##                     0.03759491
```

```
##    reconstr_discharge_disposition_id_6.SE reconstr_admission_source_id_1.SE
##                        0.03995723                              0.108937
##    reconstr_admission_source_id_7.SE reconstr_admission_source_id_17.SE
##                      0.0006734861                             0.0878212
##    reconstr_payer_code_NA.SE reconstr_payer_code_MC.SE
##            0.002047089                 0.01304637
##    reconstr_payer_code_HM.SE reconstr_medical_specialty_NA.SE
##          0.0003288569                       0.01035589
##    reconstr_medical_specialty_InternalMedicine.SE
##                              0.08295258
##    reconstr_medical_specialty_Family.GeneralPractice.SE
##                              0.02272028
##    reconstr_medical_specialty_Cardiology.SE
##                       0.008876603
##    reconstr_medical_specialty_Emergency.Trauma.SE
##                            0.0001698318
##    reconstr_max_glu_serum_None.SE reconstr_A1Cresult_None.SE
##                  0.03807583                  0.001058087
##    reconstr_A1Cresult_.8.SE reconstr_metformin_No.SE
##            0.0001195513                 5.500911e-06
##    reconstr_metformin_Steady.SE reconstr_glimepiride_No.SE
##                  2.63671e-05                 0.000202087
##    reconstr_glipizide_No.SE reconstr_glipizide_Steady.SE
##            0.0003077734                   6.236309e-06
##    reconstr_glyburide_No.SE reconstr_glyburide_Steady.SE
##            0.001608282                   0.002414192
##    reconstr_pioglitazone_No.SE reconstr_pioglitazone_Steady.SE
##              9.487483e-05                       0.0001483897
##    reconstr_rosiglitazone_No.SE reconstr_rosiglitazone_Steady.SE
##              0.001004889                       0.0007112666
##    reconstr_insulin_No.SE reconstr_insulin_Up.SE reconstr_insulin_Steady.SE
##          0.003344264             0.001336411              0.001866094
##    reconstr_insulin_Down.SE reconstr_change_No.SE reconstr_change_Ch.SE
##            0.0004420325             0.0001008356           0.0001008361
##    reconstr_diabetesMed_No.SE reconstr_diabetesMed_Yes.SE
##            8.775217e-06                 8.775219e-06
```

If we dimension the dataset and the error set, we confirm that they are both of equal size. This confirms that we have one error reconstruction value for each cell value in the data set.

```
print(dim(diabetes_ready_df))
## [1] 50883    47
print(dim(reconstruction_error))
## [1] 50883    47
```

This will yield a rich and diverse set of patient data to analyze. Some patients can easily have a feature that behaves within the norm and another that doesn't (i.e., an anomaly). This is a more granular approach than the previous row-based one and can help find patients with more complex areas of anomalous behavior.

One way to proceed with this approach is to loop through each feature and pick the top x highest reconstruction errors, pull the patient ID, and see if there are any patients that contain more than one high-error feature. Any patient with multiple high-reconstruction errors would be a candidate for further investigation. It would also list the suspicious features to kick-start the investigation. There are plenty of other ways of automating the analysis of reconstruction error. Another way that we won't cover here would be to calculate the average or standard deviation of errors for each feature and pick a feature along with an extreme range and analyze further.

To keep the code and result set workable, we will collect five patients per feature with the highest reconstruction error. Such a list could assist medical staff with finding high-risk patients, especially if the same patient appears multiple times under different features.

```
error_data_all <- c()
for (feature_id in seq(names(reconstruction_error))) {
    # build a data frame to pair feature and error values
    error_data <- data.frame(feature=feature_names[feature_id],

        value=diabetes_ready_df[,feature_names[feature_id]],
                        patient_id=diabetes_ready_df$patient_nbr,
                        error=reconstruction_error[,feature_id])
    # sort the error in descending order
    error_data %>% dplyr::arrange(desc(error)) -> error_data

    # pick highest 5 patient errors per feature
    error_data <- head(error_data, 5)
    error_data_all <- rbind(error_data_all, error_data)
}

# how many patients appear in the list multiple times?
head(sort(table(error_data_all$patient_id), decreasing = TRUE),5)

## patient_row
##  68049567  76018752 140771498   2526498   2532402
##         4         4         3         2         2
```

In the above output, we see that patient number 68049567 has four different features that appear within the highest reconstruction error range. Let's pull that patient up and take a closer look:

```
##    encounter_id patient_nbr time_in_hospital num_lab_procedures
##        82847010    68049567                4                 52
##    num_procedures num_medications number_outpatient number_emergency
##                 5               5                 0                0
##    number_inpatient number_diagnoses readmitted race_Caucasian
##                 1                6          0              0
##    race_AfricanAmerican gender_Female gender_Male age_.40.50. age_.50.60.
##                       1             0           1           1           0
##    age_.60.70. age_.70.80. age_.80.90.
```

We see that this patient had 52 lab procedures, with 5 medical procedures, and is on 5 medications. The abnormality may be in the complex medical history for a person of such a young age (s/he shows up in the earliest age bucket).

To deepen the investigation, it would be interesting to look at the other patients that have multiple high-error features or look at the data from a feature point of view, for example, the highest reconstruction errors by age group.

8.10 Using Anomaly Detection to Improve Classification Accuracy

We can also apply autoencoding in various ways to improve a classification model's accuracy. In a nutshell, we prune out anomalous rows and/or features before training the model. This is similar to removing outliers from the data before analysis. It helps the model focus on the principal behavior and not get confused or distracted by rarer behavior.

8.10.1 Base GLMNET Model

The UCI diabetes dataset we downloaded earlier is designed for classification as it contains a binary outcome of whether or not a patient was readmitted to the hospital for the same problem. Whenever the "readmitted" feature is equal to "< 30," this means that the patient was readmitted in less than 30 days and will represent our positive outcome; all other cases will represent our negative outcome.

```
# prep outcome variable to those readmitted under 30 days
diabetes$readmitted <- ifelse(diabetes$readmitted == "<30",1,0)
```

To demonstrate how the autoencoder can help improve the accuracy of a classification model, we split the data into two samples, one for training the model and another for evaluating the model's accuracy. We will use the same splits throughout all modeling examples to comparably evaluate each approach.

```
# split data set into training and testing with seed so you can reproduce the split
set.seed(1234)
split <- sample(nrow(diabetes_ready_df), floor(0.5*nrow(diabetes_ready_df)))
diabetes_train_df <- diabetes_ready_df[split,]
diabetes_eval_df <-  diabetes_ready_df[-split,]
```

We use a generalized linear model (GLMNET) to learn and score the model on how well it predicts whether a patient will be readmitted in less than 30 days. We will score the model using the area under the curve (AUC) metric. The AUC is a popular evaluation metric for binary models and yields a score between 1 and 0. An AUC score of 1 represents a perfect model where every prediction is 100% correct. An AUC score of 0.5 or lower is a random model with no accuracy whatsoever.

The first model we run uses the unchanged data set. This will be our benchmark score to determine how our data transformation using autoencoder information affects the predictions of being readmitted to the hospital.

```
x <- as.matrix(diabetes_train_df[,feature_names])
y <- as.factor(diabetes_train_df[,outcome_name])
set.seed(1234)
cvfit = cv.glmnet(as(x, "dgCMatrix"),y=y,alpha=0,family='binomial')
coef(cvfit, s = "lambda.min")_error,1)
```

The base model returns an AUC score of 0.638 in predicting whether a patient will be readmitted in less than 30 days for diabetes. An AUC of 0.638 is therefore our benchmark score.

8.10.2 Modeling With and Without Anomalous Patients

By using the autoencoder to find patients that behave differently from the norm, we can easily remove them from both the training and evaluation sets. This not only improves the model's accuracy, but also separates the minority of anomalous patients from the rest of the data for further analysis.

From a healthcare perspective, the benefit of a more predictive and more stable model is valuable in and of itself, but being able to analyze patients that behave very differently than the norm is an added source of valuable information.

There are two ways to improve the accuracy of the GLMNET model. The first way is to only model and evaluate the non-anomalous patients outright; the other is to do the same and ensemble it to the original benchmark model. Let's briefly look at both approaches.

The first step is to get the reconstruction error for our training and evaluation data. This will allow us to find the optimal cutoff to remove patients that can confuse the model's learning capabilities.

```
model_cutoff <-
sort(reconstruction_error$Reconstruction.MSE[floor(length(reconstruction_error
$Reconstruction.MSE) * .995)])

print(model_cutoff)

## [1] 0.07593834
```

Our error threshold is the cutoff point that separates the highest half-percent errors from the rest of the training set. We prune both the training and evaluation datasets of all errors above 0.07593834 and retrain the GLMNET model.

We truncate the training dataset:

```
diabetes_train_df_temp <- diabetes_train_df
# assign the reconstruction error to each row of data
diabetes_train_df_temp$error_recon <- reconstruction_error$Reconstruction.MSE
# remove all patients with a reconstruction error above threshold
diabetes_train_df_temp <- dplyr::filter(diabetes_train_df_temp,
                                        error_recon < model_cutoff)
```

Then we rerun the model with the new data:

```
set.seed(1234)
cvfit = cv.glmnet(as(x, "dgCMatrix"),y=y,alpha=0,family='binomial')
diabetes_eval_df_temp <- diabetes_eval_df
# assign the reconstruction error to each row of data
diabetes_eval_df_temp$error_recon <- reconstruction_error$Reconstruction.MSE
dim(diabetes_eval_df_temp)
```

We then truncate the evaluation dataset:

```
# remove all patients with a reconstruction error above threshold
diabetes_eval_df_temp <- dplyr::filter(diabetes_eval_df_temp,
                                       error_recon < model_cutoff)
```

Finally, we predict:

```
x <- as.matrix(diabetes_eval_df_temp[,feature_names])
preds <- predict(cvfit, x)
GetROC_AUC(probs = preds, true_Y = outcome)
```

This yields a 0.64 AUC score. This isn't a huge jump in score, but it is still better than modeling on the entire set of patients. It also suggests that further improvements could be reached with further research into why some patients behave very differently than the norm and why it hurts the model's accuracy. The **GetROC_AUC** call is a custom function that takes the vector of predicted probabilities and the vector of actual outcomes and returns the AUC score (see the GitHub repository for the full source code).

One drawback of the previous method is that we truncate the evaluation set. This is tantamount to only running predictions on a subset of patients (those with few to no anomalies). Another approach that allows predictions on the entire dataset makes use of "ensembling." This approach uses averages of multiple sets of predictions on top of each other to increase a classifier's understanding. Here we add the previous truncated data predictions with the benchmark predictions. This approach does show a slight improvement over the straight benchmark model (see the GitHub repository for more details on the ensembling approach).

```
GetROC_AUC(probs = c(full_predictions, truncated_predictions), true_Y =
c(diabetes_test_df[,outcome_name], diabetes_test_
truncated_df[,outcome_name]))
```

This approach yields a slightly improved AUC score of 0.639 over the AUC from the original dataset.

8.10.3 Modeling without Anomalous Features

If we set the h2o.anomaly built-in parameter "per_feature=TRUE," we can calculate an error sum score for each feature, remove some of the more error-prone ones, and see how it affects our model. We create a similar feature loop as we did previously to automate the summing of our reconstruction error by feature:

```
error_sums_by_feature <- c()
for (feature_id in seq(names(reconstruction_error))) {
  error_data <- data.frame(feature=feature_names[feature_id],
                       error=sum(reconstruction_error[,feature_id]))
  error_sums_by_feature <- rbind(error_sums_by_feature, error_data)
}
error_sums_by_feature %>% arrange(desc(error)) -> error_sums_by_feature

# top feature to remove
print(head(error_data_all,5))

##                              feature      error
## 1                         num_procedures 3689.36275
## 2                           insulin_Up   3363.58804
## 3                         insulin_Down   3289.44652
## 4   medical_specialty_Family.GeneralPractice   3000.30478
## 5                          age_.40.50.  2839.85166
```

The above output represents the top five features where the autoencoder struggled the most to reconstruct the data. We can gain a small improvement by rerunning the model with the datasets pruned of those difficult-to-reconstruct features.

For example, we select two features to remove:

```
features_to_remove <- c('insulin_Up','insulin_Down')
```

And rerun the GLMNET model:

```
# get score without most error-prone features
feature_names <-  names(dplyr::select(diabetes_train_df, -encounter_id,
-patient_nbr, -readmitted))
feature_names <- feature_names[!feature_names %in% features_to_remove]
x <- as.matrix(diabetes_train_df[,feature_names])
y = as.factor(diabetes_train_df[,outcome_name])
set.seed(1234)
cvfit = cv.glmnet(as(x, "dgCMatrix"),y=y,alpha=0,family='binomial')

# evaluate
x <- as.matrix(diabetes_test_df[,feature_names])
preds <- predict(cvfit, x)
print(GetROC_AUC(probs =  preds , true_Y = diabetes_test_df[,outcome_name]))
```

In the above code snippet, we remove both "insulin_Up" and "insulin_Down" and see the AUC score going from 0.6385 to 0.6386. This is a tiny improvement but still shows promise for further investigation into pruning out chaotic features to improve and stabilize or, at the very least, simplify the model. It also raises interesting questions, such as why a feature like "num_procedures" is so hard to reconstruct, and why does it attract chaotic behavior?

8.11 Conclusion

When tuning an autoencoder, the recommended approach is to have only one hidden layer. This isn't a requirement, but it certainly makes the job easier. Also, there is no one-size-fits-all recommended width for that hidden layer. Traditionally, it should be a size smaller than the original feature space (Kukačka). That said, you will need to experiment with different settings. A slight reduction over the original feature space will catch subtle anomalies, while a drastic reduction will catch many anomalies as the reconstruction algorithm will be overly crude and simplistic. Varying the hidden layer size will capture different points of view, which can all be interesting depending on the complexity of the original data set and your research goals.

I hope this brief chapter successfully illustrates that autoencoders are not just about data compression or dimensionality reduction. Unsupervised autoencoders are practical tools to highlight pockets of chaotic behavior and improve a model's accuracy. More importantly, they are a powerful tool to better understand your data.

References

Abdi Hervé, W. L. 2010. Principal component analysis. *WIREs Computational Statistics*, 433–459. Retrieved from WIREs Comp Stat: http://www.utdallas.edu/~herve/abdi-awPCA2010.pdf.

Allworth, J. 2017 *James Allworth: Founders and Motivation*. Retrieved from Stratechery: https://stratechery.com/2017/james-allworth-founders-and-motivation/.

Anomaly detection. 2017. Retrieved from Wikipedia: https://en.wikipedia.org/wiki/Anomaly_detection.

Hinton, G. E., Salakhutdinov, R. R. 2006, July 28. Reducing the dimensionality of data with neural networks. *Science Magazine*. Retrieved from https://www.cs.toronto.edu/~hinton/science.pdf.

Ghahramani, Z. 2004, Sept 16. Unsupervised learning. *Gatsby Computational Neuroscience Unit*. Retrieved from http://www.inf.ed.ac.uk/teaching/courses/pmr/docs/ul.pdf.

Ghodsi, A. 2006. *Dimensionality Reduction: A Short Tutorial*. Retrieved from http://www.stat.washington.edu/: http://www.stat.washington.edu/courses/stat539/spring14/Resources/tutorial_nonlin-dim-red.pdf.

Isabelle Guyon, A. E. 2003, 03 01. *An Introduction to Variable and Feature Selection*. Retrieved from http://homes.soic.indiana.edu/natarasr/Courses/AML/Readings/FeatureSelection.pdf.

Jinwon An, S. C. 2015, December 27. *Variational Autoencoder Based Anomaly Detection using Reconstruction Probability*. Retrieved from http://dm.snu.ac.kr/: http://dm.snu.ac.kr/static/docs/TR/SNUDM-TR-2015-03.pdf

Kukačka, M. (n.d.). *Overview of Deep Neural Networks*. Retrieved from WDS'12 Proceedings of Contributed Papers: http://www.mff.cuni.cz/veda/konference/wds/proc/pdf12/WDS12_117_i1_Kukacka.pdf.

Laurens van der Maaten, E. P. 2009, 10 26. *Dimensionality Reduction: A Comparative Review*. Retrieved from https://www.tilburguniversity.edu: https://www.tilburguniversity.edu/upload/59afb3b8-21a5-4c78-8eb3-6510597382db_TR2009005.pdf.

Lee, A. 2016, March 18. *The Meaning of AlphaGo, the AI Program that Beat a Go Champ*. Retrieved from Maclean's: http://www.macleans.ca/society/science/the-meaning-of-alphago-the-ai-program-that-beat-a-go-champ/.

Nielsen, M. 2017, January. *Deep Learning*. Retrieved from Neural Networks and Deep Learning: http://neuralnetworksanddeeplearning.com/chap6.html.

Package 'h2o'. 2017, February 22. Retrieved from cran.r-project.org: https://cran.r-project.org/web/packages/h2o/h2o.pdf.

Python or R . . . A debate. 2013, May 25. Retrieved from the Astrostatistics and Astroinformatics Portal: https://asaip.psu.edu/forums/software-forum/195790576.

Index

Note: Page numbers followed by "*fn*" indicate footnotes.